Coast to Coast Raves
for *Manhunt*...

"A gripping account of the life and times of a high-rolling spy and armaments dealer, Edwin P. Wilson."
— KIRKUS REVIEWS

"Suspense, intrigue, disguises, murders, suicides, unsavory love affairs and a star criminal ... This work of non-fiction reads like a spy novel!"
— CHATTANOOGA TIMES

"Frightening ... disturbing ... a fascinating look into the shadowy world of Wilson."
— THE LOS ANGELES TIMES

"An enthralling piece of work!"
— CHICAGO TRIBUNE

"Riveting ... provides the clearest picture yet published of the rogue CIA agent and his infamous odyssey."
— ASSOCIATED PRESS

MANHUNT
PETER MAAS

A JOVE BOOK

So it is in the Libyan fable that
an eagle, pierced by an arrow, gazed
at the feathered shaft and said, "Not
by others, but by our own plumage,
are we now smitten."

—Aeschylus, *Fragments*

CONTENTS

PROLOGUE

This is the story of a manhunt that lasted for nearly four years over three continents. It is about the murky bypaths of espionage and deception, confusion and inertia in the corridors of justice, the exigencies of foreign commitments. It is also about two engaged men, like a Western, the lawman after the outlaw, one on one, moving toward a final confrontation.

As most people did, I first read about Edwin P. Wilson in a slew of newspaper stories in 1981. He was said to be a former operative for the Central Intelligence Agency who had placed himself in the service of the Libyan dictator and godfather of international terrorism, Colonel Muammar el-Qaddafi.

Qaddafi not only was entertaining grandiose notions of military expansion and subversion throughout North Africa and the Middle East, fueled by the billions of dollars flowing in from Libyan oil deposits, but was openly supporting such terrorist organizations as Germany's Baader-Meinhof gang, Italy's Red Brigade, the Red Army of Japan and the most violent factions of the Palestine liberation movement. It was reported that he had dispatched hit teams to the United States to assassinate President Reagan.

In these accounts Wilson was portrayed as a mysterious figure, a sort of Great Gatsby of the spook world. What espe-

cially caught my eye was that he had a huge estate called Mount
Airy Farms in the fashionable northern Virginia hunt country,
an estate, I would learn, that abutted those of neighbors like the
tycoon Paul Mellon of Pittsburgh, Virginia's Senator John
Warner and his then wife, Elizabeth Taylor, and Jack Kent
Cooke, the multimillionaire owner of the Washington Redskins
football team.

He had acquired it while still in U.S. intelligence and I
wondered how this could be. I knew that CIA pay grades were
the same as those for other federal agencies and departments.
Then I discovered that the most Wilson had ever made in the
CIA was $25,000 a year and that his salary in his later employ-
ment with an ultrasecret Navy spy operation known to a select
few as Task Force 157 never got beyond $32,000 annually.

Just a decade before, I had begun work on my book *Serpico*,
the story of the brave officer who had exposed endemic corruption in the New York Police Department. But even in those bad
days, a cop who suddenly bought a house on a couple of acres
in the suburbs with a pool, say, or a tennis court would have
raised at least some eyebrows. At least some questions would
have been asked.

Less than an hour's drive from Washington, outside the tiny
community of Upperville, dominated by an Episcopal church
built by funds from the Mellon family, Wilson's Mount Airy
Farms was actually four contiguous estates, which he bought
one after another until he possessed a total of 2,338 acres of
lush, rolling, white-fenced land upon which show horses roamed
and hundreds of Black Angus cattle grazed.

And this was only the beginning. He had another farm in
nearby Middleburg, where President John F. Kennedy once purchased a retreat so that his wife could ride to the hounds, and
an additional thousand-acre spread five miles away called Apple
Manor, which he put at the disposal of key political and military
contacts who wished to hunt deer, wild turkey, grouse, quail,
partridge, even an occasional bear.

There were other holdings as well. Investment property in
North Carolina. An entire mountain in West Virginia. A townhouse in Washington. A second one in Alexandria, Virginia, in
which he installed his mistress. A beach house on the New Jersey
shore. Real estate in Mexico and Lebanon. Two country manors
in England. Quarters in Switzerland overlooking Lake Geneva.

All told, his net worth was more than $15,000,000, including approximately one million dollars in numbered Swiss bank accounts and South African gold.

Yet nobody in the dark, sensitive, security-conscious circles in which Wilson moved ever seemed to care how any of this had been made possible.

The CIA stayed silent about Wilson—where he had come from, what his role with the agency had been. But as his name continued to be embarrassingly coupled with the CIA in headline after headline, other stories attributed to unnamed intelligence sources started appearing in the media and then in a book called *The Death Merchant* by a Washington author, Joseph C. Goulden, dismissing him as a fringe player whose low-level agency contract was subject to renewal every couple of years, that he had been recognized early on as a rotten apple and promptly tossed out.

Although my previous investigative work had led me into the labyrinths of organized crime and law-enforcement and political corruption, my sole connection with the spy business was in 1960, when I was a reporter for *Look* magazine and the CIA tried to recruit me in hopes of using my journalistic credentials for its own purposes.

Still, I had developed a number of trusted contacts over the years. Through them I met others who enabled me to gain access to classified documents that detailed much of Wilson's intelligence career. I discovered that he had in fact been a highly valued agent who had not been fired at all, but rather left the CIA because he wanted to.

There was nothing in these records, however, that revealed what made him tick. How he came to supply the Qaddafi regime with weapons that killed people in England, West Germany and elsewhere; to arrange for the shipment of vast quantities of the most lethal and restricted explosives, which also killed and maimed people to an extent that remains unknown today; and to create a deadly, private network composed of both active and retired American military and intelligence personnel answerable only to him.

Beyond this were graver issues. How deeply did Wilson's corrupting hand reach into the U.S. intelligence community? How much had he compromised it? How could a man like Wilson, who at one point in his cloak-and-dagger career had come within an eyelash of being appointed to an assistant secretary-ship of the Army, have operated so brazenly? How could the CIA not have known what he was doing and stopped him? Or was he, as he would claim, simply working under an elaborate cover to serve the agency's arcane interests?

In the spy trade, where little is what it appears to be, where truth, as a matter of course, is a lie and fact fiction, anything was possible. After all, Wilson for a time had worked in the same agency division that attempted to hire me. And if he was not acting with official sanction, did he have confederates within the intelligence establishment?

It seemed incredible that he could have accomplished what he did on his own. But if he had, that presented the gravest question of all. How could it have happened? Even more astonishing, I discovered that for a long period of time the CIA, the FBI and the Department of Justice had had a very good idea of what Wilson was up to and essentially had done nothing.

2

That Wilson was a fugitive at all—holed up now, in 1981, in a villa in Tripoli, Libya, on the Mediterranean coast, apparently untouchable—was primarily due to one man, an assistant U.S. attorney for the District of Columbia named E. Lawrence Barcella, Jr.

Barcella had stumbled over Wilson by accident. As other events gradually unfolded, his pursuit became an obsession, personal in every sense of the word. The two men would meet secretly in Italy in a temporary truce. They corresponded and talked over international telephone lines, each trying to outwit the other.

Barcella's marriage would be severely strained, his life disrupted in countless ways. Vacations were wiped out. Saturday was just another workday, taking him away from his young daughter, on whom he doted. He'd wake up constantly in the middle of the night, wondering where Wilson was at that moment, what he was thinking, what he was plotting.

A friend of Barcella's had seen the movie *Butch Cassidy and the Sundance Kid* on television. In the movie, the principals, played by Paul Newman and Robert Redford, having robbed one train too many, are tracked down by a dogged sheriff whose trademark hat is a white straw skimmer. Wherever the two outlaws go, despite every stratagem they can devise, they always find themselves on some hilltop, looking back in growing amazement, alarm and anger at a shimmering white dot following in the distance, the sheriff's skimmer. It was known that one of Wilson's favorite pastimes in his Tripoli villa was watching taped movies. "Boy," said Barcella's friend, "if he's got that picture in his library, it'll really give him the willies," and Barcella laughed, pleased at the analogy.

The coincidences, the twists of fate, the ironies that permeated the story, would make even a hack writer of fictional thrillers blush.

But the cast of characters was irresistible. Among them a voluptuous redhead. An international confidence man whose hidden past I managed to unearth. A tragic drunk. A man with three missing fingers. A Mormon who neither drank nor smoked, who only smuggled guns and explosives. Shadowy players in high places, vying for power and profit. A psychopathic killer.

And behind it all, there was a grand design that drew Barcella and Wilson inevitably together, as if there never had been any other possibility.

Both were purely American products. And so dissimilar. The one, Wilson, six feet five and rawboned, with enormous hands, hands that could easily break your neck, a perfect reflection of his western, Big Sky roots. And Barcella, from the urban East, conscious of his immigrant heritage, seventeen years Wilson's junior, a shade under five ten, built like a middleweight, quick on his feet.

They shared a special quality, though. Both of them were risk takers.

THE CONSPIRACY

gruesomely dismembering him. It was big news in Washington, the first political assassination there since Lincoln's and the first ever of a foreign official, and the investigation was being intensely covered in the press. Every assistant in the office had hungered for the assignment.

But Barcella was just beginning a rape prosecution. He had a special interest in it. The victim was a young woman who worked in a pub that he and his wife, Mary, often went to, and they had come to know and like her. In his seven years in the office, it was the only case Barcella had ever asked for, and he wasn't about to give it up.

So the Letelier investigation went to Gene Propper, a youthful attorney Barcella had helped bring into Major Crimes. By April 4, although it had become evident that the Chilean secret police and right-wing Cuban exiles were responsible for Letelier's death, proving it in court was a long way off.

That afternoon, Barcella was with Propper, discussing what to do next, when Propper's phone rang. The capital's most famous reporter was on the line, Bob Woodward of the Washington *Post*. He was, said Woodward, working on a new lead regarding the Letelier murder, a lead that involved a former CIA agent named Edwin P. Wilson and three Cuban bomb experts, one of whom was known to have been in Washington the previous September, two days before Letelier's car blew up.

"Who's Wilson?" Barcella asked when Propper filled him in on the call, and Propper said, "You got me. I've never heard of him."

It turned out to be a classic instance of law-enforcement infighting and self-serving leaks. A small cabal of FBI supervisory agents specializing in terrorist activities were out to crack the Letelier assassination on their own. One of them ran across a retired CIA bomb expert who said a funny thing had happened. Around the time of the murder another ex–agency man, Ed Wilson, tried to hire him to fashion explosive devices in Libya. Wilson also had displayed an extremely sophisticated detonator and said that he had plenty more.

When Wilson's name was run through FBI computers, the file showed that he was the subject of an ongoing probe. Three Cubans in Miami, trained by the CIA, had reported that Wilson had approached them about an assassination overseas that the Libyan government desired. It also disclosed that the Justice

Department's foreign agents registration section was looking into whether Wilson was an unregistered Libyan agent. Supporters of Letelier, meanwhile, were charging CIA complicity in his death. The FBI supervisors made what they thought were discreet inquiries about Wilson to the section, in hopes of connecting him with Letelier. But Letelier was too hot an item, and a source Woodward had in the Justice Department contacted him immediately about the new development.

After Propper got hold of the file on Wilson and talked it over with Barcella, neither of them saw much of a tie-in with Letelier, especially since the Cubans were quite open about the Libyan murder contract. It hardly seemed likely that they would bump off Letelier and then place themselves in the middle of a similar conspiracy.

Still, every avenue had to be explored, and Propper phoned a lawyer in the foreign agents registration section and said he'd like to talk to Wilson if it wouldn't bollix up the Libyan matter. No problem, the lawyer said. The section didn't think it had a prosecutable case against Wilson anyway.

Within minutes Woodward was on the phone again, demanding confirmation that Propper was going to interrogate Wilson about Letelier. Propper hedged as best he could. At Barcella's suggestion, he had also requested files on Wilson and the three Cubans from the CIA, and when Woodward found out about that as well, Propper, livid at all the leaks, at last said yes, he intended to have a chat with Wilson.

Woodward's front-page story in the *Post* on April 12 began: "A former CIA explosives expert and three Cuban exiles will soon be sought by federal authorities for questioning in the investigation of last year's Embassy row bomb-murder of former Chilean Ambassador Orlando Letelier, according to informed sources."

The next paragraph read: "Edwin P. Wilson, the former Central Intelligence Agency operative, and the three Miami-based Cuban exiles came to the attention of federal officials when they learned that Wilson was under FBI investigation in an unrelated assassination plot abroad."

On April 20 Propper interviewed Wilson in Washington and was convinced that he had no link to the Letelier bombing. But nothing would become more meaningful to Wilson, or would come to haunt him more, than the fact that his name stuck in Larry Barcella's head. And what stuck most was a chance remark Propper made after seeing Wilson. "I'll tell you one thing, Larry," Propper said. "When that guy claimed he wouldn't know a detonator from a coffeepot, he was lying, for sure."

2

Woodward's story triggered all sorts of subterranean waves. Two days after it was published, a young man named Kevin Mulcahy, obviously quite emotionally distraught, came to see Woodward. He identified himself as a former CIA employee who had gone to work for Wilson. He said that Wilson and still another ex–CIA man, Frank Terpil, had entered into a secret partnership not only to supply explosive devices and technical expertise to Qaddafi's Libya but to ship arms to the Palestine Liberation Organization.

According to Mulcahy, Wilson had two key high-level contacts in the CIA, Theodore Shackley and Thomas Clines, and he cited other agency personnel, past and present, who were part of Wilson's apparatus. Mulcahy even said that Wilson had once tried to introduce him to Carlos Ramirez, the infamous "Jackal" who had masterminded the massacre of Israeli athletes during the 1972 Munich Olympics. He also said that after breaking with Wilson seven months ago, he had brought his allegations to both the CIA and the FBI with no apparent results.

Woodward was tempted to follow up, but the Letelier murder had been his main interest and any possible Wilson connection with it was fading fast. Mulcahy wasn't the most stable guy he'd met. Besides, his Justice Department source said that it seemed as if any crimes Wilson might have committed regarding Libya had all occurred outside U.S. jurisdiction and nothing could be done about them. It was a dead issue.

Wilson, who was in Tripoli when Woodward's story broke, rushed back to Washington. It was the first time his name had ever appeared in print. He retained William O. Bittman as his lawyer for a $5,000 down payment. Bittman was a natural choice, having represented another spook who had been a pivotal figure in the Watergate scandal, E. Howard Hunt. In righteous indignation Wilson had Bittman threaten the *Post* with a libel suit if he was mentioned again in the same breath with Letelier.

As for Libya, he said that he was just an ordinary businessman trying to make an honest buck. It wasn't his fault that Qaddafi was such an unpopular fellow. He remained in Washington for a week. He made arrangements for the secret demonstration of a U.S. day/night-vision TV camera that had an image-intensification tube which was under strict export control. The demonstration, for the benefit of Libyan military intelligence, would take place the following month at Wilson's Mount Airy estate. He also had a private laugh with his friend Tom Clines, then the director of CIA training, over how everyone was barking up the wrong tree concerning Letelier. And confident that he had nothing more to worry about, he returned to Tripoli.

The story, though, led to another big Woodward front-page break—the past existence of a hitherto covert Navy intelligence group, Task Force 157. And once more, up popped Edwin P. Wilson. The Navy, after recently disbanding the task force, had refused to grant its contract employees civil service credit for their time, and one of them phoned Woodward's office to say that he'd read the piece about Wilson and that Wilson had been in 157 as well. Ben Weiser, a reporter working with Woodward, took the call and when he asked what "157" was, he learned that the task force had been created to coordinate a watch on Russian naval passage through ocean "choke points" like the Danish Straits and the Dardanelles, to recruit spies to work foreign ports and to scan shipping to detect Soviet nuclear cargoes. It also had its own secure communications system, one that was used by Henry Kissinger, distrustful of the CIA, when President Nixon sent him on his secret trip in 1971 to open relations with China.

· Another reader who first found out about Ed Wilson in his morning Washington *Post* was President Jimmy Carter's new director of the CIA, Admiral Stansfield Turner. What got Turner's attention was a line halfway through Woodward's story saying that there was "some evidence that Wilson may have had contact with one or more current CIA employees." When he arrived at his Langley, Virginia, office, he demanded to know who these employees were. To his chagrin, it required no big search. Just about everybody, it appeared, except him, knew about them. One was William Weisenburger, whose job was to acquire exotic equipment for the agency and who had supplied

Wilson with ten miniature detonators of the most advanced
design. A second CIA man, Patry Loomis, had been discovered
only a few months earlier, while operating under deep commercial cover in the Far East, to be working on the side for Wilson.

Weisenburger, Turner was told, had already received a reprimand, and although the inquiry regarding Loomis was still
going on, he probably would get the same treatment. "That's
pretty mild, isn't it?" Turner asked. "Shouldn't we be getting rid
of them?" But to his amazement, Turner found a solid wall of
opposition, from his top deputy and a longtime CIA professional, Henry Knoche; from the chief of clandestine affairs, William Wells; and most surprisingly, from the inspector general,
John H. Waller. Weisenburger, they all said, had simply been
duped into doing a favor for an old friend and Loomis was just
moonlighting, not unheard-of among agency personnel. It
wasn't such a big deal. CIA relationships were complex. This
wasn't the Navy.

Turner, however, was looking for a way to make his presence felt in the agency. The day of freewheeling covert "cow-
boys," as he put it, was over, and he ordered the firing of both
Loomis and Weisenburger. He convened five hundred CIA officials in the "bubble," the Langley auditorium, and advised
them, among other things, that Wilson was persona non grata.
He then sent a "book cable," a CIA message, to agency stations
around the world, warning them not to have any dealings with
Wilson, who had been abusing his past affiliation with the
agency, and ordering them to report back to Langley about any
approaches Wilson may have made.

As Turner probed further, he learned of Wilson's close ties
to Shackley and Clines. Theodore Shackley occupied one of the
agency's most sensitive positions. He was associate deputy director in the Directorate of Operations, second in command of
all the CIA's global clandestine "dirty tricks." Turner also knew
that if Gerald Ford had defeated Carter in the 1976 elections,
Shackley would probably be sitting in *his* chair. In a private
meeting, Shackley told Turner that his connection with Wilson
was purely social, that while he had spent weekends at Mount
Airy, it was mainly because his wife and Wilson's were such good
friends. He had never spoken to Wilson about the slightest
professional matter. Turner didn't believe him, but no criminal
charges had been brought against Wilson. The most he felt he

could do at the moment was to take Shackley out of clandestine operations and appoint him deputy head of the National Intelligence Tasking Center, whose mission, to coordinate U.S. intelligence gathering, sounded more important than it really was.

Turner found Thomas Clines even less credible. During the investigation of Loomis, Clines had been spotted at a table with Loomis and Wilson in a Tysons Corner, Virginia, coffee shop one morning, not far from Langley. Clines claimed it was happenstance. He had dropped in for a solitary breakfast, saw the two men and sat down with them. Since the inspector general, who came out of the clandestine branch himself, had exonerated Clines of any purposeful wrongdoing, Turner's hands were pretty much tied.

In gathering information for this book, I asked Stansfield Turner if he had taken any action at all against Clines. He recalled with some satisfaction that he had been determined at least to remove Clines from the Washington scene and had ordered him assigned to a "small Caribbean nation."

"Which one?" I inquired.

"I can't tell you. It's classified."

"Admiral," I said, "I believe I have a record of every post Clines served with in the agency and there's no Caribbean nation mentioned." After I had ticked them off, I added, "I've got everything else. What difference does it make?"

"I'm sorry," Turner said. "I can't help you."

I contacted one of my agency sources the next day and told him about my encounter with Turner. "Oh, right," he said, "it was Jamaica. Except Clines never went."

"He never went?"

"No."

Clines had been removed as head of the CIA's Office of Training all right, but he ended up in an equally sensitive spot as the agency's Pentagon liaison. And Turner still didn't know it. It was a perfect illustration of how the "Company" could run rings around a director not considered part of the club who threatened the status quo, even a former Rhodes scholar fresh from commanding NATO forces in southern Europe.

On bulletin boards at CIA headquarters anonymous notices would go up likening Turner to Captain Queeg.

. . .

3

Larry Barcella read with mild interest yet another Woodward article, which said Turner had fired two unidentified "mid-level agency employees" because of their connection with Wilson in the sale of explosives and other materials overseas, including Libya. But it wasn't his problem. The Justice Department and the FBI were supposedly on the case. Then, after the revelations about Task Force 157, Wilson's name dropped out of sight.

Besides, Barcella had a lot more on his mind. That June an infant girl that he and Mary had adopted arrived home. She was christened Laura. Barcella was ecstatic. Hardly a week passed without his bringing in a new batch of photographs to show around the office. "Hey, Larry," one of the other attorneys said, "I can just see you when she starts dating."

"What do you mean?" Barcella exclaimed in mock horror. "The first boy who comes up my front steps marches right back down."

It would not be till the end of the year that he would cross paths with Wilson again, in a most unexpected way. In the meantime, Barcella wasn't the only one who remained unaware of precisely what Wilson was up to.

TWO

On April 2, 1977, the same day Woodward got his original tip about a possible tie between Wilson and Letelier, Doug Smith drove his blue Ford four-wheel-drive pickup out of the Fontana, California, bunkers of a major explosives dealer, J. S. Brower and Associates, several miles east of the main Brower offices in Pomona, and headed across the arid wasteland toward Los Angeles International Airport.

In the back of the pickup were cases of what appeared to be one-gallon cans of DAP, a glazing compound for windows that can be found in any neighborhood hardware store. The cans actually contained a whitish puttylike substance called Composition C-4. Ninety percent of C-4 was a chemical combination called RDX; the rest was binding material. Aside from the components of a nuclear reaction, RDX was the most powerful explosive on earth, the chief ingredient in conventional U.S. military bombs and shells.

It was produced in only two places in North America, a munitions plant in Tennessee and a commercial factory in Canada. Export licenses for RDX were rigidly controlled. Commercially, its offshoot, C-4, was in demand for demolition projects because of its malleability and the way its force could be directed. These same features made it a favorite for terrorists to use in blowing up a building or a car, or for turning ordinary household items—an ashtray, a lamp, a radio—into instruments of death.

RDX's versatility didn't stop there. It could be manufactured in sheets, usually a foot square and a quarter-inch thick, with an adhesive backing. The sheets were pliable and could be cut to any desired size or shape. A classic terrorist tactic was to mail one, wired to a miniature detonator, in an envelope. When the recipient opened the envelope flap, he or she was torn apart.

Besides the bulk C-4, Smith's pickup was carrying two cases of these sheets in drums supposedly containing a paint thickening agent, along with a thousand sophisticated space-age detonators the size of a wristwatch stem winder. Also in the drums, which included instruction manuals, were four Smith & Wesson nine-millimeter pistols. All told, the load weighed in at eleven hundred pounds.

When Smith reached the airport, he drove straight to the Lufthansa cargo facility. He spoke to two men in the office and told them that the Lufthansa regional cargo sales manager in Washington knew about the shipment and they should check with him if there were any questions. The following day the C-4 and the handguns departed Los Angeles without a customs export declaration, without an airway bill of lading, without a trace of paper of any sort. After the freight arrived in Frankfurt, Germany, it was transferred to another Lufthansa flight to Libya.

Smith, meanwhile, returned to the Pomona headquarters of J. S. Brower and Associates and telexed the phony address he had used for the shipment—David Well Oil Supply Co.—to its true consignee in Tripoli, Edwin P. Wilson.

Exactly six months later, on October 2, a chartered DC-8, recently converted to cargo use, sat on the tarmac at Houston Intercontinental Airport all day long. The loading had been a mess. The main door of the jet, which had come in from Miami the night before, hadn't been altered yet to accept containerized packaging. So instead of quickly forklifting 856 five-gallon black cans labeled oil-drilling mud inside the DC-8, the loading crew had to place them on a conveyor belt and store them individually on board.

To make matters worse, it was a Sunday and there had been a scramble up and down the freight line to find enough hands to help out. A can had fallen off the belt and split open. It was tossed into a nearby dumpster. One of the men who had been recruited noticed the residue left on the tarmac. It was the oddest drilling mud he'd ever seen. When he kicked it, it was rather like clay. Drilling mud was pretty fluid. And the color, kind of white-gray instead of brown-gray, wasn't right either. But he said nothing. He was glad to get the extra money and it wasn't any of his business.

The cans had been trucked from California a few days before, from J. S. Brower and Associates, and in every can, under three or four inches of real drilling mud, was tightly tamped Composition C-4.

Around midnight, the DC-8 finally took off from Houston, its declared destination Lisbon, Portugal, laden with a staggering twenty-one tons of C-4. It was the largest private shipment of the explosive in history and it was going to the center for world terrorism, Colonel Qaddafi's Libya, on orders from Edwin P. Wilson.

Despite the strict controls on C-4, Jerome S. Brower had acquired it with no trouble at all. Brower was a reputable and respected explosives dealer, considered to be a peerless demolition expert, During the Korean War, he had led a commando team nicknamed "Ali Brower and his thirty thieves," whose specialty had been blowing up bridges. He had been called upon many times by governmental agencies, including the Bureau of Alcohol, Tobacco and Firearms, for his advice. He had counseled a number of police department bomb squads, and he had often responded to their requests for emergency aid in disarming or removing unstable explosives. However one looked at him, Jerry Brower seemed to be a patriotic, civic-minded American in a dangerous business, as the three missing fingers and part of the little finger of his left hand attested. And now he was working for Wilson.

In gathering together such a huge amount of C-4, Brower had been extra careful, ordering it over a period of months from three different supply depots in New York, Louisiana and Texas. And to avoid any personal connection with the flight, he flew separately from Los Angeles to join the DC-8 during its two-hour Lisbon stopover. Already on board was Brower's attorney, Edward Bloom, who had paid for the plane in Miami and at the last minute decided to make the trip for the excitement. Brower wanted to know what the terrible smell was, and Bloom explained that the DC-8's previous charter had been South American meat runs.

In Tripoli, after the plane was unloaded, Brower met with Wilson and gave him the invoice. He explained that while there were fifty pounds of C-4 in each can, the drilling mud on top added another ten pounds of weight. Wilson thought about this for a minute and said that, well, he'd promised the Libyans more C-4 than had been delivered. Couldn't Brower write up a second invoice that read sixty pounds of it per can?

For Wilson, who was charging the Libyans twenty dollars a pound for the C-4, the invoice change immediately raised his profit on the shipment by $171,200. And just to tickle the fancy of the Libyans, he told them that the explosive had been stolen from U.S. military installations.

It was the kind of dealing Wilson loved. Better than an orgasm, he'd say.

2

The forces that shaped him, what he was and would become, were in motion long before he joined the CIA. The agency afforded him the opportunity to act on them.

There hadn't been a time in his life when he was not thinking about money. These days, as you fly over it, the terrain around Nampa, Idaho, where Wilson was born on May 3, 1928, is a startling verdant oasis springing out of seemingly endless vistas of mountain-ringed high desert sagebrush north of the Snake River. Massive irrigation has made Canyon County one of the richest agricultural areas in the nation.

But back in the Great Depression, things were quite different. As a fourth-grader, Wilson used to hang around the auction yard on Saturday when farmers brought in their calves. The farmers were anxious to get back to their fields, so young Ed would bid on the spot for a calf, offering a quarter. A farmer would demand a dollar and a quarter. After haggling, Wilson would acquire the calf for thirty-five or forty cents. Then he would sell it for seventy-five cents, even a dollar. Some Saturdays he cleared as much as five or ten dollars. The third of four children, with an older brother and sister and a younger brother, he had at that tender age become the dependable family breadwinner. He knew this to be true. His mother had told him so.

He attended a rural two-room schoolhouse on Black Cat Road. His teacher, Reta Fletcher, remembered him well as an outgoing, diligent student, not intellectual but, you know, smart. She also remembered that even then he spoke of how he was going to better himself. She'd see, he said. A neighboring farmer, Chester Eggers, said he was "kind of a goer and quite a forceful fellow." In Nampa High School he joined the Future Farmers of America.

His father was a dirt-poor homesteader from Iowa, attracted to Idaho by the new irrigation projects under way there. Wilson professed to have despised him, but his real feelings were far more confused. He saw him as an impractical dreamer, unable to provide for his wife and children. Still, he was forced to recognize how popular his father was in the community—a low-keyed, friendly man with a sly sense of humor. Just about everyone who was a member of the congregation at the local Nazarene church could recall the Sunday morning when Wilson's father emerged after services to find a turkey perched on the radiator cap of his car. How he had grabbed it and presented it to the minister, saying if this bird was that bent on being at church, it was certainly ready for a greater glory. Nothing brought forth the dichotomy of Wilson's attitude more than his father's death in 1968 at the age of seventy. At the wake, he saw a packed funeral home—adults somber and teary-eyed, children openly crying—and attempted to reconcile his emotions by allowing that while his father might have been esteemed for his readiness to lend a helping hand to others, he sure hadn't done much for his own kids.

He expressed no ambivalence about his mother. She was tough, hard and practical, he would say, qualities he admired and felt were characteristic of himself. She was Canadian, from Calgary, a nurse who had met his father during a nursing assignment in Idaho and bowled over by his engaging manner had married him immediately. He liked to point out that he drew physically from his mother, a big-boned woman five feet ten, instead of his rather slight and stoop-shouldered father.

One year his father trekked the family across Idaho and Montana to Devils Lake, North Dakota, where he failed at running a tire sales and repair shop. Wilson never forgot the bitter winter cold and the misery of their life. He had a newspaper route. Sometimes he got lucky and was able to roll a drunk.

They returned to Nampa at the outset of World War II.
Wilson, his mother, his brothers and sister pitched in to work
a sixty-acre farm, raising grain and some livestock, while his
father traveled around the state, buying and selling cattle. Wilson's older brother, Wilbur, joined the merchant marine and
whenever a school vacation coincided with his brother's return
from a voyage, Ed hitchhiked to California to see him and listen
spellbound to his latest adventures.

The Nazarene sect, a fundamentalist offshoot of Metho-
dism, operated a college in Nampa and he went to it for a year.
But in 1947, after the spring planting, he took off for California
again. His brother helped him get a card in the Sailors Union
of the Pacific and he shipped out as an ordinary seaman to
China, Japan and the Philippines, returning home only to help
with the crops.

It was a crucial period for him. Fights occurred all the time,
on ship and in waterfront dives throughout the Far East. Wilson
was a strapping nineteen-year-old by then with enormous fists,
and he learned what he believed was the bottom-line tenet of life
—the survival of the fittest. He didn't win every fight he was in,
and there was one he never forgot. An ex-logger in the crew had
been picking on the ship's alcoholic carpenter. Wilson decided
to challenge the bully and ended up unconscious on a Tokyo
dock. It wasn't losing that he remembered. It was what happened when the carpenter came to him a day later, while he was
still lying in his bunk trying to recover, and asked why he had
gotten into the fight. After Wilson told him, the carpenter said,
"Gee, he wasn't bothering me that much." It was the best lesson
he ever got, Wilson liked to say. Wiped out any last vestige of
idealism in him.

At sea he also developed a curious, almost pathological,
hatred of homosexuals. The first incident happened one night
when he was awakened in his bunk by a groping hand. He came
out of the bunk and reached for a light, but by the time he turned
it on, everyone in sight was apparently asleep. The next time it
happened, Wilson grabbed the hand and held it until he got the
light on, and then methodically beat the fellow to a pulp. That
was the way you had to handle faggots, he always said. Beat the
living hell out of them every chance you got.

He tried a logging camp in northern Oregon for a few
months, but the snow and cold and isolation became too dispir-

iting. There had to be a better way, he thought, and he took a bus to Portland and enrolled in the University of Portland, a Catholic school run by the Holy Cross order. It was, he said, the first time he had seen men wearing "dresses."

Ed Wilson had sixty dollars in his pocket. He got a job at a local laundry as a combination night watchman, janitor and maintenance man, arranging his academic schedule so that he attended classes in the morning, slept in the afternoon, took additional classes at night, arrived at the laundry at nine P.M., slept for a couple more hours and then did his cleanup and maintenance duties till eight A.M.

He returned to Nampa to put in the crops, borrowed $300 as a down payment on a small grain harvester and ran it through the farm country. By the time he was back in college, he had cleared $2,000. He kept his job at the laundry, but now at least he could afford a secondhand car to get to it, and anticipating some sort of corporate career, he elected a major in industrial psychology. He had no social life. Occasionally he would bed down with a whore. The next summer Wilson borrowed money for a bigger self-propelled combine and earned $5,000. The third summer, recruiting his younger brother, Robert, he gambled on two combines and netted $10,000.

He graduated from college in 1951, but the Korean War was raging, and Wilson's Nampa draft board was breathing down his neck. He applied to both the Army's Counter Intelligence Corps and the Marine Officers Candidate School. The Marine acceptance came through first and he was sent to Quantico, Virginia. In superb physical shape, he breezed through OCS. Money remained his chief preoccupation. Every weekend he got off from training, Officer Candidate Wilson would hop the cheapest night flight to Detroit, buy two new cars at factory prices, drive one, towing the other, back to Quantico, where he sold them at a profit, undercutting nearby dealers. Sometimes he would double the number of cars he delivered by taking along a fellow candidate he had befriended named Howard Wickham.

As an infantry second lieutenant, he was stationed in Japan, then Korea. The fighting was over by the time he arrived and he spent most of his time leading patrols along the demilitarized zone between North Korea and South Korea. In early 1955, promoted to first lieutenant, he tumbled down a mountainside

and tore up his knee so badly that he was flown back to the
Marine hospital at Camp Pendleton, California. After three
months of treatment, he was told he would be discharged with
a ten percent disability. He hitched a ride on a Navy plane to
Washington, hoping to wangle a transfer to the Marine Air
Wing.

On the flight, Wilson started telling a civilian passenger
sitting next to him about his past life, and how he was trying to
retain his commission and hoping that maybe the knee injury
wouldn't count as much being a pilot as it did in the infantry.
The man listened and finally said that if things didn't work out
with the Marines, Wilson ought to give some thought to the
CIA. The agency might be in the market for someone like him,
the man said, without identifying himself.

He gave Wilson a phone number and a contact name, Peter
Tomley, to call. The suggestion appealed to him. During his
days as a seaman, he had devoured spy novels and imagined
what it would be like to be a secret agent infiltrating ports like
Hong Kong and Singapore. It was the reason he had applied to
Army Counter Intelligence. And when he was informed that the
Marines had more pilots than they knew what to do with, he
made the call and was directed to 2400 E Street in northwest
Washington, where CIA headquarters then was located in a
fenced-in cluster of yellow buildings near the Potomac.

He filled out his personal history statement, underwent a
battery of medical and psychological tests, scoring well as the
kind of adaptive, nonreflective, self-reliant, action-oriented per-
sonality-type the CIA especially prized, and waited while a
lengthy security check was conducted, which determined,
among other things, that he was "a person of good character,
of the highest integrity, opposed to Communist ideals, and loyal
to the U.S."

A last hurdle remained, the forbidding visit to Building 13,
one of a number of barrackslike structures left over from World
War II on the mall by the Washington Monument that the CIA
also was occupying until its massive new complex at Langley was
completed. In Building 13, an exhaustive polygraph examination, designed to ferret out whatever intimate secrets might still
remain hidden, was administered to every CIA applicant.

When Wilson was asked if he'd ever had any homosexual
experiences, he answered no and felt his blood pounding, the

sweat on his palms, and fancied the pens measuring his physiological response going right off the graph paper. He would explain later that he had been thinking about the groping hand in his shipboard bunk. In a fury he rejoined his group, about twenty men in all, and after the CIA security officer in charge asked if anyone had anything else to say, Wilson snarled, "Yeah, how do you get out of this goddamn place? I don't think I passed the goddamn Building 13, and as far as I'm concerned, I don't give a shit." The security man wanted to know what the problem was, and when Wilson told him about the homosexual question, he laughed and told Wilson not to worry, he'd passed, that just about everybody in the room was in the same boat. Ed Wilson never forgot the incident. From then on, whenever he was trying to convince somebody about something, he'd always say, "I swear it. I'll take a polygraph on it."

After promising to remain single for at least two years, he signed a secrecy agreement, vowing never to reveal his intelligence activities, and was sworn into the CIA on October 27, 1955. He was now a member of the Company. He did not know what he would be doing, only that he would have a civil service rating of GS-5 with a starting salary of $3,670 plus an expense allowance. It was not even half of what he had made running a combine during his college summers.

But Wilson figured quite correctly that he was entering a fascinating new world filled with unimaginable possibilities.

THREE

He was caught up immediately in the aura of the CIA. It was like putting on a magic coat that made you invisible and invincible.

Within weeks of being sworn in, Wilson stood with the others at a remote Air Force base in the Nevada desert north of Las Vegas, listening as the legendary director of the CIA himself, Allen Dulles, told them that they were embarking on a mission that would revolutionize the gathering of intelligence, that would forever change its nature.

Behind Dulles as he spoke, so ungainly on the ground with its long, drooping wings, was what the Russians would come to call the Black Lady of Espionage—the high-altitude U-2 spy plane, whose existence then was the agency's most closely held secret.

Wilson had been assigned to the same CIA branch that had investigated him for six months and had given him his lie-detector test, the Office of Security. And now he was a member of a special sixty-man detachment that would guard the planes and keep tabs on the pilots, the support crews and their families. Wilson was one of the earliest recruits, and his status and responsibilities were upgraded almost at once when nine veteran security officers died in a crash on the way to Nevada from Washington.

Since the U-2s would be operating from bases overseas, he was given a fake job cover as an international representative for Maritime Survey Associates, with a mail-drop address at 80 Boylston Street, Boston, Massachusetts.

Every three weeks Wilson got time off from his training. He would either drive or fly to San Diego to see Barbara Hagen, a girl he'd met on a blind date while his knee was being treated at Camp Pendleton. Born and raised in New Jersey, she had come out to visit a relative in the Marine Corps and decided to stay on as a lab technician at San Diego State College Hospital. Practically a nurse, like his mother, Wilson would think.

There were other pleasing comparisons. Like his mother, she had nothing flighty about her. And like him, she'd had to work her way through college, Rutgers University, to obtain a degree. When she asked him what he was doing, he told her about his seaman's background and used his Maritime Associates cover. The job was going to keep him away for long stretches at a time, he said, but he was confident he was headed somewhere.

Four U-2s were based near Adana on the southern coast of Turkey, and Wilson went with them. Among the pilots he watched over was Francis Gary Powers, whom the Soviets would finally manage to shoot down three years later.

Whenever he could, on courier trips back to the States bringing U-2 photographs of Russian missile sites, he continued to see Barbara. In mid-1957 she told Ed she couldn't wait for him any longer. Unaccustomed to women he hadn't paid for, Wilson was flabbergasted. He had no idea she wanted to marry him. And pleased and excited that someone desired him, he asked the Office of Security for permission. The answer was no. In desperation, he told Barbara what his real job was. That mollified her and she got work in Washington to make it easier for them to see each other when he came in on a flight.

Finally the agency gave its approval and they were married in her hometown, Flemington, New Jersey, on September 28, 1957. Wilson's friend from his Quantico days, Howard Wickham, was his best man. He and Barbara had a three-day honeymoon before he returned to Turkey. The following February he learned she was pregnant. He began pressing for a domestic assignment and in January 1959, three months after their first son, Karl, was born, Wilson was transferred to the CIA's Washington field office.

Mostly he did security investigations. For a time he guarded a KGB defector who had turned in the most important Russian spy the United States had yet nabbed, Colonel Rudolf Abel. There was a nice irony to this: Abel would eventually be traded back to the Soviets for the captured U-2 pilot, Gary Powers.

The CIA was engaged in widespread illegal domestic mail intercepts and wiretaps, and one day while tapping the phone of a foreign affairs specialist for *Newsweek* magazine, Wilson found himself recording a call with Vice President Nixon. It was a heady power trip. "You'll never guess who I was listening to today," he said to his wife.

Years later, when Wilson was regularly in the headlines, he would be described as having played an important role in the Bay of Pigs invasion. The closest he came to it, though, was as a security man for an Air Force colonel who went to Alabama to enlist pilots from the state air national guard to support the invasion. When the Bay of Pigs took place, Wilson actually was undercover as a graduate student at Cornell University.

2

It was a dramatic turn in his intelligence career. He'd seen the Office of Security as a dead end for a man of his ambitions. What he coveted was entry into the CIA's clandestine services, especially its International Organizations Division, which ran labor operations, penetrated student groups and infiltrated the media.

Labor was a big-ticket item for the CIA. The agency, working through friendly leaders in American organized labor, had achieved a genuine triumph in creating and funding free trade unions against their Communist-dominated opposition in post–World War II Europe.

With his union background in the merchant marine and his track record in security, Wilson argued that he had ideal qualifications and persuaded a covert staff officer to run interference for him. In September 1960, just after his second son, Eric, was born, he got what he wanted.

His status in the agency also changed. Covert agents working under deep commercial cover were usually placed on contract. This gave the CIA a case for "plausible deniability" if questions were ever raised about whether the operative was an employee. And it gave the agency a way to beat budgetary staff limits, which didn't apply to contract personnel. Many of these contracts were for a specified time or task, but Wilson's was a permanent career contract, subjecting him only to the same performance scrutiny that every staff officer periodically received, and providing the same medical and pension benefits. Barring across-the-board cutbacks, Wilson was in the CIA for as long as he wished.

The CIA sent Wilson to the School for Industrial and Labor Relations at Cornell. He specialized in international labor studies. It was tough, he remarked to a friend, "competing against all those New York Jews." After a year of on-campus courses, he had a fellowship to go abroad, preferably under trade union auspices. Wilson approached Paul Hall, the president of the Seafarers International Union of North America, for a job. The Seafarers had been carefully selected. Wilson had kept up his membership in its Pacific branch and he arrived now with legitimate academic references. Best of all for the union, Wilson could accept a modest salary—$193.72 a month plus expenses—since Cornell supposedly would be picking up the rest of the tab. Hall had no idea the CIA was involved.

Wilson left with his family for Belgium in September 1961. He rented a house in the village of Schotenhof outside Antwerp, one of the continent's busiest ports, and within a short drive of Brussels, headquarters for the agency-backed International Confederation of Free Trade Unions. As Hall's personal representative, he moved quickly into important European labor circles and made sure to write chatty reports back to Cornell about attending conferences in Geneva, Paris, London and West Berlin.

For his other life, in the CIA, he began monitoring cargoes being shipped out of Antwerp for Castro's Cuba; he set up a network of informants to identify key Communists on the Antwerp docks; he infiltrated left-wing unions to foment trouble, urging them on to even more radical acts that would produce police crackdowns; and on a sophomoric level that gave him great glee, he would make life miserable for visiting Soviet-bloc labor delegations by seeing to it that pests like ants and roaches were let loose in their hotel rooms and that the toilets were plugged up. He also took on hazardous assignments, packing a

pistol on trips to Marseilles for agency payoffs to Corsican mob-
sters to keep the Communist dockworkers in line.

Through all this, money remained a concern. In March
1962 he sent a hurt letter to Paul Hall complaining about the
cancellation of an agreement allowing him to take $25 a week
out of expenses as a salary supplement. "As indicated when I
first requested a job," he wrote, "some possible salary remuner-
ation in the form of expenses because of foreign taxes was and
is still desirable." Wilson, who had been raised to a GS-7 grade,
was getting $5,740 annually from the agency. He also had invei-
gled the CIA into giving his wife a part-time secretarial contract.

Wilson returned to New York when his Cornell grant ran
out. Hall, pleased with his work for Seafarers in the international
labor community, upped his pay and dispatched him to Washington to help out with the union's lobbying on Capitol Hill. Six
months later, after he had gotten to be known around town, the
agency arranged his transfer to the International Department of
the AFL-CIO, which functioned for organized labor in America
as a kind of miniature U.S. Department of State. Unlike Hall, its
leadership, including the son-in-law of AFL-CIO president
George Meany, knew exactly where Wilson was coming from. He
was first sent to Latin America to help fight left-wing union-
organizing drives. Then he went to the Far East.

In 1963 he was in Saigon when the president of Vietnam,
Ngo Dinh Diem, was overthrown and assassinated. An important Vietnamese labor leader and supporter of Diem, Tran Quoc
Buu, whom the CIA thought might be turned into a collaborator
to serve its interests, wound up in jail. As the AFL-CIO's representative on the spot, Wilson was ordered to get him out. He
went right to the top, demanding and receiving an audience with
Ambassador Henry Cabot Lodge. Buu was promptly released
and went on to become everything the agency had hoped.

3

Then, in the summer of 1964, the CIA sent Wilson down
a path that profoundly altered his life professionally and personally. He was assigned to Special Operations, which combined
some of the activities of his old division with covert paramilitary
missions around the globe.

The groundwork for his new role was painstakingly laid.
First Langley had the AFL-CIO recommend him as an advance

man in Hubert Humphrey's run for vice president. The choice of Humphrey on the Democratic ticket had come at the last minute and his campaign manager, a Washington lawyer named Martin McNamara, was glad to get all the help he could.

Wilson stayed close to Washington, advancing Humphrey appearances chiefly in Maryland and Pennsylvania, which kept him in close contact with McNamara. After the election, he asked a favor of McNamara. He had spoken about his merchant marine past and said he wanted to start up his own business in the ocean freight forwarding field. Would McNamara mind doing the legal paperwork? McNamara wasn't surprised. He had found Wilson a gregarious, fast-moving, very sociable fellow, smart and ambitious, and he agreed to incorporate Wilson's new firm, Maritime Consulting Associates.

So if anyone ever bothered to check the history of Maritime Consulting, it would appear quite aboveboard. It was actually a CIA proprietary, one of the many front companies the agency had to disguise its black arts. Special Operations had a logistics branch for land, sea and air support. Ed Wilson would be in charge of the sea end of things. Some proprietaries were shells; others, like Maritime Consulting, were designed to be fully operational. The CIA paid for office space, staffing and office equipment, including a telex, at a cost that would eventually reach over $100,000 annually, and picked up the tab for all the travel and entertainment expenses Wilson got so adept at submitting.

Then he asked McNamara for another favor, to introduce him to key people at the Department of Agriculture. Congress had authorized mammoth grain shipments to underdeveloped countries. Wilson needed a piece of the action to enhance his legitimacy, and he got it. As further cover, he went to his friend and best man, Howard Wickham, and recruited him to be Maritime Consulting's figurehead president. Wickham by now knew that Wilson was in the spy business and he'd do anything, he said, to help his country.

As it did with all intelligence officers and career contract employees engaged in clandestine missions, the CIA assigned Wilson a pseudonym in agency files to protect his real identity. These pseudonyms consist of a first and last name with a middle initial. Wilson's was Greek, which added a nice shipping touch.

His job was to bring in cargoes wherever the CIA wanted

its participation untraceable, in Latin America, Africa, the Middle East and Southeast Asia. He sent incendiary, crowd-dispersion and harassment devices to Chile, Brazil and Venezuela. Arms to the Dominican Republic when another Castro-like takeover was feared. Advanced communications gear to Morocco. Weapons of all kinds to Angola. A whole range of high-tech electronic equipment to Iran. More arms for a CIA-backed coup in Indonesia. Military parts and supplies to Taiwan and the Philippines. Logistical support for the so-called secret war the CIA began to wage in Laos. He also arranged for boats—flotillas of them, if required—such as the ones used in continuing raids against Cuba.

In the countries receiving agency consignments, he hustled other business. The agency was delighted. It only deepened his cover. Sometimes Wilson would nudge up the costs of these transactions, even those ordered by the CIA. There was minimal auditing and little thought given to what he was doing, as long as he delivered the goods. Proprietaries were not set up to make money, although occasionally it happened. Wilson had protection on another front. If the Internal Revenue Service nosed around, the fact that he was running a cover CIA operation took care of that.

4

The best part, however, was his case officer, Tom Clines.

Every deep-cover agent like Wilson had one, the link to Langley. He and Clines hit it right off. And through Clines, many more doors would open. Oddly, they had met previously, in the late summer of 1960, when neither knew the other was CIA. Clines had just returned from a tour in Germany as Wilson, preparing to go to Cornell, was selling the small house he owned in northern Virginia. He had stopped at his realtor's and there was Clines, dabbling in real estate on weekends.

When he became Wilson's case officer, he also was working toward a degree in business administration under CIA auspices at American University. He was a big, bluff, genial man, two years younger than Wilson, who had practically grown up in the CIA, starting out as a mail boy in 1949. He was promoted to courier and then moved into personnel work. In 1958 he was sent to West Germany as an administrative man.

After the Bay of Pigs fiasco, he was assigned to the CIA

station in Miami, which, under the cryptonym JM/WAVE, sponsored hundreds of sabotage raids inside Cuba, as well as a series of assassination attempts against Castro. Clines was the "control" for a string of Cuban exiles, who idolized him as a tangible symbol that the ball game wasn't over, that Cuba would yet be liberated.

Privately, though, Clines, who never could learn Spanish, was contemptuous of most of them and regaled Wilson with endless tales of their ineptitude. No wonder, he'd say, that the Bay of Pigs had flopped. The story Wilson most remembered was one Clines told him about how this Cuban kid had begged to be sent in on a raid. Finally Clines had said okay. The next morning when Clines arrived at a supermarket parking lot in Miami's Little Havana to pick him up, the kid was standing on top of a car, letting everyone within shouting distance know that he was going in. Clines didn't say anything. He drove the kid down the Florida keys to a spot several miles from the real boat rendezvous and dropped him off. "What'd he do?" Wilson asked, and Clines said, "Who cares?" and the two men laughed over their drinks.

At least Wilson found it cheering that Clines wasn't earning all that much more than he was. It was a fact of agency life. Holdovers from the rather romantic days of the OSS during the Second World War were in the main monied Ivy Leaguers. But now the CIA was decidedly middle-class. In the ranks, salaries were tied to Government Service grades that applied as well to someone working, say, in the Department of Commerce. When Wilson was starting up Maritime Consulting, the highest grade, a GS-18, earned $25,382, with pensions effective after twenty years.

Every so often, Clines would touch Wilson for a loan, fifty here, a hundred there. After all, Wilson had his proprietary expense account—and Clines was the one who wrote up his evaluation reports.

FOUR

Within the CIA's tightly knit covert side, word of a master stroke got around fast. And after the Congo, Ed Wilson had it made.

In 1965 the agency-backed forces of General Joseph Mobutu were locked in combat in the former Belgian Congo, now Zaire, against rebel troops supported by Russia and Red China. It was the first all-out East-West confrontation on the African continent.

The core of the agency's ground forces were mercenaries recruited from South Africa, Rhodesia and Kenya. Air cover came from vintage B-26 bombers and T-28 trainer jets converted to fighters, flown by Cuban pilots left over from the Bay of Pigs.

The Russians and the Chinese, meanwhile, were airlifting weapons and medical supplies from Algeria and Gamal Nasser's Egypt into the Sudan and Uganda, where they were trucked into the Congo. When the Cuban pilots closed off the overland routes, shipments were ferried at night from Tanzania across Lake Tanganyika.

Everyone agreed that the new Navy patrol craft called Swift boats would be ideal to interdict the arms flow. Built by a company in Louisiana, they were originally designed to service offshore oil drilling rigs in the Gulf of Mexico, but the

Navy had adapted them for duty in the rivers, bays and estuaries of Vietnam. High-speed, with a shallow draft and aluminum hulls, they were fifty feet long and packed three heavy machine guns as well as an eighty-one-millimeter mortar. The problem, though, was how to plop them down in a lake in the middle of Africa.

Wilson came up with an audacious solution. Why not slice them in half, even thirds, so they'd fit in C-130 cargo planes, and weld them together again on the shores of Lake Tanganyika? He consulted the manufacturer, Stewart Seacraft, and the answer was yes, it could be done. Three of the Swift boats were flown in that way. To man them, Clines recruited Cuban skippers and crews who had been on hit-and-run missions out of Florida, and the last Congolese rebel supply line was cut.

After this, Clines was able to engineer some rapid promotions for Wilson and by 1966 he was a GS-11. Meanwhile Clines, always short of money, continued to get regular loans from Wilson. Clines liked the high life and was constantly hustling big deals, mostly in real estate, that never seemed to materialize, trying to impress people by grabbing checks and being out on the town with an array of girl friends.

The promotions meant more pay. But by now Wilson had begun to learn how to make the most of his schizoid existence as an agency deep-cover man on the one hand and an apparently legitimate shipper on the other, and prestige was becoming equally important to him.

Wilson's fortunes were rising elsewhere. Barbara Wilson, as upwardly mobile as he, had gotten into real estate herself. Unlike Clines, though, she bought small, ramshackle houses, fixed them up, with Wilson doing much of the refurbishing at night, and rented them to Washington's transient military population for enough to handle at least the mortgage payments while their value increased. And they had acquired the first substantial home of their own, a rambling place with fourteen acres in Vienna, Virginia. Vienna has since become a bedroom suburb of Washington, but it was then considered pretty far out in the country, and Wilson was able to buy it for $60,000.

2

He began expanding his contacts in the CIA.

The most important was Theodore Shackley. Clines was the

connection. Clines had been with Shackley when he was chief of station in Miami during its anti-Castro heyday.

Before that, in Germany, Shackley had been part of the team that surreptitiously engineered the famous tunnel between West Berlin and East Berlin so the agency could tap Russian phone lines. It then ranked as one of the CIA's finest exploits until it was belatedly discovered that the KGB had known about the tunnel almost from the beginning, but elected to do nothing for months in order not to blow its informant, a mole Moscow had buried deep inside MI-6, the British Secret Intelligence Service.

Wilson was mightily impressed to be socializing with the likes of Shackley. The whispers accompanied Shackley wherever he went. This was a fellow on the move, a surefire candidate for the CIA's directorship some day. He was a tall fair-skinned man who peered through thick horn-rimmed glasses. People usually thought of him as cold and distant, although his admirers said this demeanor was simply the expression of a keen, analytical, no-nonsense mind. And he was the most secretive of men, as elusive as he was well known.

Behind his back, he was called the Blond Ghost. Nobody seemed to know, for instance, what college he had attended, or indeed if he had ever gone to college at all. Rumors abounded that he was an orphan, that the agency had become his surrogate family, his whole life, and Shackley did nothing to discourage this talk. As Frank Snepp, a CIA analyst who had once served under Shackley and heard the rumors, said, "You just don't go up to your boss and ask him if it's true he was an orphan."

Years later, after Shackley was effectively forced into retirement from the agency because of his relationship with Edwin P. Wilson, he wrote a book extolling covert action and thus himself.

I called a friend of mine at his publisher's and asked him to look in Shackley's publicity folder, hoping for a few vital statistics. He called back in astonishment. He had never seen one so bare. There was a list of about ninety academicians and businesspeople to whom Shackley wanted the book sent, and a notation that he was one of America's most distinguished and respected intelligence officers, a three-time recipient of the CIA's highest decoration, the Distinguished Intelligence Medal.

That was it. Not even the most nominal information was included, a birthplace or birthdate.

After I finally obtained a record of his agency career, I learned that he had been born in Springfield, Massachusetts, on July 16, 1927. His parents separated when he was a boy and he moved to Palm Beach, Florida, with his mother. His father died when Shackley was twenty-three and a senior at the University of Maryland, from which he graduated with a B.A. in political science and history. Not a great deal to hide, unless one desired to create a sense of mystery, to make others wonder, keep them off balance.

In 1966 Shackley was on his way to another sensitive post, to be station chief in Laos, where he would direct some twenty-five thousand Meo mountain tribesmen in a covert war that at the time most Americans never heard of. These nomadic tribesmen in the northern part of Laos, outside the mainstream of its national life, had initially been organized by the CIA into counterinsurgency cadres to resist the Pathet Lao, the Laotian equivalent of the Viet Cong. But the operation was drastically enlarged: the Meos were structured into battalion-strength units, complete with a general, and were dragged directly into the Vietnam morass. This got the attention of the regular North Vietnamese army and before it was over, by which point Shackley was long gone, ten thousand Meos had fled to Thailand, all that remained of a population that once numbered a quarter of a million.

Clines was transferred to Laos to work for Shackley, as he had in Miami. This meant a new case officer for Wilson, but Maritime Consulting had achieved a momentum of its own that made it practically autonomous, and agency review was perfunctory. Under its commercial cover tons of equipment and supplies were sent in to support the secret war, and Wilson himself visited Vientiane, the Laotian capital. Shackley especially prized the electronic beepers that Wilson shipped in. These beepers would be planted in Communist Pathet Lao units by infiltrating Meo tribesmen, or perhaps secreted in a flashlight or medical-aid kit left along a trail frequented by the Pathet Lao. Spotter planes picked up the beeps and ordered in air strikes.

One of the ace spotters who operated closely with Shackley and Clines was a much-decorated Air Force officer named Richard V. Secord, a West Pointer and veteran combat pilot in

Vietnam. Like their ties to Wilson, his would bring about unexpectedly early retirement, in Secord's case from a career that had reached rarified Pentagon levels and promised even better things ahead.

3

Hubert Humphrey's old campaign manager Martin McNamara hadn't seen Wilson since he'd helped him start up Maritime Consulting. Then, in 1969, McNamara spotted him in a Washington restaurant lunching with a man named Robert Keith Gray. Well, well, mused McNamara, Ed's really moving into the big time.

Gray had been appointments secretary to President Eisenhower. A bachelor of fastidious taste and manner, he already was a superstar lobbyist and power broker, heading up the Washington office of Hill & Knowlton, one of the largest public relations firms in the country. In Ronald Reagan's 1980 election campaign he played a key advisory role, reporting directly to campaign manager William J. Casey, whom Reagan later appointed as his director of the CIA. He then would go on to form his own firm, Gray and Company, with an unforgettable address on its gray stationery, which lacked both a street and number—just The Power House, Washington, D.C.

At the time McNamara spied Wilson and Gray together, Wilson, with the agency's blessing, was about to dissolve Maritime Consulting in favor of another, broader-based proprietary called Consultants International. Over a decade later, when Wilson began making such unsavory news, a Washington reporter trying to unearth whatever he could about the fugitive discovered that Robert Keith Gray was listed as a Consultants International director. In an interview, Gray was quoted as saying that he barely knew Wilson, his acquaintance with him so passing that it wasn't worth mentioning. Being listed on the board was news to him; it was done without his knowledge.

This didn't quite jibe with what McNamara had seen. I'd also heard that Gray had sponsored Wilson's membership in Washington's chic George Town Club, where he could rub shoulders with other wheeler-dealers like Tongsun Park, the South Korean who became famous for spreading wads of cash on Capitol Hill, and Peter Malatesta, a flamboyant local figure who'd been an aide to Vice President Spiro Agnew.

Finally, Gray agreed to see me. His headquarters had once been an electric generating station. But an interior decorator had been hard at work. Now a reception area rose three stories high, boasting exposed brick and beams and a burnished oak floor. Potted plants arched gracefully over deep leather couches. There was the hum of metaphorical electricity everywhere. Clocks showed the hour in various parts of the world. Behind a glassed-in enclosure, television screens monitored the three networks and a cable news channel. Above, in other glassed-in, cantilevered offices, people busily conferred, telephoned, bent over computers.

In Gray's office, overlooking the floor, there were photographs of him with every president since Eisenhower, all warmly inscribed. He was a slim, small man, sixty-two, exquisitely tailored, with closely cropped white hair. His eyes were vaguely hazel and, for me, expressionless. He said that he was sorry he wasn't going to be of more help about Wilson and reiterated his comments in the interview I had read. "We were elevator buddies," Gray said. "He seemed very likeable."

"Elevator buddies?"

"Yes," he said as if I were retarded. "Sometimes we rode up and down together in the same elevator."

I suggested that the two of them having had adjoining offices in one building might be a coincidence, but to have it occur in a second one as well was stretching fate.

Gray shrugged. At last he said, "He was always trying to get business from me. Referrals. As far as I was concerned, he was just another five-percenter. I didn't take him seriously."

Had Gray sponsored his club membership?

"I might have. I can't recall."

According to records in my possession, Gray had accompanied Wilson on a two-week trip to Taiwan in 1969. Wilson had already shipped in a number of cargoes for the CIA, including such covert items as torpedo tube replacements for Taiwanese submarines. Now he was going there himself to supervise the arrival of air-filtering machines for the fortified caves on the outer Taiwanese islands of Quemoy and Matsu, and Gray went along with him to try to sign up Taiwan as a public relations client.

"Two weeks with Wilson in Taiwan?" I said. "That's some elevator trip."

"I was a guest of the government," Gray insisted, as though it was happenstance that they were on the same plane. "There was a general and an admiral, too."

"Didn't you talk? Can you give me any anecdotes about Wilson?"

"No."

"Did he ever hint that he was in the CIA, or the intelligence community?"

"No."

About twenty minutes had elapsed. Gray's intercom phone buzzed. He looked at his watch. "I'm sorry," he said. "I have to run. I have an important meeting at the Turkish embassy."

He departed so quickly that I didn't have a chance to ask a last question. Gray had claimed practically no knowledge of Wilson. Yet ten years before, in the course of a top secret Navy review of Wilson's intelligence career, Gray had described him as a person of "unqualified trust" with whom he'd been in contact "professionally two or three times a month" since 1963.

I attempted to see Gray again, without success. After all, why should he bother with me? He was on a first-name basis with most of the key officials in the Reagan administration and was said to be especially close to Edwin Meese, the president's confidant who was about to be appointed attorney general of the United States. He also had a galaxy of former Democratic officeholders working for him. Besides, an FBI agent had already questioned him about Wilson. Gray had given him essentially the same answers as he had to the reporter who first interviewed him, and nothing more had happened.

In a world like this, it was easy to see how Ed Wilson came to believe he could do just about anything he wanted to.

4

Gray wasn't the only connection he cultivated.

He also worked Capitol Hill, becoming a familiar face around the offices of such senators as Strom Thurmond of South Carolina and John McClellan of Arkansas. He was after more commercial business, all the while dropping thinly veiled hints that he served U.S. intelligence interests.

As the line between his covert CIA activity and personal profit increasingly blurred, he managed to make it seem almost unpatriotic to turn him away. He made a specialty of being a consulting expert on containerized cargo shipments. He got chummy with another powerful senator, Mississippi's James O. Eastland, and through him became the representative of the state's main outlet to the sea, Gulfport.

According to a letter in Pentagon files, Eastland wrote to the chief of the U.S. Army Materiel Command in 1969, "I regret not expressing to you sooner my sincere appreciation for your courtesy to Mr. Edwin P. Wilson," adding that he was "most hopeful of the full utilization of this [Gulfport] asset for the movement of substantial quantities of military cargo in containers."

Wilson was quick to exploit less prominent government employees. Senator Eastland introduced him to his "good friend" Paul Cyr, once an intrepid agent behind the lines for the OSS during World War II and now congressional liaison for the Army Materiel Command. As soon as he discovered that Cyr was in financial trouble because of severe drinking problems, Wilson put him on the payroll of Consultants International while he was still working for the Pentagon, and through him got inside information on the Army's shipping needs.

In 1970 Wilson's net worth was in excess of $200,000. By replacing Maritime Consulting with Consultants International, he had moved out of pure shipping into more generalized deal-making. The CIA continued to subsidize his operation and he made sure to fulfill agency commitments and keep up his contacts.

By then Theodore Shackley, after his Laos tour, had been appointed chief of station in Saigon, which, like Miami in its time, was the biggest one going, and Wilson would pop over to see him every so often.

Shackley remained as aloof and mysterious as ever to those under him. His wife and daughter stayed in Hong Kong most of the time. His house had characterless agency-supplied furnishings. A subordinate who regularly went there in the evening to brief him recalled that he would always find a lamp shining in his face, as if he were undergoing an interrogation. No books were visible; just memos and reports. But Shackley appeared to relish the trappings of power, and in Saigon he always had a big security detail and zipped through the streets with a motorcycle escort, like a proconsul.

If Shackley was close to anyone, to the naked eye at least, it was Erich Fritz von Marbod, from Wenatchee, Washington.

An army parachutist at sixteen, then a graduate of the Harvard School of Business, he had progressed rapidly through various Pentagon planning positions, among them international affairs and intelligence, which had brought the two men together. While Shackley was the Saigon station chief, von Marbod became comptroller of the Defense Security Assistance Agency and because of Vietnam they were thrown together once more. In appearance and demeanor they could not have been more dissimilar: Shackley tall and austere; von Marbod a reddish-haired, bantam-rooster type, jovial, backslapping. But they both were on the way up. Von Marbod would become the arbiter of all military assistance to Vietnam.

Tom Clines returned to Langley as a senior operations officer. He'd go on to attend the Navy War College. The agency underwrote his master's degree in international affairs at George Washington University as a prelude to his joining the CIA's International Communism Branch, which devoted itself to analyzing the worldwide aspirations of the Kremlin. In Washington, relations between Wilson and his old case officer changed dramatically. Clines often volunteered to drive Wilson around in a beat-up Volkswagen he had. Finally Wilson told him he couldn't afford to be seen in a car like that, and gave him the cash for a new one.

5

For Edwin P. Wilson, the future looked golden. And toward the end of 1970, he began negotiating the first major acquisition in what would become his Mount Airy Farms estate in Upperville, Virginia.

But suddenly and unexpectedly the smooth road Wilson was traveling got very rocky. Richard Nixon had always been paranoid about the CIA. He blamed the CIA in large part for his presidential defeat by John Kennedy—for letting Kennedy get away with his campaign oratory about a missile gap when in fact there was no missile gap, for telling Kennedy about the Cuban invasion plans, so Kennedy could make speeches about the need to do something about Castro, while Nixon, bound to secrecy as the vice president, was forced to remain mute. And now, as the president, under intense pressure to terminate the Vietnam War, Nixon was convinced he wasn't getting sufficient advance notice about what the enemy was planning next. All they had at

Langley, he ranted to his aide John Ehrlichman, was "forty thousand people reading newspapers."

James Schlesinger, then the assistant head of the Office of Management and Budget, was ordered to examine the CIA from top to bottom. He concluded that intelligence cost-control was a joke and that U.S. intelligence estimates more often than not wound up as bland compromises between quite disparate viewpoints. Some programs had to go, and among them were most of the proprietaries, including Wilson's, which had assumed unacceptable lives of their own.

Eager to keep him, the agency wanted to bring Wilson back to Langley for retraining as a staff case officer. His first assignment would be in Vietnam, where American involvement was at its critical stage. But that would mean no more fat subsidy for Consultants International, no more freedom to wheel and deal on the side, no prospect of gentleman-farming in Virginia. This wasn't the vision Wilson had conjured up for himself. All he had to do was look at Tom Clines, continually strapped for money, always asking for a handout, to see that.

He tried hard to preserve his old status, and when he failed, he still managed to cut a pretty fair settlement. Pension benefits were quite a way off, and what he needed was a quick fix to tide him over, so he got a year's pay as severance. Ever conscious of a dollar, he arranged to receive it in two annual installments to save on taxes. And he was even permitted to keep using the Consultants International name as if nothing had changed. A lot of people he'd been dealing with, in arms and technology, wouldn't know that he wasn't with the agency any longer.

Then, in the middle of this, he got a break, and his problems were over. Clines was first to tip him off. Wilson officially left the CIA fold on February 28, 1971. Two months later, on April 30, he was back in business with another U.S. intelligence operation.

A month after that, on June 1, he closed on his initial Mount Airy property. The purchase price was $342,000.

FIVE

That same spring in Washington Larry Barcella was sworn in as an assistant U.S. attorney. His father, the youngest of eleven children of immigrant parents and the first to go to college, wept silently as his son took his oath of office.

For Barcella, it was the cancer that had made him different, had given him such a special view of life and of himself. He was seventeen then, a senior in high school in Birmingham, Michigan. He had come home from football practice one evening and his mother noticed a swelling on the side of his neck. He said that it must have come from the new helmets the team had been issued. But the swelling persisted and grew larger. The family physician removed the nodule, and after a biopsy, his parents were informed that it was malignant.

They took him to the Memorial Sloan-Kettering Cancer Center in New York for further examination and tests. Incisions were made in his feet and in his groin for the insertion of tracer dye. He sat outside a doctor's office at the center while his mother and father heard the results before he was called in and told only that he was seriously ill and was in for a long siege of treatment. While he had been waiting, he had gone through some papers on a desk that said he had lymphoma sarcoma and a life expectancy of eighteen to twenty-four months.

When he returned home, he looked up the words in a dictionary and discovered that they meant cancer of the lymph glands. He denied the prognosis to himself. He was too young, too invulnerable. There were too many games to be won, too many girls to chase. Within his family the nature of his illness was unspoken.

He underwent cobalt radiation three times a week at Edsel Ford Hospital until his system could tolerate no more. Afterward, the cancer went into miraculous and apparently complete remission. For five years he had a blood test every third week, first from the physician who had initially excised the lump, then at Dartmouth College and during his first term at Vanderbilt Law School in Nashville, Tennessee.

Right after he had entered Vanderbilt in 1968, his draft board told him that, barring any information of an exceptional nature that he might care to provide, his student deferment would be lifted. He returned to the hospital that had treated him, gave his name and asked for his records. A nurse fished out a folder, glanced at the cover and then angrily said, "I don't find this a bit funny. *Who* are you?"

Barcella insisted that he was who he said he was and produced his driver's license. The nurse looked at it, bemused, slapped down the records and walked away. When Barcella picked up the folder, he understood why she'd been so upset. Underneath his name was stamped the word "Deceased."

It was a moment of liberation that forever affected him. He would live what amounted to a second life in a manner that fulfilled him, unfettered by conventional concerns about either failure or getting ahead.

He was precisely what Edwin P. Wilson didn't need.

2

Barcella was born on May 23, 1945, in Washington, where his father, a reporter, had been transferred by United Press. Unlike Wilson, he had no inner conflicts about his father. He adored him. His father was a son of a brickmaker who had immigrated to America at the turn of the century and settled in Hamden, Connecticut, near New Haven.

After high school, his father got a job on the New Haven *Register* to earn enough money to go to college, and two years later, having applied for and won a partial scholarship, he entered and graduated from Dartmouth. He was hired by United Press and married Louise Berniere, the daughter of a railroad construction foreman.

Her roots were also in the northern Italian lake country around Milan, but her people, as was not uncommon in the region, were relatively tall, with fair skin, blue eyes and blond hair. Barcella, with his smooth olive complexion, teased his mother that the only physical feature he had inherited from her side of the family was a receding hairline. From both sides, however, came a voluble, emotional warmth, marked by a deep-seated work ethic and a sharply drawn sense of right and wrong.

In Washington, when Barcella finished his junior year in high school, his father, with the financial burden of a daughter already in college and a son nearing college age, accepted a public relations post with General Motors and the family moved to Birmingham. Barcella remembered that his anger cut two ways—anger at the move and, knowing how much his father loved being a newspaperman, anger at the sacrifice he had made.

At Dartmouth—there really had never been any question that it would be Dartmouth—he spent his time partying, became a champion in beer-drinking contests. With the shadow of cancer still hovering over him, why not live it up? He might die next week, he figured, next month. Who gave a fuck?

One day his father visited him. They walked around the campus, but now, instead of exuberantly pointing out his old dorm or reminiscing about some merry prank, he spoke quietly about how much of an outsider he had been at first, how little shared experience he had with the other students, the ethnic slurs he experienced. But finally, he said, none of that had mattered. He'd been given an opportunity. That was what counted. A man could do whatever he wanted. To waste an opportunity, though, was unforgivable.

Barcella never forgot it.

Toward the end of his second year at Vanderbilt, he went out with a lovely slender blond sophomore undergraduate from Albany, Georgia, named Mary Lashley, the daughter of a rural mail carrier and a high school science teacher. She wore a crinoline petticoat and Mary Janes and had bows in her hair. She had just turned nineteen, and Barcella thought she was the most naive girl he'd ever met. "Do you keep a kiss list?" she asked, and he said, "What's that?" and she said, "You know, how many dates you've kissed," and Barcella said, "Well, how many?" and she said, "Twelve. How about you?" He hadn't kept count, he said, maybe two or three hundred, and her eyes widened and she said, "*Really?*"

She also was the smartest woman he had encountered in his life, a math major with a straight *A* average who had one of the highest aptitude test scores recorded in Georgia. They got engaged on June 14, 1969, when she came to Washington to visit him and his family. Her parents were appalled, especially her teacher mother, who had dreamed great things for her daughter. They wouldn't be getting married for another year, Mary said, and she'd double up on her classes to get her degree. Her grades would suffer terribly, her mother argued, but she went ahead anyway, and still got nothing but *A*'s.

The wedding was on June 1, 1970, in Albany. The cultural clash was memorable. The ceremony was held in a Methodist church with a minister and a Catholic priest officiating. On both sides of her family, Mary Lashley's ancestors had been in America since the early 1700s. Her mother, the keeper of the family tree, excitedly told Barcella that with the census now being made public through 1900, she could track down the whereabouts of even more relatives. That wouldn't do him much good, Barcella replied. In 1900 all of his people were still on the boat.

Their three-day honeymoon driving north to Washington would be their only vacation for the next four years. Larry went to work immediately in the U.S. Attorney's Office for the District of Columbia. Mary still lacked four credits for a diploma and she enrolled over the summer at Georgetown University to finish up and then was graduated magna cum laude. She would go on to study for a master's degree and then a doctorate and would become an award-winning economist, but at that time, in 1970, in the nation's capital, the best job she could land, despite her outstanding academic credentials, her Phi Beta Kappa key, was as a secretary in an accounting firm.

Barcella was one of a handful of law school graduates to be taken on, and it had a special meaning that he was hired without the help of his father's many political contacts. His father had been returned to Washington by General Motors as the head of its office there, and earlier that year had suffered a heart attack.

Barcella was sure it was because of the pressures of his work. And as his father stood watching misty-eyed while he was being sworn in, after first serving as a law clerk, Barcella felt that a debt that could never truly be repaid had at least been honored.

In Washington, where the U.S. Attorney's Office handled both federal and local crime, a newcomer like Barcella normally progressed through a structured indoctrination—misdemeanors, grand juries, appellate work, felonies. But almost at once he came under the wing of a veteran prosecutor named Harold Sullivan, who was in charge of the newly created Major Crimes Unit.

The post gave Sullivan the chance to put into practice his theory of what a prosecutor ideally should be. Prosecutors had two ways to go. They could be in on cases from the beginning, even make them, or they could just sit back and conduct trials, which was the route most of them took. Obviously, he told Barcella, thousands of cases simply happened, inundating both the police and prosecutors, and they had to be processed, but to have a real impact on crime, a prosecutor had to isolate patterns, to target and attack key criminals. It was vital for the prosecutor to be in at the start. Police identifications could be screwed up, witnesses mishandled, warrants wrongly sworn. And there was still another critical payoff. He would know his case inside out.

Barcella was fresh in the office, preparing motions and doing legal research while boning up for his bar exams, when he met Sullivan. They hit it off instantly and began talking at length on Saturdays, when Barcella came in to use the library. Sullivan would often be the only other person around, and finally one day he said, "What are you doing tonight" and Barcella said, "Nothing special," and Sullivan asked if he was interested in the investigative as well as the courtroom aspect of the job. "Sure I am," he said, and Sullivan said, "How would you like to see how an undercover operation closes out?"

"Are you serious?" Barcella said. "What do I have to do?"

"Be at the Morals Division of the Metropolitan Police Department at three this morning."

"*Three A.M.?*"

"That's right," Sullivan said. "You think you're working in a bank?"

Headquarters was absolute bedlam when he arrived. The

operation was a big drug bust and Barcella felt as though he were in the middle of a television cop show. He picked up a ringing phone. "What is it?" Sullivan said, and Barcella said, "It's one of the sergeants. They need another search warrant."

"Well, write it up."

"Me?"

"Yes, you."

He was hooked for good, and over the next year and a half he stayed in Major Crimes at Sullivan's side, helping to put together the prosecution of drug cases, murders, organized armed robbery rings. It was, he would reflect one day, as if he had gone straight into basic training to track down Edwin P. Wilson. As if, somehow, it had all been ordained.

The excitement of working with Sullivan made a sudden career decision that much easier to resolve. Nixon was just beginning his second term as president when John J. Sirica, the chief judge of the federal district court, summoned Barcella to his chambers. "I know your father," Sirica said, "and I've heard good things about you." Sirica said that a high-level administration figure—he didn't specify who—had asked him to suggest a bright young Italian lawyer to work in the White House, and he was thinking of recommending Barcella. "It could be a hell of an opportunity. Give it some thought. Talk it over with your dad."

Discussing the offer with his father helped Barcella crystallize his feelings about himself and his values. He had promised to stay at least three years in the U.S. Attorney's Office. "I gave my word," he said, "and I'm not going to break it, no matter what." So he wrote a letter to Sirica saying how flattered he was, but that he had to fulfill the personal and professional commitment he had made to himself and the office.

Three years later, after Sirica had presided over the Watergate trials, Barcella happened to bump into him in a courthouse corridor. "Well, young man," the old judge said, "that was a pretty smart move not going over there." Instead of the hoped-for Italian, the man who had ended up getting the job he had spoken about was Egil ("Bud") Krogh; along with such as Gordon Liddy and Howard Hunt, Krogh became part of the White House "plumbers" group engaged in the illegal wiretapping of reporters. That evening, when Larry told Mary what Sirica had said, she asked, "What do you think would have happened if you had taken the job?" and Barcella said, "I guess I would have just quietly resigned. But I think I've changed. Now I would blow the whistle."

As a fledgling assistant, he couldn't remain in Major Crimes forever, and he went into misdemeanors, where he learned to be fast on his feet in court because there was practically no time for trial preparation. But when he was subsequently given a choice between felonies and appellate work, he picked the latter. The U.S. Attorney was startled by his decision. Given the option, hardly anyone passed up felonies. But Barcella said that he felt uncomfortable about his expertise in legal research and needed to sharpen his skills in drawing up briefs. All the while he hung around Sullivan whenever he could, and Sullivan said not to worry, he'd be back in Major Crimes.

On the afternoon of January 19, 1974, Barcella was watching on television as Notre Dame was about to spring one of the great upsets in collegiate basketball, snapping a record-winning streak that UCLA had compiled over three seasons of play. During a commercial break, Barcella's father called to say, "Some game!" Sports had always been a great bond between them. When Barcella was a kid, his father would take him out to the press box at Griffith Stadium whenever their favorite team, the Boston Red Sox, was in town, and on Sundays in the autumn they would go together to watch the Washington Redskins. Barcella hung up, and then, right after the final buzzer sounded in the Notre Dame game, the phone rang again. He said, "Phenomenal, wasn't it, Dad?" But it was his mother. "Please come!" she said. "Something's happened to your father!" By the time he arrived, a medical team and the police were there. His father was dead from another heart attack.

In less than two years, he was grieving again when Harold Sullivan also died of heart failure, although everyone knew the real reason was that he had worked himself to death. Barcella was then trying felonies, and shortly after Sullivan's funeral, the new U.S. Attorney, Earl Silbert, called him in. He said he was naming Sullivan's deputy, Don Campbell, as the head of Major Crimes, and he wanted Barcella to be number two. Barcella was hesitant. There were other qualified people who had been in the office longer than he. There could be plenty of resentment. "Come on," Silbert said, "everybody here knows you were Harold's prodigy. You're the logical choice. No one's going to complain about anything."

His first case in Major Crimes made national headlines in February 1975. It was a sting, originally cooked up by a Washington detective and a squad supervisor in the local field office of the FBI. Undercover cops and federal agents posing as members of a Mafia fencing operation set up business, in a warehouse complete with hidden videocameras, to receive stolen goods. After the boom was lowered, 107 convictions were obtained and upwards of $6 million in property was recovered.

But a case that defined the kind of prosecutor Barcella was never made the papers at all—one that at the time, when he was still trying ordinary felonies, seemed to be an open-and-shut auto theft. A guard at the Lorton, Virginia, penitentiary had reported that his car had been stolen. Around five o'clock in the afternoon, according to the guard, he had stopped at a red light on his way home when someone slid into the back seat, announced a stickup, took his wallet and gun, told him to get out of the car without turning around and drove off with it. The same day the theft was recorded, a man named Donald Robinson had been spotted trying to start the missing car by crossing the ignition wires.

Robinson gave the standard story. The car had been lent to him and he'd misplaced the keys. He said he had met the guard in a Washington bar. The guard had gotten so drunk that he asked to be driven home, and since he had no way of getting home himself, the guard told him to keep the car overnight and return it in the morning. Then it turned out that Robinson had three prior felonies, including two auto thefts, and as a result faced life in prison. He had been indicted a couple of months before, and now Barcella would be prosecuting him. His own lawyer wasn't even fighting the charge; all he wanted was to plea-bargain a lesser sentence.

Something bothered Barcella, though. He couldn't put his finger on it at first. The gun, for instance, hadn't been found, but it might already have been hocked. Then he saw what it was. While he was driving the guard home, Robinson had said, he'd been stopped and given a warning about speeding. That was an unnecessary detail if he was lying, and Barcella told the detective on the case to check it out. Maybe the cops had radioed the area dispatcher that they were flagging a car and had passed on the license number.

Barcella asked the defense lawyer if he could speak to his

client, and the lawyer, anxious to get down to plea bargaining, said, "Sure, why?" and Barcella said, "I don't know. I just have this funny feeling."

Robinson came in with a hangdog look. He repeated essentially the same tale. When Barcella asked what happened to the gun, he seemed to revive a little. He hadn't seen any gun. Never! Finally he blurted, "Hey, look, man, you ain't going to believe this, but it's the God's truth." The guard, after some heavy drinking, had gone upstairs with a prostitute who was sitting with them. Her name was Star, he said, and when the guard staggered down, he was mumbling about how he'd been robbed by Star and wanted to be taken home. Then he threw in another detail. The guard had given him a matchbook with his address written on the inside.

There wasn't any mention of a matchbook in the original police report. Nor was one included in the list of items taken from the defendant. Barcella called in the case detective and told him to find out from the arresting officer if he recalled seeing a matchbook. A day or so later, the detective said, well, yes, there had been a matchbook, but nobody knew where it was. At the time it hadn't seemed very important. Next the detective told Barcella that the car had indeed been stopped on the night in question. The cop involved remembered that there were two men in the front seat and that the passenger, half-asleep, kept saying, "It's okay. It's my car. I'm letting him drive me." Then it was established that a whore with the street name Star frequented the bar that the guard and Robinson had been in, that there were rooms for hire above the bar and that Star's specialty was the Murphy game—rolling drunk customers.

At this point Barcella had put in almost as many hours on the case as he would have on a first-degree murder. "What are you working on," another assistant kidded him, "the crime of the century?" He had the complainant brought in. At first the guard was amiable, but as Barcella's interrogation grew more pointed, he got surly. "That son of a bitch has two priors," he said. "You believe him over me?" Then he said, "I want a lawyer," and Barcella said, "I don't blame you. You know what I think. I think when you sobered up in the morning and found your service revolver missing, you decided to lay it off on Robinson. You're some piece of work."

The Robinson case was dismissed and the guard was charged with perjury. When news of what had happened got around, Barcella earned a singular reputation for fairness. "Just don't cross him" was the word.

SIX

Any last-minute reservations Wilson had about leaving the CIA evaporated after Tom Clines told him about Task Force 157, Wilson hadn't ever heard of it. Hardly anyone in the Office of Naval Intelligence knew about it either. There was no special significance in the name. The task force's first executive officer, Commander Donald Nielsen, had picked it from a list of available numbers the Navy kept.

By 1971, when Wilson signed on, the task force was housed on the ninth floor of an office building in Alexandria, Virginia. Its original mandate, to observe Russian naval movements, had expanded to include developing a supersecret communications system, placing espionage agents in foreign ports and launching a series of extremely sophisticated oceanic spy missions.

To cloak these missions, Task Force 157 became the first military intelligence operation to make regular use of proprietaries and it went to the CIA for advice in setting them up. In an interview, Commander Nielsen told me that the word came back from Langley, "Ed Wilson is the man you need." Then Nielsen left the task force for another assignment.

For Wilson, the timing couldn't have been better. He agreed to a career contract at the same pay grade he had had in the CIA, with salary, health insurance and pension benefits, and formed two new commercial fronts, World Marine Inc. and Maryland Maritime Co. He also was to build a network of overseas agents to collect intelligence, particularly in North Africa and the Middle East. The subsidy for these proprietaries—"housekeeping," as they say in spy talk—was about a third of what Wilson had received from the agency for Consultants International. But if the CIA's expense auditing was minimal, the Navy's was virtually nonexistent in an operation totally unprepared to deal with someone like Wilson.

Once he had incorporated World Marine and Maryland Maritime, all he had to do was put up a couple more signs in the 1425 K Street offices of Consultants International, which he continued to run as part of his deal with the Navy. Besides, he had gotten so chummy with the head of Task Force 157, Captain Paul Adams, any normal controls over him became academic.

Wilson's first 157 case officer, W. Don Randol, recalled how he found this out right away. Randol had joined the task force at its inception. He'd been posted overseas in Germany, and Wilson had been in place for several months before Randol returned to headquarters. Wilson was pleasant enough, but always breezed by him with a wink to see Adams. When Wilson was around Washington, he and Adams had private coffee sessions nearly every morning. Most of the time, though, Wilson would be off on another mysterious world trip. First class, naturally. And often Adams would be with him. Substantively, Randol had little idea of what Wilson was up to at any given moment.

When Task Force 157 wanted a spy ship, Adams accompanied Wilson to Ireland, where he bought a trawler under his World Marine cover. In a covert arrangement with the shah of Iran, the trawler was to fly the Iranian flag, cruising the Persian Gulf to scan for nuclear weapons Russia might be bringing into countries friendly to Moscow, principally Iraq, and to ascertain the nuclear capability of the Soviet fleet in the Indian Ocean.

World Marine also handled the shipment of all the sensitive gear that was installed on the trawler. For his part in the venture, Wilson charged $500,000. He was quite amenable when Randol suggested there ought to be some sort of a breakdown in the purchase and outfitting figures. Wilson's new bill read $250,000 for "product" and $250,000 for "service," and it went right through.

To many on the 157 staff, Adams appeared bewitched by Wilson's swashbuckling ways, as if he were James Bond come to life. In private meetings with Adams, Wilson had proposed a plan whereby, in case of war with Russia, the United States would covertly take over the entire Swedish merchant fleet, with the permission of a presumably neutral Sweden. When word about this got around the office, everyone thought it was looney. But Adams, apparently bemused by the boldness of it all, loved the scheme. Wilson claimed to have the contacts to pull it off, and a conference was actually held with Swedish government officials, although nothing ever came of it. The point wasn't lost on the others, however. Ed Wilson was beyond control.

And Adams was absolutely dazzled by his Mount Airy home. Wilson, the instinctive high roller, had lost no time in turning his initial purchase into a showplace. It was a mile south of the highway out of Upperville, down a country lane. About half of the original 478 rolling acres was devoted to fields of corn and grain and pastures upon which horses and Black Angus cattle grazed, and the rest was forested, dotted with towering oaks and stands of hickory and cottonwood trees.

A long curving drive led up to the three-story main house, set on the crest of a gentle rise and built in the Georgian manner, with four fireplaces, seven bedrooms, a basement containing a pool room, a sauna and a steam bath, and on the ground floor, in addition to the paneled living and dining rooms and a library, a huge kitchen lined with handcrafted cherrywood cabinets. Of the kitchen, an appraiser familiar with stately residences in the area said, "To be honest, I have not seen a kitchen quite as elaborately finished as this one is."

There was a tennis court, lighted for night play, and the heated swimming pool complete with a waterfall. There was the restored smokehouse, three miles of graveled roads, four ponds stocked with fish, a four-bedroom tenant house, an eight-stall horse barn, a two-story machine shed with a walk-in freezer, and a big brick cattle barn.

Barbara Wilson oversaw the interior remodeling and decorated the house with antiques, Early American paintings and Persian rugs her husband shipped back from the Middle East. She was excited and gratified by their new life-style. Wherever she turned, there was abundant evidence that she had made the right choice to be with him, neighbors now to the Mellons, the drabness and struggle of their early days a fast-receding memory. It was her happiest time, although one day she would remember it as the beginning of a personal nightmare.

Once, on a visit to the estate, Don Randol, looking around in awe, asked how he had been able to manage it, and Wilson with his deep-throated laugh said, "Hell, if you think this is big, you ought to see my mortgage." The quip only added to his mystique. Where did he come from, what were his resources, how high did his connections reach? Some on 157's staff speculated that the CIA had planted him in their midst, to spy on them.

Within a year, in May 1972, he purchased an adjoining 530-acre estate called Elmwood and put it under the Mount Airy Farms umbrella.

As his overseer, he hired twenty-eight-year-old Douglas Schlachter, who looked like Barney Rubble in the television cartoon comedy series *The Flintstones.* Underneath his ingenuous façade, though, was a canny, observing mind. Schlachter had come down from a rural part of Long Island to help his brother run a Texaco service station at Bailey's Crossroads near Wilson's old house in Vienna, Virginia. Wilson used to buy gas there and took a liking to Schlachter. He was perfect for Wilson's needs, good with machinery, had a nice feel for the land, was a hunter and fisherman and, as it turned out, an enthusiastic cook. "You stick with me, buddy boy," said Wilson, "and I'll make you a million."

Whatever else Schlachter would say about Edwin P. Wilson, he could not deny that he delivered on his promise.

2

In 1973 Wilson decided to try for a quantum career leap. He'd get out of the intelligence business entirely and go for a major federal post. Through Paul Cyr of the Army Materiel Command, he met Mississippi's other powerhouse senator, the chairman of the Armed Services Committee, John Stennis. Although a Democrat, the conservative Stennis didn't have many problems getting along with the Nixon White House, and he backed Wilson for a slot that had opened up in the Pentagon.

The job was assistant secretary of the army for installations and logistics, and the kickback possibilities were enormous: worldwide shipments of military weapons and supplies, base

construction, procurement, housing, even commissaries and
post exchanges. The new deputy secretary of defense, William
Clements, who subsequently became the governor of Texas,
had a fellow Texan, an oilman named John A. Hammack, screen
the field. Wilson made it right down to the wire before he lost
out to another candidate with more corporate backing in the
private sector than he could muster.

But Wilson was practical. He had gotten on well with Hammack, and when the Texan returned to Dallas, Wilson used him
in the most highly classified project he undertook for Task Force
157. To fire a missile accurately—one from a submarine, for
instance—you have to allow for the earth's gravity pull along its
trajectory. A strategic area that remained unmeasured was the
Mediterranean off North Africa, along the coasts of Morocco,
Algeria, Tunisia, Libya and Egypt. Wilson bought a small
freighter in West Germany and had it refitted to measure mag-
netic fields.

The cover story for the ship was that it was searching for
undersea oil deposits, and to make this look good, the task force,
on Wilson's recommendation, retained Hammack to provide
the necessary equipment. After the months-long survey was successfully completed, Wilson received a lot of kudos. He also
made a lot of money. He had seen to it that the oil-exploration
part of the covert project was actually completed, and he sold
the data at a fancy price to several petroleum companies.

3

At Mount Airy Wilson kept a perpetual open house. If he
was away, his wife would play hostess on weekends, enjoying the
role immensely, while Doug Schlachter took care of the outdoor
side of things.

Former vice president Humphrey would come on occasion,
congressmen like Silvio Conte of Massachusetts, New York's
John Murphy, Charles Wilson of Texas, Michigan's John Din-
gell, senators like Thurmond and Stennis, all came there to
enjoy the elaborate barbecues, the riding, the hunting and
fishing. But the people Wilson most wanted to charm and se-
duce were Capitol Hill aides, anonymous generals and admirals,
civil service employees at the highest government grades, GS-
17s and -18s. These were the people who made the Washington
world turn. No one was more important to him than a GS-18.

Politicians and political appointees could come and go, but GS-18s stayed on, savvy insiders, executing policy if not indeed forming it, awarding contracts.

Others gathered at Mount Airy as well. One was Theodore Shackley. His wife and Barbara Wilson took to each other instantly. Shackley's daughter loved to ride. Wilson practically gave Shackley a horse for her—charging a hundred dollars, so technically no one could ever say it was a gift—and boarded it as well.

Shackley was not happy. In 1972 he'd been brought back to Langley from his prestigious Saigon station to head up the CIA's Latin American Division. Theoretically, promotion from station chief to division chief was highly desirable. But Shackley's assignment was to clean up an ugly mess that had left the agency reeling.

An intelligence officer named Philip Agee, after serving in a number of Latin American stations, was writing a book that not only was critical of the CIA but also took almost ghoulish pleasure in identifying scores of undercover agents he had been associated with or knew about. It would take forever to get the Latin American Division back in shape. Meanwhile there would be intelligence coups elsewhere, a parade of people passing him by.

But his old friend from his days in Vietnam, the Pentagon's Erich von Marbod, helped bail him out. With his expertise in financial and logistical management at the Defense Security Assistance Agency, von Marbod had become a favorite of James Schlesinger's, Nixon's budget man. Then for a brief period in 1973, during Shackley's time of purgatory in the Latin American Division, Schlesinger was named director of the CIA and Shackley soon found his career back on course as chief of the agency's hotshot Far East Division.

Next Schlesinger was appointed secretary of defense and he made von Marbod his comptroller. By 1974 von Marbod was the absolute boss of all military assistance to Vietnam. In the final days of the war, he was sent into Saigon by Schlesinger himself to prevent huge stores of U.S. hardware from falling into Communist hands. He did as much as was humanly possible; the cool eye in the middle of a maelstrom, he moved in and out of the doomed city, dressed in a khaki flight suit, a pistol at his waist, a machine gun slung over his shoulder, directing the removal by sea and air of everything that could be saved, issuing orders to destroy what could not be taken out. His performance, everyone agreed, had been spectacular.

Wilson met von Marbod through Shackley and Clines, and von Marbod often was at Mount Airy; he, too, had a daughter who liked to ride. Clines, of course, in between trips to CIA stations to conduct seminars on Moscow's latest global maneuvering, was always around.

Shackley and Clines also introduced Wilson to Richard Secord, back from flying missions during the CIA's secret Laotian war. Now an Air Force colonel in Washington, he first served as the Pentagon's desk officer for Laos, Thailand and Vietnam, and then as executive assistant to the head of the Defense Security Assistance Agency.

All of these CIA and Department of Defense officials, with the exception of Clines, appeared to be men of extraordinary ability. Von Marbod had rung in Shackley on key White House-level meetings about Vietnam, and President Gerald Ford was impressed with his succinct briefings. Inside the CIA, Shackley was odds-on to be the next director of the agency when Ford was elected on his own. Von Marbod would become the Pentagon's ace troubleshooter, appointed by Schlesinger to the newly created post of senior U.S. defense representative to Iran. Secord would go to Iran as well, getting his first general's star, as chief of the U.S. Air Force Military Advisory Group.

All were achieving increased power and prestige, which brought them more and more into contact with others who had not only power and prestige but wealth as well. Yet they remained inescapably tied to fixed government pay scales. Whatever else they felt about Ed Wilson—and certainly von Marbod and Shackley perceived him as their intellectual inferior—they knew he could do something they couldn't, which was make money. As they relaxed by his pool at Mount Airy, there was tangible evidence all around them.

4

On February 28, 1975, Wilson added the neighboring 479-acre Max Welton estate to his Mount Airy holdings for $369,000.

He figured he was on a roll, like a craps player with a hot hand, letting it all ride, his downside covered by 157. But then the task force wasn't there for him anymore. Donald Nielsen, 157's former executive officer, now a captain, had returned to replace Paul Adams as the task force commander. Wilson immediately tried to cozy up to him as he had to Adams, but Nielsen wasn't buying.

A good part of it was due to Wilson's closeness to Adams. Adams had resigned from the Navy after leaving 157. Nielsen learned that Wilson had gotten him a job heading up the Athens office of an American shipping company. Nielsen didn't know what this meant, but he didn't like the sound of it. Then Adams approached him and asked to be retained at a thousand dollars a month to keep an eye on ship movements in the Athens port of Piraeus. When Nielsen said that kind of information was readily available at the Lloyd's central registry list in London, Adams replied, "Come on. Grow up. We're all friends, aren't we?"

And the more Nielsen looked into Wilson, the more unhappy he got. Naval attachés around the world reported that while Wilson came on strong as an intelligence man, his main interest was in business opportunities, and he was spending an inordinate amount of time in Iran, which wasn't exactly a prime 157 responsibility.

What baffled Nielsen was how the CIA could have given Wilson such high marks. Twice he requested a reading on him from the agency and twice the word came back—he was triple-A. On June 27, 1975, Nielsen ordered a complete investigative review of Wilson under the Navy's top secret classification, "Yankee Blue." Nothing derogatory was uncovered, which meant a clean bill of health.

One of the people interviewed about Wilson was Robert Keith Gray, who "provided only favorable information" and recommended him "for a position of trust." Nielsen knew how influential Gray was. Still, he had this gut feeling that Wilson was bad news.

Wilson had repeatedly invited Nielsen to Mount Airy, and finally one day Nielsen went, taking along his four-year-old daughter. Wilson had the delighted child led around on a pony, and later, over drinks, told Nielsen that the pony was hers, just like that, but it was an offer Nielsen refused. Nielsen also met Shackley and Clines, and he couldn't get the idea out of his mind that Wilson was doing stuff for Shackley.

Then Nielsen saw a way out of his dilemma. Wilson might be a great support-and-logistics man, adept at making deals, expert at moving funds through the international banking system so they couldn't be traced. But his 157 contract required him to set up a minimum of eight to ten overseas offices, putting agents in place to collect information, and not one office had materialized.

Nielsen pointed this out to him in the summer of 1975. No problem, Wilson said. He'd get right on it. But by late September, nothing had changed, and Nielsen decided to cancel his original contract and give him a temporary one, good for six months, till April 30, 1976. Nielsen, aware of the political clout Wilson appeared to wield, told Admiral Bobby Ray Inman, the director of Naval Intelligence, that he was kicking Wilson out. Inman said he couldn't care less. Because of 157's special status outside the normal chain of command, Nielsen had a chilly feeling that Inman's attitude also applied to the task force.

Wilson's initial reaction to the news was to try to sweet-talk Nielsen out of it. When he failed, he turned ugly. He said he was bringing in a lawyer to sue for breach of contract, but Nielsen called his bluff, sure that someone in Wilson's position wouldn't want this to get around. Then Wilson told Nielsen he'd see to it that the task force was snuffed, that he would replace it with his own outfit. After Nielsen got reports from 157 personnel overseas that Wilson was telling them the same thing, he turned off the spigot on his expenses. If Wilson wanted to do any more traveling, he'd have to pay for it himself.

In midwinter 1976, faced with the imminent termination of his contract, Wilson attempted to make good on his threat. Through a senior aide to Senator John McClellan, he arranged to have lunch with Inman; he informed the admiral that he knew about his reservations regarding 157 and said that Inman had every right to be concerned.

Wilson suggested creating an entirely new operation, to be run by him. He also said he knew that Inman was having some budgetary problems. If Inman backed him, he'd get all the congressional money Naval Intelligence needed. Inman was outraged by the proposal and Nielsen's worst fears were realized. Inman used it as the excuse to torpedo Task Force 157 for good. The whole project had gotten out of control, he declared. There were too many potential abuses.

Inman went on to be director of the National Security Agency and deputy director of the CIA, and he was interviewed many times about the lunch after Wilson started making headlines. He was quoted as saying that the approach so reeked of bribery that he not only ended up dissolving 157 but also passed on Wilson's name as an obvious grafter to the FBI. But while the FBI is nonpareil at record-keeping, not a scrap of data about this could be located in its files, either on paper or in a computer. What happened was what Wilson counted on. If someone got into trouble in the intelligence community, the problem was swept under the rug and the culprit, if the transgression was bad enough, was simply let go.

The last thing you had to worry about was a criminal prosecution.

SEVEN

Wilson met Frank Terpil at a 1975 Christmas party for current and former intelligence operatives in the Bethesda, Maryland, home of an ex–CIA officer named Fred Wells.

The two started chatting and exchanged business cards. It turned out that Terpil's office was only a couple of blocks up from Wilson's. Terpil obviously knew who Wilson was, which fed Wilson's ego.

He told Wilson that he had a really good hook into Libya through Colonel Qaddafi's first cousin, Sayed Qaddafadam, who was handling military procurement out of the Libyan embassy in London. Maybe they could do something together. If they combined their connections, there were millions to be made, Terpil said.

When he checked out his agency record, Wilson figured Terpil wasn't in his league. Twelve years younger. A high-school education. He'd been in the CIA from 1965 to 1972 as a courier and then a communications man before he'd been phased out under a cloud. It was an accumulation of things. His last station had been in India, where he was suspected of using diplomatic pouches to smuggle gems. The final straw came when he was caught in an elaborate money-changing scheme involving Indian rupees in Afghanistan while he was supposed to be on duty in New Delhi.

But Wilson was beguiled by the burly, slightly balding, fast-talking Terpil when he stopped by the Consultants International office. His Brooklyn street talk had Wilson laughing from the beginning. Wilson didn't have to worry about his experience in gun-running, he said. He'd been at it since he was a teenager. He'd gotten a submachine gun from another kid, whose father collected guns, and sold it at a profit to a man who turned out to be an undercover cop, and he was arrested. But, said Terpil, guffawing, the important thing was he had beaten the rap, claiming that he thought he was dealing in a museum piece. After the CIA, he moved around overseas selling surveillance devices, using contacts he had made while he was in the agency. Now he had a sales company called Intercontinental Technology, a subsidiary of Stanford Technology, Inc.

That especially impressed Wilson. Stanford Technology, in the heart of California's Silicon Valley, was run by Albert Hakim, a shadowy Iranian citizen of Palestinian origin, who dealt in sophisticated electronics and had sold a surveillance system to the shah's secret police, Savak. Wilson had tried to sell the Iranians the same sort of thing, using the good offices of General Secord in Teheran, but despite Secord's best efforts, Savak wasn't in the market for any more, at least for the moment.

Terpil told Wilson he was tired of working for someone else. What he wanted was a partnership now that he had come up with a Libyan connection. The connection was this Pennsylvania guy, he said, Joseph McElroy, who had been one of the first entrepreneurs to cash in on the money-flush OPEC oil nations in Africa and the Middle East. McElroy began supplying them everything from Pampers to pistols. Gradually Libya became his big customer, and from Pampers, it was more and more pistols.

Terpil had been with McElroy when he delivered fifty Smith & Wesson revolvers to the Libyan embassy in London at Sayed Qaddafadam's personal request. But he had made his score, upwards of $20 million, according to Terpil, and he wanted out. Terpil had first come across him on a flight to London, and the two had gotten friendly. In a couple of weeks, McElroy was going with him to London to meet with Qaddafadam, and then to Libya for more introductions, so Terpil could pick up some, if not all, of his business.

At the time Terpil was making his pitch, Wilson was shipping under his Consultants International banner an array of riot-control equipment to Brazil and Argentina; M-1 rifles and Colt .45 handguns to Haiti; a communications network for Morocco; night-vision scopes to Saudi Arabia, Jordan, the United Arab Emirates and Pakistan. He was doing just fine, except that after his lunch failure with Admiral Inman, he was weeks away from losing his 157 subsidy, which had made everything else clear profit. And he sensed the first tendrils of a cash-flow problem coiling around him. He had overreached himself in his land acquisitions. If he unloaded his most recent addition to Mount Airy, the Max Welton estate, he'd still be in reasonably good shape, but he couldn't bring himself to do it. All those acres were a testament of who he was, what he had become. He told his wife that surrendering any of them would be like cutting off his balls.

So Wilson was considerably more interested when Terpil returned from Libya. "They're hot to trot," Terpil said. He'd met with Qaddafadam in London, and in Tripoli with the chief of Libyan military intelligence and security, Major Abdullah Hajazzi. What they yearned for were clandestine explosives, especially C-4, or *plastique*, as the Libyans called it—explosives that could be inserted in toothpaste tubes, pens and pencils, telephones and radios. There were certain people whose removal Colonel Qaddafi desired, Terpil quoted Hajazzi as saying, people he'd feel "more comfortable about if they were not around."

And Wilson didn't have to accept Terpil's word for it. Joseph McElroy confirmed that Qaddafadam also had inquired about getting a Redeye, the hand-held, heat-seeking U.S. Army missile, which would be ideal, say, for knocking off a terrorist-targeted airliner.

Now it was Wilson's turn to come up with some connections. Early in May, after he officially left 157, he and Terpil flew to California to see Jerome S. Brower in his Pomona office. Along with his splendid war record and civic-minded cooperation with police bomb-disposal squads, Brower was the president of the Society of Explosives Engineers. A U.S. Senate subcommittee was planning legislation to counter terrorism and the Bureau of Alcohol, Tobacco and Firearms had recommended him as an adviser on how to go about chemically tagging various explosive components so they could be tracked to their source.

Although Wilson didn't know Brower personally, he had heard from a Consultants International sales representative on the West Coast that Brower was anxious to expand his explosives manufacturing and supply business. During the meeting, both Wilson and Terpil mentioned their past intelligence activity. Without getting into specifics, they sounded him out on his willingness to sell them explosives on credit for "an operation" in Libya. Brower didn't ask too many questions. He'd be very interested, he said.

Wilson and Terpil formed a new firm, Inter-Technology, to handle the venture under the cover story of clearing Libyan land and waters of minefields left over from World War II so that oil exploration and drilling could proceed safely. Neither of them knew much about the technical side of explosives, but Wilson said he had just the fellow to recruit. On the recommendation of Tom Clines, he had hired a former part-time CIA employee, Eula Harper, to be his secretary at Consultants International. Her husband, John, also ex-CIA, had been an agency demolitions man for twenty-five years and once worked with Clines in Miami.

Wilson confided to Harper that the mine-clearing part of the operation was a sham, but then in the best spook tradition he invented an equally false story. The real purpose was to help Libya develop an antiterrorist training program. Ed Wilson was enormously pleased with himself. For anybody with qualms about fooling around with booby traps and timers, the explanation made everything palatable. Obviously, to defuse a terrorist bomb, one first had to have the knowledge and wherewithal to put it together.

The Libyans wanted all sorts of detonators, but the ones they wanted the most were miniaturized American-made programmable time-delay detonators, the kind that could be set to go off in one hour or in three months. Even Wilson was stunned by the number—500,000 of them. But oil money kept pouring into Libya, and in a frenzy of buying, Colonel Qaddafi had already concluded a $12 billion military aid pact with Russia to supply him with planes, tanks, missiles and artillery. It was, Wilson chortled, like selling coals to Newcastle.

Harper figured the programmable timers would cost around thirty dollars apiece, and probably less if that many were ordered. Wilson promptly marked up the price to the Libyans to $62.50 per unit. On this one item alone, he and Terpil stood to clear better than $1.5 million.

A secret proposal, dated June 30, 1976, was presented to Qaddafi's Libyan Arab Republic for the "design, manufacture, implementation and detonation of explosive devices [to be used] in conjunction with Psychological, Espionage and Sabotage activities."

Terpil brought Harper to Tripoli to review it with Major Hajazzi and Captain Abdullah Senussi, his chief assistant. Senussi was a little down-in-the-mouth. He had recently dispatched a terrorist team either to kill or to kidnap Habib Bourguiba, the president of Tunisia, whose stance against Israel wasn't strong enough for Qaddafi's tastes, but Bourguiba had escaped unscathed.

Hajazzi didn't blink at the prices being quoted. He had, however, an unexpected demand. He wanted an immediate demonstration test of the detonators, and Wilson, fearing unknown competition, told Harper to get on it pronto.

Harper contacted William Weisenburger, the CIA's man for exotic equipment, and told him he needed ten sophisticated timers right away. Weisenburger said he could get them from the American Electronics Laboratory in Falls Church, Virginia, which often filled agency needs, but because of the urgency and short notice, they would cost $8,000. Wilson okayed the cash disbursement and Eula Harper paid Weisenburger. It was a nice piece of change for Weisenburger since the actual price American Electronics had charged him was $1,800.

In mid-July Harper showed off the timers in Libya. Three of them malfunctioned. But Wilson did some fast talking. These were rush-order prototypes. What the Libyans ought to be thinking about were the timers that worked. As soon as the bugs were eliminated, all the rest would be like them, and on July 22 in Tripoli the secret proposal finally was agreed to. Senussi signed for Libya, and Terpil signed on behalf of Inter-Technology. For the record, should anyone ever look into it, a separate contract for mine-clearing was signed by Ibraham el-Kanuni, a former security officer whose letterhead proclaimed him to be the exclusive Libyan importer of explosives for "mine clearance, blasting excavation and fireworks display."

What upset Wilson even more than the malfunction of the timers was how much they had cost him. He told Harper to find another source. Harper went to a second supplier for the CIA, Scientific Communications, a Texas outfit with an Arlington, Virginia, office, and contracted for a thousand of them for $40,-000. He said they were to be used to open and shut valves in oil fields and refineries overseas. He didn't say what country. The potential order, he added, could reach 500,000. Wilson wasn't happy with this new price either. Through Harper he met another former CIA technician named Edward Walsh. If he had the financing, Walsh said, he could produce similar devices much cheaper, but it would require a couple of months to gear up. Wilson told him to go ahead. In the interim he'd cover himself with Scientific Communications.

The next step was to arrange the explosives part of the package. On August 9, Jerome Brower flew in to Washington. He stayed overnight with Ed and Barbara at Mount Airy, the grandeur of it not lost on him, and met with Wilson, Terpil and the Harpers at Inter-Technology. Also present was Walter Doerr, the local cargo manager for Lufthansa, the only airline that had routes both in the United States and Libya. Doerr pointedly announced that Lufthansa wouldn't accept either illegal or hazardous shipments and then made himself scarce.

On the list Harper gave to Brower was a variety of explosives, blasting caps, time fuses, primers, firing reels and igniters. Brower had no problem with two of the explosives, Triex and Quadrex, both of which he manufactured. Each was a so-called binary explosive—that is, had two components which if shipped separately were not volatile—and Brower was sure he had a technical out if any legal trouble developed.

Brower was even willing to go along with Primacord, a detonating cord with a C-4 core. Stretched on the ground and ignited, it could dig a trench a foot deep, and wrapped around critical supports would topple a building instantly, but arguably it could be used for any number of industrial purposes as well.

Where he drew the line was pure C-4 in bulk or sheet form. He wanted to see what happened on this first shipment. After several calls back and forth to Pomona, he estimated a price of

$36,595 for the other items on the list. In the actual delivery, though, he tossed in additional quantities of Triex and Quadrex, which brought the total to $54,000. On August 13, with invoices supplied by him that did not accurately reflect its contents, the shipment left California on a Lufthansa flight, without being inspected, and arrived in Tripoli, where it was unloaded by Libyan soldiers.

The secret proposal called for an instructional team of explosive-ordnance experts, and within twenty-four hours John Harper took off for Tripoli. He was to receive $96,000 a year, along with a $250,000 paid-up life insurance policy. He'd have two assistants at $48,000 each. Keeping it in the family, he chose his son Wayne as one of them.

Wilson picked the other, his Mount Airy Farms manager, Doug Schlachter. While Schlachter knew practically nothing about explosives, Wilson trusted him and wanted him there to keep an eye on the Harpers and to report back on the reaction of the Libyans. He had enthralled Schlachter with his espionage tales. Better yet, Schlachter believed that his employer was still engaged in covert intelligence and that Libya was just another assignment in Wilson's curtained world. He'd seen von Marbod, Secord, Shackley and Clines often at the farm, and he had over-heard snatches of conversation between Wilson, Shackley and Clines about Libya.

And, indeed, from the start Wilson told them that he was going to be doing business there. But relations between Washington and Tripoli were near the breaking point and he decided he needed some more protection. What better way than to have it whispered that he was really building a clandestine spy network in Libya? When Qaddafi overthrew the Libyan monarchy of King Idris in 1969 and took power, the CIA's initial estimate was that he could be turned. He was, after all, a fervent Moslem and apparently staunchly anti-Communist. That hope, of course, had long since gone by the boards.

Now Ed Wilson could be a vital new source for the agency, relaying information to Shackley and Clines, in the guise of an "undisclosed businessman," about what was going on inside Libya, inside Qaddafi's crazy head, what new adventures he was concocting, what the Soviets were doing there—perhaps Wilson could even snag some advanced Russian weaponry.

Wilson came away from these talks convinced that his flanks

were covered in the best possible way. Everyone knew President Ford was going to put Shackley in as his next CIA director as soon as the elections were over. Out at Mount Airy they would kid him a little about it, at least as much as anybody could kid around Shackley, and he would display a thin, mirthless smile.

Wilson's other concern was to do anything he could to ingratiate himself with the Libyans. Nestled unforgettably in his mind was a remark by Major Hajazzi that the explosives contract was only the beginning, that if everything worked out, there'd be many more areas of mutual profit. Qaddafi already had announced that betrayers of the Libyan revolution were under a death sentence wherever they resided, and Hajazzi mentioned that number one on the hit list was Umar Abdullah Muhayshi, a member of Qaddafi's original revolutionary circle who had broken with him over his military spending spree. After leading a failed coup attempt, Muhayshi fled to Egypt, where he lived under the protection of Qaddafi's archenemy, President Anwar Sadat. What was worse, Muhayshi was constantly on radio programs beamed across North Africa, calling Qaddafi a maniac.

The sky was the limit on Muhayshi's head, Hajazzi said, and Wilson picked right up on it. Maybe he could help out.

2

The man Wilson had in mind for the job was Rafael Quintero, an anti-Castro Cuban. At the age of nineteen, Quintero had been one of the earliest recruits for the Bay of Pigs, and under his CIA case officer, Carl Jenkins, was part of an advance team sent in before the invasion.

After the landing failed, he hid out in Cuba for six weeks before making it back to Florida, where he was promptly jailed by immigration officials for leaving the United States without a permit. That was when he met his new case officer, Tom Clines, who arranged his release, debriefed him, doubled his pay from $200 to $400 a month and, to Quintero's delight, told him that there was plenty of fight left in the agency and that he'd be going back into Cuba.

Over the years Quintero had been on a number of sabotage and assassination missions. He was absolutely devoted to Clines, would go anywhere and do anything Clines wanted, and for once even Clines was touched.

He had used Quintero to recruit Cubans to man the Swift

boats Wilson had airlifted into the Congo, and when Clines left
for Laos, he asked Wilson to do what he could for him. Wilson
was happy to oblige, and to Quintero's lasting gratitude, he
fixed up some boat charters so the Cubans could continue sporadic incursions against the Castro regime on their own once the
CIA station in Miami effectively closed down.

Now, after his meeting with Jerry Brower in Washington,
Wilson phoned Quintero and asked if he could fly up. He had
a "business proposition" for him. Quintero checked with his
agency guru, Clines, and Clines said Wilson still pulled a hundred percent. Wilson and Terpil met him at Washington's National Airport and drove him to a parking lot in nearby Crystal
City, Virginia. In the car, Terpil showed him some photographs
of a man dressed in both Western and Arabic clothes. The guy
had to be terminated, Quintero was told. The job would be
worth a million dollars. Quintero automatically assumed it was
an authorized hit. He'd round up the right people.

Then all of a sudden Wilson had a lot more on his mind
than Muhayshi. Doug Schlachter reported that old man Harper
was going bonkers. When Schlachter and Harper and his son
arrived in Tripoli, Captain Senussi took them to their bomb
factory site. The explosives Brower had shipped over were
stored in the basement of a building behind what turned out to
be the summer palace of the deposed King Idris, about twenty-
five miles south of Tripoli in an irrigated green belt between the
Mediterranean and the desert. The palace, in which they lived,
was surrounded by groves of orange trees.

Schlachter settled right in. He was laid back to begin with,
a country boy curious about any new experience and excited to
be on what he thought was a top secret intelligence assignment.
Soldiers toting machine guns patrolled the grounds and no one
was permitted to leave, but that didn't bother Schlachter either.
He started learning Arabic from the guards. He did the cooking
and tried his hand at the Libyan cuisine.

Harper's son appeared relatively content, earning more
money than he had dreamed of. But Harper himself began to
crack under the isolation. They had come into Tripoli "black,"
skipping passport control and so on, their baggage unopened,
and Harper had smuggled in vodka. He began drinking heavily,
ranting that Wilson and Terpil had stuck them in the middle of
nowhere, while *they* were living the high life, raking in millions.

But there was something else unnerving Harper that Schlachter wasn't aware of; Harper had handled explosives for the agency all right, but he was a logistics and storage man. Actually making devices wasn't his strong suit. One evening after Harper had downed a few vodkas, he picked up a flowerpot without warning and aimed it at a Libyan guard. There was another guard behind Harper with a machine gun over his shoulder. Schlachter foresaw a horrible tableau unfolding, as if he were watching a movie, the bullets spitting from the gun, slamming into Harper and him. He leaped forward, knocked the pot out of Harper's hand and finally got him into bed. The next day Captain Senussi paid a visit. Senussi didn't bring up the incident, but Schlachter noticed how much friendlier he was toward him.

Wilson had to find a replacement for Harper, and on September 3 he called an ex–CIA operative, John A. Ward, who had been a "render safe" explosives expert in the counterterrorist section, and met with him at the Holiday Inn in Tysons Corner, a well-known agency hangout near Langley. He had gotten Ward's name from Tom Clines. But even though he offered Ward $90,000 tax free plus expenses, Ward turned him down. He wasn't much interested in working in Libya; moreover, his father was seriously ill and there was no way he could leave his side.

Wilson asked if he could suggest anyone else, and Ward gave him the name of another "render safe" man, Edward Gainor. Wilson sought out Gainor the next day, showed him a sample time-delay detonator he had received from Scientific Communications and this time pushed hard on the antiterrorist training angle, implying that there was more here than met the eye. Still, Gainor declined. But he did call the CIA's Office of Security to see what was what, and a member of the agency's clandestine directorate who was temporarily attached to the inspector general's staff came out to interview Gainor about Wilson's visit.

Wilson then contacted Quintero again. He said that the job they had talked about was still on, but that there were new elements to it. Did Quintero know somebody who was a good explosives man? As it happened, Quintero said, he had already recruited two brothers, Rafael and Raoul Villaverde, who worked with him in the old days, and Raoul had been to Cuba dozens of times, blowing up bridges, sugar mills, power stations, you name it. Wilson gave Quintero a $30,000 advance and told him to stand by with the Villaverdes. He'd be back in touch.

On Labor Day weekend Wilson flew to London to pick up Terpil, and the two of them went in to Libya. Wilson told Major Hajazzi that he was sorry about the Harper problem, but these things happened. When Hajazzi expressed annoyance about the bomb-making delay, Wilson got testy himself. All the tension Libya was creating with America wasn't helping one bit. Then he told Harper he was through, and on September 9 he telephoned Quintero from Tripoli and instructed him to round up the Villaverde brothers. They would meet in Geneva.

Back in Washington, though, the first thread in Wilson's intricate weave was beginning to unravel.

EIGHT

Kevin Mulcahy wore a wooden prosthesis on his left leg below the knee. He liked to say sometimes that the amputation occurred after he was wounded in Vietnam. It had actually resulted from a motorcycle accident.

In May 1976, when Wilson hired him, Mulcahy was thirty-three, divorced and months behind on child-support payments for his two kids. A onetime altar boy and eagle scout, he was a good-looking black-haired Irishman with an intense manner that could be captivating one minute and abrasive the next.

His background could not have been more CIA. His father, with twenty-eight years in the agency, was a senior officer in administration; three brothers and a sister were agency employees. Mulcahy himself had worked for the CIA from 1963 to 1968 as a computer and communications man following a hitch in the Navy's air wing as a radio operator.

But drinking had ruined his marriage and altered his judgment. It was triggering unpleasant gossip at the agency as well, so he quit, grandly announcing that he was fed up with the low pay; he was going to make a bundle in the computer world. Instead he ended up in Alcoholics Anonymous. Seemingly rehabilitated, he threw all of his energy into counseling at a northern Virginia treatment center for victims of drug and alcohol abuse, devoting himself particularly to troubled young people.

Mulcahy had rented a house from Barbara Wilson in Vienna, near where the Wilsons once lived. He said that he hoped to use the place as a sort of halfway house for some of the youths he'd been dealing with and that sparked her interest. The older Wilson son, Karl, had shown increasing signs of distress. His father was constantly away and Barbara, with her social life, wasn't exactly up for mother of the year. But at least she recognized that her son had a problem, which was more than Wilson did, and she asked Mulcahy's help.

He first met Wilson at a buffet dinner at Mount Airy Farms in early 1976. As the two chatted, Wilson asked some questions about his past. Mulcahy said that among other things he'd worked for the government, but he didn't get into details. As was his habit, though, Wilson made it clear that he had been with the agency and implied that he remained active in the intelligence community. There was a Donald Mulcahy over at Langley, he said. Any relation? It was as if Wilson already knew, so Mulcahy said, "Yes, he's my father," and added that he also was ex-CIA. "That's the best kind of family," Wilson said, punching Mulcahy lightly on the shoulder, "an agency family." Mulcahy didn't mention how estranged he and his father had become.

He continued counseling Karl. Then at the end of April, when Wilson's forced exit from Task Force 157 became effective, he and his wife dropped by Mulcahy's house. Mulcahy was despondent. County officials were closing down the treatment center because of a funding cutback. Barbara Wilson thought to cheer him up and insisted he come with them to Mount Airy for supper.

Wilson was noodling around a different idea. With Mulcahy's father so well known and respected at the agency, it would add another layer of credibility to Consultants International if he brought Kevin in. That evening he offered to hire him as his administrative aide. A thousand a month to start, with more to come. And after a year or so, he said, if Kevin wanted to return to his youth work, he'd even donate the house Mulcahy was currently renting.

It looked like a no-lose proposition, and Mulcahy, with his hyperkinetic enthusiasm, hurled himself into his new job, spending upwards of eighteen hours a day on it, learning the intrica-

cies of export licenses and end-use certificates, finding suppliers
for contracts calling for everything from canned goods to computer equipment. And guns and ammunition.

Mulcahy found out about that at the end of his first day in
the office. Wilson had to pick up his farm manager, Doug
Schlachter, at National Airport and Mulcahy went with him. He
said he used Schlachter sometimes for special assignments and
that Schlachter was on his way back from a sensitive purchasing
mission in Ohio. There were many facets to his business, Wilson
mused out loud. He hoped Kevin wouldn't be offended, but one
of them was arms sales. Mostly legal, and always in the best
interests of the United States. Still, he'd try to keep Kevin out
of that part of things as much as possible. It amused Mulcahy
that Wilson thought of him as a great humanitarian because of
his counseling. He told Wilson not to worry, he was a big boy.
Wilson said he was glad to hear it.

Mulcahy acquitted himself so well that three weeks after he
had started at Consultants International, Wilson said he wanted
him to meet a guy named Frank Terpil, and they walked the
couple of blocks to Terpil's office at 1625 K Street. Terpil had
been in the agency, Wilson said, and now they were going into
an export operation together. If Mulcahy got along with Terpil,
he could be in on it too. He'd spoken to Terpil about him.

Mulcahy did not take to Terpil's casual, streetwise amoral-
ity, but he concealed his feelings. It was Ed Wilson's towering,
macho figure, his overwhelming self-assurance, that seduced
him. His first assignment for Terpil was an arms shipment. He
would later claim that the shipment involved machine guns and
silencers for Zambia, that it was the sinister significance of the
silencers that caused him to ask the Bureau of Alcohol, Tobacco
and Firearms about Wilson and Terpil and that when the BATF
said both men were clean, he was convinced it had to be an
agency operation.

It hadn't been quite like that, though. On May 26 Mulcahy
phoned the bureau's district office and said he wanted to talk
about a gun deal. At seven o'clock the next morning, two agents,
Gene Reagan and Jimmy Jones, met Mulcahy in a cafeteria a
block from Terpil's office. Mulcahy said he wanted a reading on
the legality of a business transaction he was engaged in.

The arms in question were MAC-10s, small, lightweight,
easy-to-hide, highly reliable machine guns with enormous fire-

power that were favored by bodyguards as well as terrorists around the world. The agents advised him that if these were the only weapons being shipped and if proper procedures were followed, there was no problem.

Mulcahy didn't mention Zambia, just that the guns were going overseas. Nor did he say anything about silencers. When Reagan and Jones ran a routine check on Wilson and Terpil, it turned up the fact that Wilson was a major property owner in the area, in fact, Mulcahy's landlord, but nothing derogatory about him or Terpil. Mulcahy also showed them one of Terpil's invoice orders for several pistols from a Maryland dealer. According to Mulcahy, the guns were for an Iranian or Turkish citizen, he couldn't remember which.

This tidbit got their attention. But Mulcahy suddenly became anxious. He was certain the pistols were out of the country by now, and he would be in a real jam if any talk of this got back to Terpil. The two agents assured him that they would hold off for a while so he couldn't be tagged as their source. Then, when they did visit the dealer, they discovered that the guns had never been delivered. Terpil had failed to come up with the firearms license he said he'd applied for.

Toward the end of June Wilson told Mulcahy that he and Terpil had decided to make him president of Inter-Technology at a salary of $50,000 a year. That was when Mulcahy found out about the contract with Libya. It was going to be big, Wilson said. Mulcahy could count on commissions and bonuses above his salary, and on top of everything, the agency would be the beneficiary of an intelligence bonanza. The way Wilson put it, it sounded like a grand alliance of patriotism and profit.

Now all the seeds for an easy rationalization were there for Mulcahy to nurture. Since he had seen the BATF agents, he'd been present at the Rough Rider Lounge at McLean, another favorite CIA watering hole, with Wilson, Harper and Schlachter when they once met with William Weisenburger about the timers. He had heard Weisenburger introduced as the agency's electronics expert and himself described as Donald Mulcahy's son. "You must know Kevin's dad, Don," Wilson had said, all so aboveboard. And he had been present at Ted Shackley's home in suburban Bethesda and heard Wilson telling him they soon would be off again to Libya. Mulcahy knew who Shackley was and what people around the agency were saying about where he was headed.

But Kevin Mulcahy also was present at the August 13 meeting with Jerome Brower, during which the shipment of quantities of restricted explosives to Libya was discussed for hours, with nobody from the CIA on hand. In the fast company he was keeping, far removed from trying to help troubled teenagers, he was drinking heavily once more.

And in August, after the first batch of Brower's explosives had been sent and the Harpers and Schlachter were in Libya, Mulcahy flew to London to be with Terpil at an arms trade show. He met Qaddafi's cousin, Sayed Qaddafadam, and heard Qaddafadam express his desire for a Redeye missile and Terpil reply that he'd get Kevin right on it. There was a constant round of partying. One night Mulcahy was found in a corridor of his hotel stark naked, yelling and pounding on doors. It took all of Terpil's persuasion to keep the night manager from calling the police, and he shipped Mulcahy back to Washington in the morning.

Wilson, not having been on the scene, just told Mulcahy to watch his step in the future. Then Mulcahy got into a bigger mess. Wilson had entrusted him with a $4,000 payoff, to be conveyed personally to Paul Cyr, his old contact in the Army Materiel Command. Consultants International had been retained by the Control Data Corporation to help it get Defense Department business, and Cyr was feeding Wilson inside information. Mulcahy stopped off in a bar and had a couple of drinks. He picked up a young woman. There were more bars and more drinks. Mulcahy remembered bringing the woman home. When he woke up in the morning, she was gone. So was the cash—and his car, which was finally located at Dulles International Airport.

Now Wilson was enraged. He didn't buy Mulcahy's story. Mulcahy better produce the money by the time Wilson got back from a trip he was taking to Europe and Libya. Kevin began brooding that he not only was finished with Wilson and Terpil but also could wind up somehow holding the bag on this whole thing.

On Labor Day, with both of them out of the country, he let himself into the Inter-Technology offices. He had to be careful. The telex was monitored by various members of the staff seven

days a week, including holidays. But he found what he was
looking for—the secret proposal to Libya spelling out a training
program for *selected students in covert sabotage operations, employing
the latest techniques of clandestine explosive ordnance,* instructing them
in such arts as *constructing and detonating bombs, audio surveillance
and surreptitious entry methods, disguise techniques and clandestine communications.*

He pulled scores of additional documents out of the files
and copied them. All the next day, Tuesday, September 7, 1976,
he studied the papers at home, drinking more, and late that
evening he called the duty officer at Langley, identified himself
and demanded to be patched through to Theodore Shackley. It
was about Ed Wilson and it was urgent. When Shackley came on
the line, Mulcahy said they had to meet right away, and Shackley
agreed to receive him.

Mulcahy showed Shackley the secret proposal. What was
going on? Had Shackley been aware of it? Was this an agency
operation?

Later he would blame Shackley for writing a report dismissing him as a crazed, babbling alcoholic who shouldn't be listened to. But this wasn't the case. Shackley submitted a deftly
balanced, very matter-of-fact memo. He was either covering
himself or delivering a meticulous, straightforward report. The
report said that Mulcahy appeared to have been drinking. On
the other hand it characterized his charges as serious allegations.

On September 8, Mulcahy phoned BATF agent Gene Reagan. He had to see him. After his interview with Mulcahy the
previous May, Reagan had said to contact him if anything more
developed on Terpil, and he assumed that was the reason for the
call. Reagan told him that he was all wrapped up in an arms raid
for that night. How about tomorrow? This was important, Mulcahy said, but all right. The raid didn't take as long as Reagan
expected, so he drove by Mulcahy's house. The lights were on,
the front door open, the stereo playing, but no Kevin.

Then the next morning Mulcahy called Reagan again. He
had decided, he said without further explanation, to go to the
FBI.

NINE

At that same time in Washington a man Wilson never heard of, named Herbert Springer, was looking to have his wife killed. Unfortunately for Wilson *and* Springer, Larry Barcella got the case.

An informant had phoned in the tip and at first it was like hearing that your neighborhood butcher was an ax murderer. Springer's clothing store was practically around the corner from the federal courthouse. He sold uniforms to the police and robes to all the judges. But the informant was one of the best Barcella had. He'd inherited him from Harold Sullivan.

But then it turned out that Springer and his wife were in the middle of an ugly divorce. Barcella sent a detective pretending to be a hit man to see Springer, who said he didn't care how it was done, except that it had to appear to be an accident. The job was worth $10,000.

"Ask him how a fake suicide sounds," Barcella said, and the detective reported back that Springer was ecstatic about the idea. Should have thought of it himself.

Springer's wife agreed to cooperate. She lent Barcella her diamond ring. Her Cadillac was driven to a spot overlooking the Potomac River. The driver's door was left open, the motor running. Once a police boat was in place to start dredging opera-

tions, Barcella planned to have the media alerted. He didn't
have to bother. A local television news team happened by and
filmed the search.

The lead item on the evening news was about the apparent
suicide of a prominent clothier's wife. Springer was shown the
ring as evidence of her death and the delighted widower, as he
supposed himself to be, paid off and was immediately arrested.

But what seemed to be an airtight case was suddenly in
trouble. In Washington, attempted murder was classified as a
major felony only if it included bodily assault. Otherwise it was
carried on the books as a misdemeanor. But the time Barcella
had spent doing appellate work paid off. The District of Columbia had been carved out of Maryland in 1801, and Barcella
recalled an obscure, catchall statute that said that any crimes
under Maryland law that had not been specifically codified as
felonies in the district could be prosecuted. Solicitation to commit murder not only was a felony in Maryland in 1801 but still
was one.

The statute had never been invoked before, but Springer's
conviction was upheld. And it opened the way for Barcella's
relentless pursuit of Wilson. Indeed, without it, Wilson never
would have become a fugitive in the first place.

2

On September 8, 1976, in response to an urgent call from
Kevin Mulcahy about a serious criminal matter, two FBI agents
from the Alexandria field office visited him.

He told them that Edwin Paul Wilson and Francis Edward
Terpil, both ex-CIA, were operating a terrorist training pro-
gram for the Libyan government under the corporate shield of
Inter-Technology, Inc.

He explained that he had been made the figurehead president of Inter-Technology and he showed them a copy of the
secret proposal he had filched over Labor Day weekend.

He told them that John Harper, another former CIA employee, had entered into a contract with Inter-Technology to
teach explosives techniques in Libya under the guise of clearing
mine fields, that William Weisenburger, currently employed by
the CIA, had sold sophisticated timers to Wilson, as had a corporate CIA supplier, Scientific Communications.

He said that Wilson had two important connections at the CIA. Thomas Clines and Theodore Shackley. Something, the distraught Mulcahy said, had to be done about all of this.

As a result of his emotional meeting with Shackley, Mulcahy also had another visitor—Thomas A. Cox from the CIA's Office of the Inspector General. The report Cox prepared for the agency focused on the secret explosives training proposal, the contract with Harper and the alleged participation of Weisenburger in obtaining time-delay detonators. Cox added that Mulcahy was drinking throughout the interview.

Meanwhile, once the nature of the information Mulcahy had given to the FBI was processed, it was routed to agent William Hart, the bureau's liaison with the CIA in the Alexandria office. When Hart tried to follow up, Mulcahy was nowhere to be found.

He'd gone to a detoxification center in the Shenandoah mountain country to dry out. But he was scared, too. He had told John Harper's wife, Eula, that he'd been to the FBI and she said, "If Ed finds out about this, he'll have you killed."

Fearful that an investigation might embroil her family, Eula Harper began laying down an exculpatory track record. She called the local representative of Scientific Communications and advised him that the timers the company had shipped to Wilson were actually ticketed for Libya. She then contacted the CIA and said that her husband and son were in Libya under the illusion that they were engaged in a mine-clearing endeavor, that she had now discovered otherwise and wanted to know if it was an agency operation. She was told that it was not.

On September 9, the head of Scientific Communications called the CIA as well. He said that 500 timers had been delivered to Wilson, with another 500 on the way, and requested guidance. He spoke to, as he put it, a "high" officer at Langley, whom he believed to be Clines, and was told that it was okay to go ahead and complete the order.

3

When Rafael Quintero approached Rafael and Raoul Villaverde about the hit that Wilson wanted, Raoul was the one who raised some questions. What bothered him in the beginning was the huge amount of money involved. Quintro was touting $750,000 or even a million. That didn't add up. The most Raoul ever got from the CIA for going into Cuba on missions like this was $300 a month.

But Quintero said, "I checked with Tom Clines and Tom Clines says Wilson is still kosher." And that was good enough for Raoul Villaverde. As far as he was concerned, Clines *was* the CIA, and Clines was tight with Ted Shackley, and Shackley, in Raoul's opinion, "was one of the best agents in the intelligence community in the whole United States." Maybe, he thought, this terrorist Quintero was talking about was so hot that a bunch of governments were putting up a bounty to knock him off, using the Company to do it. Maybe it was Carlos, the "Jackal." Then Raoul smiled broadly and said what they all were really thinking: "It's been a long time. It feels good going back into operations."

Neither of the Villaverdes knew anything about Terpil, but Quintero told them he also was ex-Company. Raoul had a vague recollection of Wilson's helping out on boat charters in the 1960s. "He is," said Quintero, "a very important man in Washington. He has a big farm in Virginia, and senators and secretaries of the government and foreign dignitaries visit his house. He makes large financial contributions to elected officials and he is very close to the main people in the Company."

On September 15 Quintero and Rafael Villaverde arrived in Geneva, where Wilson and Terpil met them. From the start it was bad. The first thing Terpil said was, "Do you have the tools?"

"What tools?" Rafael said.

"You know, for the hit," Terpil said, and Villaverde said, "I don't have nothing. I thought we were here to talk."

"Well, no problem," Terpil said, "we'll go to the Libyan consulate and get them." When Rafael heard that, he whispered to Quintero, "This doesn't sound so kosher to me." Then they learned that the target wasn't Carlos, after all, but a Libyan hiding in Cairo.

Raoul Villaverde flew in the next day and the three Cubans had lunch with Wilson and Terpil. Terpil was slugging down one gin and tonic after another. He said they had to go into Cairo that weekend to do the job. Raoul said it was impossible, they had to have time to prepare. Well, said Terpil, Raoul still had to teach the Libyans about explosives. And for the price they were paying him, he better be good. There were some really good Russians and Chinese in Libya.

"Fucking Russians and Chinese are there?" Raoul asked, incredulous. He half rose from his chair. "We're not working with fucking Communists!"

"Those Chinks," Terpil said, giggling, as if mesmerized by his own words, "they can booby-trap a coat hanger, so, like, you take a coat off it and it's the last coat you'll ever try to put on."

Wilson tried to shut Terpil up. Whatever else these Cubans were, they were fanatically anti-Communist. Rafael Villaverde had gone in with the Bay of Pigs brigade and had been a prisoner until President Kennedy arranged the release of the men who had been captured. Like Quintero, Raoul had infiltrated the island ahead of time and escaped on his own. And there was yet another Villaverde brother, caught in one of the post-invasion sabotage raids, who was still being held in a Castro cell.

Finally Wilson got up from the table. The Cubans followed, leaving Terpil mumbling to himself. "It's not as bad as it looks," Wilson told them. Then he went back to chew out Terpil, but Terpil waved him off. "Who needs those dumb spicks, anyway?" he said.

"It smells like Watergate," Raoul Villaverde said when he was alone with his brother and Quintero. "They're using the Cubans again." They decided to have Quintero tell Wilson that, despite what Terpil had said, they were willing to go along with the operation because of their confidence in him, but first they had to get their affairs in order in Florida and create cover stories to explain a prolonged absence.

Quintero and the Villaverdes departed for Miami in the morning. And on September 19, Quintero flew to Washington to report what had transpired in Geneva to Thomas Clines.

4

In Geneva, Wilson knew within seventy-two hours about Kevin Mulcahy's contact with Shackley and the follow-up interview conducted by the CIA's Thomas A. Cox..

Right then, though, nobody was aware that Mulcahy had also been to the FBI. Wilson called Mulcahy's family, which was ready to believe anything about him, spoke to his mother and told her that Kevin was a sick degenerate who was spreading scurrilous stories in the agency about him and his associates, many of whom he could not control, and that if her son kept it up, his life would be in severe jeopardy.

Wilson had brought John Harper out of Libya and parked him in another Geneva hotel, and the day after the calamitous lunch with Quintero and the Villaverdes, he told him he could go home. If Harper breathed a word of what he'd been doing, Wilson said, he could kiss the world good-bye.

Wilson also met with Brower, who had arrived to collect on the explosives he had shipped from California in August. He told Brower that he'd spoken to the Libyans about building a C-4 manufacturing plant, and they were really interested. Then he revealed all his problems with John Harper. Harper's kid was still in Libya making bombs, but he couldn't cut it by himself, Wilson said, and anyway it wasn't a good idea to keep him on. This whole deal, and all that money, could be blown unless some first-rate explosives people were found fast. He needed four of them and he was willing to pay them a hundred grand each, Swiss bank accounts and so on, and Brower said he'd come up with the men.

While he was meeting with Brower, Wilson received word that his mother had died in Vancouver, British Columbia, and he and Brower flew back together. Wilson got off the plane in Seattle. After the funeral, he telephoned Clines and found out that Quintero had been in to see him.

There was no way for Clines to avoid officially reporting it. Quintero—or the Villaverdes—might be talking to others about the assassination approach or the explosives assignment in Libya. But in his two-and-a-half-page memorandum for the record regarding his meeting with Quintero, he did as much as he could to downplay Wilson's role.

It was "Frank" who had told Quintero that the assassination target was a Libyan defector, who insisted that the Cubans go immediately to Egypt, who wanted them to get the necessary "equipment" from a man named "Mohamed," who proposed that Raoul Villaverde go to Tripoli to train Libyans in demolition work, who said that "Chinese and Soviets were in Libya with many sophisticated devices."

And in a confidential report to the inspector general, Clines made the distinction between Wilson and Terpil still clearer. *Rafael Quintero, he wrote, thought that he was involved in an Agency operation from his first contact with Mr. Ed Wilson even though Mr.*

Wilson stated it was not . . . Later he realized things were not proceeding
properly but he was sure that Mr. Wilson would do nothing against the
interest of the United States Government . . . After the first meeting in
Geneva, Mr. Quintero became concerned—the picture looked like some sort
of set-up to embarass [sic] *the U.S. Government. Frank was playing the*
pivotal role in this entire matter.

On September 21—the same day that Orlando Letelier was
murdered—Wilson returned to Washington so Clines could
write another memo. He wanted to lodge an official complaint
against Kevin Mulcahy. Mulcahy was a dangerous drunk. Because of Mulcahy's past employment with the agency, Wilson
had done his best to try to put him back on his feet. Had hired
him at a handsome salary. But none of this had worked.

He recounted Mulcahy's drunken spree in London. He said
that Mulcahy had stolen a large sum of money from him. He had
no choice, finally, except to fire Mulcahy, and now Mulcahy was
seeking revenge, fabricating wild charges against him, palming
off documents like the so-called secret proposal, which, while it
featured Frank Terpil's typed name at the bottom, bore no
signature. Anyone could have faked it. Wilson demanded that
the boom be lowered on Mulcahy. What he was doing was inex-
cusable.

Wilson also learned from Clines that Mulcahy had been
talking to the FBI. But weeks, then months, passed without
anything happening. Wilson decided he was home free. His
complaints to Clines about Mulcahy must have turned the trick.

THE INVESTIGATION

TEN

Fifteen months after Mulcahy had gone to the FBI and the CIA, eight months after the Bob Woodward story in the Washington *Post* linking Wilson to the CIA and the Letelier bombing, Larry Barcella, with some time on his hands, happened to wander into the office of Don Campbell, the chief of Major Crimes, and Wilson's life would never be the same.

It was the doldrums between Christmas and New Year's, 1977. Earlier that year, Barcella had gotten more deeply involved in the Letelier case, but the fascist regime in Chile had thrown up the barricades and the investigation was at a standstill.

As Barcella chatted with him, Campbell was catching up on correspondence and memos. He reached for a stapled sheaf of papers, glanced at the top page and started to toss it aside when he suddenly said, "Hey, wait a minute. What do you make of this?"

Barcella read the covering letter. It was a notification from the Justice Department that it had decided to decline prosecution of Edwin P. Wilson and Frank Terpil. Based on an FBI investigation, which was attached, the bureau could find no grounds that offered hope of a successful case in court and the Justice Department's foreign agents registration section had concurred.

The notification was routine. The Justice Department always did it as a matter of courtesy whenever an investigation, however tangentially, touched on the jurisdiction of any U.S. Attorney's Office. Hardly ever did anything come of it.

Instantly, though, Barcella recalled the crack Gene Propper had made after seeing Wilson the previous spring, that if nothing else, Wilson had been lying when he said he wouldn't know the difference between a detonator and a coffeepot.

"Let me look this over," he said and with growing indignation began to read some of the details of the cynical conspiracy Wilson seemed to be masterminding with his sidekick Frank Terpil, one that apparently made skillful use of loopholes in existing law at every turn. If Wilson could get away with this, how many others would be doing the same thing? Or already were.

The FBI report included interviews with Rafael Quintero and the Villaverde brothers about the assassination Wilson and Terpil wanted carried out. Barcella thought about the obscure statute he had invoked in order to prosecute Herbert Springer for plotting to kill his wife. Although Quintero's original meeting with Wilson had occurred in Virginia near National Airport, Wilson had made calls to him from Washington and later had given Quintero $30,000 within the confines of the District of Columbia. At least this provided a jurisdictional hook.

On the other hand, it was reaching pretty far—allegations about a murder conspiracy against a Libyan defector nobody ever heard of who was said to be living in Egypt.

The next day Barcella showed the report to Propper and said, "Tell me what you think," and after studying it Propper told him, "Maybe there's something here."

"I'm with you," Barcella said.

2

For Wilson, meanwhile, Qaddafi's money was rolling in. To celebrate, he had added, for a million and a half dollars, the 707-acre Bollingbrook estate to his Mount Airy Farms showplace in Upperville. He had already purchased a $300,000 townhouse at 1016 22nd Street in northwest Washington for the expanding operations of his old CIA cover, Consultants International—operations that included, for the sake of both profit and legitimacy, an exclusive contract to ship 125,000 barrels of Indonesian crude oil a day to a refinery in Puerto Rico, commissions on a $20-million package for prefabricated housing in Guatemala *and* an order for a thousand Colt Cobra .38 revolvers and a million rounds of ammunition for the same United States–backed Chilean dictatorship that was behind the murder of Orlando Letelier. Working for Wilson in the townhouse were several former members of Task Force 157, along with a number of retired high-ranking military officers.

In Tripoli, it had been a real eye-opener when Doug Schlachter went to pick up the first payment of $350,000 at Libyan intelligence headquarters. Captain Senussi received him, ushered him into a vault-lined room and pulled out a drawer packed with hundred-dollar bills.

Upon learning that the money was for deposit in Switzerland, Senussi asked if Swiss francs wouldn't be more convenient, and Schlachter said he guessed so, and another drawer was pulled out that was filled with them, and then, as Senussi and his subordinates stood around laughing, Schlachter was shown other drawers loaded with French francs, German marks and British pounds. "So you see," Senussi had said, "we have whatever you want."

Best of all, Wilson no longer had to split the profits with anyone. Frank Terpil was out of the picture.

Schlachter was the one who discovered that Terpil was skimming the cash payments. As much as ten percent would be missing when the money reached Switzerland. Terpil claimed that it was because of the bribes he had to give to various officials, notably Major Hajazzi and Captain Senussi. Wilson had Schlachter inform them of this, and Terpil was told that it would be beneficial to his health if he left the country.

It was just as well, Wilson thought. He'd soured on Terpil ever since the meeting with the Cubans in Geneva. His original estimate of Terpil had been correct: for all his up-front charm, he was basically a two-bit player unable to hack it in the big leagues. Terpil at least was a realist and, $2 million richer, departed Libya immediately. The next Wilson heard of him was when he showed up in Uganda as the supplier of weapons, explosives and instruments of torture to the bloody despot Idi Amin. "That's where he belongs," said Edwin P. Wilson. "With a bunch of asshole niggers."

Wilson didn't like to spend any more time in Libya than he

had to, so he decided to depend on Schlachter to maintain a
local presence. Senussi had told him about the incident with
Harper and the flowerpot in the palace of King Idris and expressed his gratitude for what Schlachter had done. Still, Wilson
couldn't get over how his former farm manager and the Libyans
cottoned to one another.

They liked him and he actually seemed to like them. Wilson
had observed it firsthand; right in front of him, Senussi had
asked Schlachter if he desired some forbidden English whisky,
and Schlachter grinned and said that he didn't care, but maybe
"Mr. Ed here" would enjoy a bottle or two.

Schlachter would even roll up for the night in a rug as if he
were, as Wilson described it, "some goddamn camel driver."
Suddenly Doug Schlachter was indispensable. Wilson made him
a sort of junior partner, and within two years the country kid,
who had been pumping gas in a Virginia service station when
Wilson met him, would bank more than $1 million in a Swiss
account.

When the Woodward story broke in 1977, Wilson was in
Libya waiting for the first shipment of C-4 concealed in cans of
DAP from Jerome Brower's munitions bunkers. While he had
not told the Libyans he'd been in the CIA, he had made it
clear he possessed high-level U.S. intelligence contacts, and
for a moment, he feared that he might be viewed as a double
agent. But the Libyans didn't appear to be disturbed at all by
Woodward's disclosure about Wilson's agency background. In
fact, they found it amusing, as if the joke was on Washington.

Besides, Wilson was producing for them. Brower had come
up with four explosives men, who had begun to teach trainees
how to construct booby-trap devices. There was no record of
entry in their passports. Each got $35,000 tax free, travel ex-
penses for vacations home, paid-up insurance polices and a
$10,000 bonus at the end of a year. Now the C-4, five hundred
pounds of it, was on hand. And Wilson promised the Libyans
that there would be a lot more, tons of *plastique*, more than
enough to implement all of Qaddafi's destabilizing schemes in
Chad and Niger, Tunisia and Morocco, in the Sudan, Ethiopia,
Jordan, Egypt and Lebanon, and to make possible terrorist
strikes throughout Europe—in Italy, Germany, France and England, in Northern Ireland.

The C-4 was the critical point in Wilson's relations with

Libya. Brower had already shipped in his binary explosives, Triex and Quadrex, as well as magnesium powder for incendiaries and aluminum stearate for napalm. But what the Libyans hungered for was the real thing, programmed to blow up a car, to topple an apartment house, preferably in Israel, or to send through the mail, to make Muammar el-Qaddafi an unrivaled source for unexpected death. And once Major Hajazzi was able to finger a chunk of C-4, to smile at the prospect of the bodies it would dismember, he was as good as his word about additional contracts.

Nothing drove the Libyans wilder than the thought of eight Hercules C-130 transports that had been purchased right before Qaddafi took power and were still sitting on an airfield in Marietta, Georgia, originally embargoed by the Nixon administration. Qaddafi would even put President Carter's brother, Billy, on the payroll in an unsuccessful attempt to get the planes released. Eight other C-130s were already in Libya, but to support the adventures Qaddafi had in mind, spare parts to keep them in the air were crucial. So now Ed Wilson would deliver all those restricted parts for $8 million—and for another $1 million annually, pilots to fly the planes and ground crews to service them.

He also got an order for five long-range surveillance vans, designed for desert patrols and equipped with the day/night-vision TV cameras that he had demonstrated at Mount Airy for Libyan intelligence officers. The image-intensification tube, which was under strict export control, was hand-carried into Canada, where it and the rest of the equipment was assembled, and then flown by charter to Tripoli. The completed prototype van cost $60,000; the charge to the Libyans was $900,000.

He entered an agreement to provide veteran U.S. Special Forces personnel, the Green Berets, to train commando teams. The Libyans paid $100,000 a year per Green Beret; Wilson in turn recruited each of them for half as much. Then Qaddafi had a grander vision, a 3,500-man mobile strike force, and Wilson would bring in more than a hundred ex-Berets, Marine black-belt karate masters and American and British pilot instructors for Libya's fleet of American-made CH-47 Chinook cargo- and troop-carrying helicopters.

He contracted to outfit the strike force with everything from combat boots to helmet liners, along with tents and backpacks,

M-16 automatic rifles and ammunition, fragmentation, smoke and illumination grenades, various types of mortar tubes and shells, a full range of sidearms, light artillery and heavy machine guns. The weaponry end of the deal alone added up to $23 million.

Relations between Libya and Anwar Sadat's Egypt, tense at best, were rapidly deteriorating. The Libyans wanted to know about Egyptian missile and troop placements, about any new tactics and strategy, and Wilson would get this intelligence for them—from inside the Pentagon.

And when they asked for a few handguns to be delivered to Libyan embassies here and there, he threw them in at no extra charge.

3

Wilson was still with Task Force 157 when he met Patry Loomis, a young CIA careerist who had worked in Vietnam under Theodore Shackley. Personable but otherwise unremarkable—just the profile-type the agency valued—Loomis was being prepared for an undercover tour in Indonesia as an aircraft salesman for Fairchild Industries, and the agency's Office of Training had sent him over to Wilson to learn the finer points of commercial covert activity.

Loomis's wife, Joanne, a pretty, full-bodied blonde, was an avid horsewoman, and Wilson had the couple out to Mount Airy a number of times. He told Loomis he'd be in the Far East one of these days and maybe they could do something together, and Loomis, gaping in awe at the estate, as so many others had done, said to be sure to look him up.

In the fall of 1976, Joanne returned to Washington, unhappy with life in Indonesia, unhappy with her marriage. Wilson hired her as his executive secretary and began an affair with her. His own relations with his wife, other than on requisite social occasions, had by now become venomous. He blamed Kevin Mulcahy on her. He wasn't, he raged, going to be tied down to some dried-up menopausal woman. Barbara Wilson said nothing, physically afraid of him, afraid, too, of his power, and of losing her status as the lady of the manor.

Then, in early 1977, with Brower's explosives people in place in Libya and Frank Terpil gone, Wilson went to Asia to drum up more business. In Jakarta, he was told by Loomis that the Indonesian police were in the market for large amounts of security and surveillance gear. He opened negotiations and guaranteed Loomis a fat fee if the deal came off. But Loomis made the mistake of using Wilson's business card with his own name written on it. The local CIA station chief found out about this and had Loomis transferred back to Langley. He was told that the worst he could expect was a reprimand—until Woodward's article appeared and Admiral Turner fired him along with William Weisenburger.

Loomis also was a former Green Beret, and Wilson put him to work recruiting the cadre of retired Special Forces personnel he needed in Libya. Loomis asked around and got the name of a master sergeant, Luke Thompson, who had participated in many CIA covert operations in Southeast Asia, including the assassination of suspected Vietcong sympathizers and secret search-and-destroy attacks in Cambodia.

He phoned Thompson at his home in Fayetteville, North Carolina, where the Special Forces headquarters at Fort Bragg was located. Loomis identified himself and said that he was calling from Washington about an "employment position" that required Thompson's expertise in putting together an "A" team, the Green Beret designation for a self-contained, high-powered attack-and-demolition unit. He added that the mission was "abroad" and the money would be "good."

All the buzzwords Loomis had used—"Washington," "overseas," "money"—spelled CIA. Thompson went by the book and contacted military intelligence at Fort Bragg to check the legitimacy of the offer.

That same night—July 20, 1977—two intelligence officers came right over to see Thompson. One of them then called Langley about Loomis's credentials. But wary of delving too deeply into what appeared to be a sensitive mission, he only asked if Loomis was employed by the agency. The answer from Langley was yes. Technically, it was correct; although Loomis had been dismissed, his ninety-day termination clause hadn't run out yet. Langley made no effort to find out what had prompted the inquiry.

So Fort Bragg military intelligence told Thompson, "You can proceed as you desire." He rounded up three retired Green

Berets, and Loomis and another former Special Forces man, Kenneth Conklin, now a lawyer, who was doing legal work for Wilson, flew down from Washington and met with them at the Sheraton Motor Inn in Fayetteville.

Conklin and Loomis assured them that while they couldn't talk about the specifics of the mission, all bases had been touched. It was perfectly legal. Thompson and the others would not be mercenaries, simply advisers to a foreign military service, and that violated no U.S. laws. Thompson was still on active duty, with another year to go. Loomis told him to put in for some leave time and an early retirement would be arranged. Thompson's thirty-day leave was approved at once, further convincing him that it was a sanctioned operation.

In Washington Joanne Loomis got passports for the men and gave them each $1,000 for expenses. The next day, July 27, exactly a week after Loomis's call, they were on their way to Zurich. They had a description of Wilson—he'd be wearing a gold Rolex watch, they were told—and were instructed to wait for him in the airport's international zone. He took them to a coffee shop. All of them would later recall how enormously impressed they were by him; he was their kind of guy—tough, down-to-earth, authoritative. He told them they would be going into Libya. "I want you to ingratiate yourselves with those people. Get in tight with them, whatever it requires." And Thompson remembered thinking that this sounded like an infiltration mission. They'd be paid $4,500 a month, Ed Wilson said. There would be no signed contracts. "If I welsh, you'll come looking to kill me. If you welsh, I'll be coming after you. That's our contract," Wilson told them. "You got any questions?"

"Who are we working for?" Thompson asked.

"Me," said Wilson, and they appreciated how professionally cryptic his response was. Nothing more than necessary. No elaborate explanations. No pep talks. And the truth was, this was no weirder than dozens of agency ventures they had known about.

They entered Libya without visas, toting war bags and training manuals. Ibrahim el-Kanuni, the explosives importer, was there to escort them past immigration. He presented a card that said he was the director of Middle East marketing for the Delex International Corp., Washington, D.C., which reinforced their sense that this was CIA. Washington! It must be a CIA cover.

Delex, in fact, was one of an intricate network of companies Wilson had created to distance himself from the Foreign Agents Registration Act. In none was he listed as an officer. He was just another sales representative, working on commissions.

They were booked into a seafront hotel. Doug Schlachter took them to a briefing by Hajazzi and Senussi. It gave Thompson the willies to think that their job was to train Libyan commandos. He had more misgivings when he saw the bomb factory at the King Idris palace. When Thompson's leave was up and he had to depart, Schlachter said to be sure to see Wilson in Washington about getting early retirement. But Thompson first returned to Fort Bragg to report what he had seen and heard to military intelligence. Now he was told that it was a "civilian" matter and was ordered to inform the FBI's Fayetteville office. After his interview, though, that seemed to be the end of it. Loomis had been right. There was a huge loophole in the U.S. Neutrality Act. It might be illegal to enlist in a foreign military service, but there was no law against "advising" one.

Luke Thompson went ahead and put in his retirement papers. Wilson, however, never pulled the promised strings to have them processed quickly. Thompson had served his purpose. If additional Special Forces personnel were required, they could be contacted through the men already in Libya. Ironically, Thompson proceeded to recruit still another retired Green Beret for Wilson. "I don't know exactly what's going on over there," he said, "but it pays heavy dust." And that was the lamentable bottom line for these men, who wore their patriotism on their sleeves. The dust, as they called it, was what mattered.

ELEVEN

As Luke Thompson was telling the FBI what he had seen in Libya, an eighteen-wheeler pulled away from the old brick magazine of Technical Explosives, Inc., in the mangrove swamps of Jefferson Parish, Louisiana, and headed for California.

It was carrying 7,500 pounds of C-4, all that Technical Explosives had in stock, ordered by J. S. Brower and Associates. A state trooper car preceded it. Louisiana law required that a shipment of this nature and size be guarded to prevent it from falling into the wrong hands.

"What in the world do you need so much for, Jerry?" the general manager of Technical Explosives had asked, and Brower said, "Keep this to yourself, but it's to simulate nuclear blasts for an Army research project." At the state line the troopers waved good-bye. There was no pickup escort in sight, despite advance warning. "Well, that's Texas for you," one of the troopers remarked.

At Goex, Inc., in Cleburne, Texas, south of Fort Worth, the trailer truck halted to pick up an additional 28,000 pounds of C-4, the entire amount Goex had on hand. That same day, from the Plattsburgh, New York, facilities of Canadian Industries, Ltd., 18,500 more pounds were forwarded to Brower, also with police protection. Brower was about to command almost every pound of C-4 that was commercially available in the United States, and nobody had noticed it.

Under the supervision of his trusted lieutenant, Doug Smith, who had driven the first delivery of *plastique* across the California desert the previous April, unloading the explosive and repacking it into 856 cans of oil drilling mud took a month. It had come in fifty-pound cardboard boxes, and in case any government inspectors came around, each box, once emptied, was refilled with ordinary putty, which looked exactly like C-4, and then was stowed in Brower's Fontana bunkers.

On September 26, 1977, a tarpaulin-covered flatbed truck carrying 42,300 pounds of the newly packaged C-4 left Fontana for the Houston Intercontinental Airport. A man named Reginald Slocombe, whom Wilson hired to run still another of his many companies, Aroundworld Shipping and Chartering, was in charge of the logistics and had picked Houston because it had less security control than other possible choices, such as Los Angeles or Chicago. Wilson found admirable qualities in Slocombe. Besides being a knowledgeable freight forwarder, he was a devout Mormon, a bishop in the church. And it was after Brower had gone down to Houston to survey the layout and had seen vast amounts of oil drilling equipment being readied to go overseas that he got the idea of how to disguise the cargo.

To pay for the explosives, Wilson forwarded funds to a secret account Brower maintained in Liechtenstein. Money was then transferred to a second account in Switzerland. Brower sent Edward Bloom, seventy-three, his attorney and friend, to pick it up. And now, as the flatbed headed for Houston, Bloom and Slocombe were in Miami, dickering for a DC-8 charter to ferry the C-4 to Libya. Bloom forked over $82,000—in cash. The plane's pilot was the son-in-law of a famous member of President Nixon's inner circle, Bebe Rebozo. And in the first hours of October 3, when the lengthy process of loading the cans on a conveyor belt had been completed and the DC-8 finally took off from Houston, Reginald Slocombe alerted Wilson by phone. Slocombe used Wilson's own code name, "Angus," after the cattle he had at Mount Airy, and said, "This is R-man. The bird has flown the coop."

In Tripoli, Jerome Brower was happy to oblige Wilson's request that he fake the invoice to show that each can of supposed drilling mud contained sixty instead of fifty pounds of

C-4. Brower had done a little thieving of his own. Although he
had delivered slightly in excess of twenty-one tons of *plastique*,
he had actually purchased twenty-seven tons, the cost of which
was covered up in his total billing price to Wilson. The extra six
tons remained in California. Brower figured that Wilson would
be back for more of the stuff sooner or later, and if not, he'd
eventually sell it somewhere else. Either way, it would be all
profit.

In the meantime, Colonel Muammar el-Qaddafi sat on a
mountain of C-4, the largest illegal shipment of it in history.

2

That same last week in December 1977, when by chance
Larry Barcella saw the Justice Department notification that it
was declining to prosecute Edwin P. Wilson, Wilson was making
good on his promise to start passing on to Libyan military intelligence the deployment and capabilities of Egyptian armed
forces. He also supplied U.S. contingency plans in the event of
war in the Middle East, which included the use of the 82nd
Airborne Division.

Wilson's source was seventy-one-year-old Waldo H. Dubberstein, a member of the Directorate for Foreign Intelligence
in the Pentagon's equivalent of the CIA, the Defense Intelligence Agency. Dubberstein was in charge of the DIA's desk for
North Africa, the Middle East and South Asia. After a distinguished academic career, he had been in Army intelligence during World War II and then was in the CIA for twenty-four years
before retiring in 1970 as a GS-15 senior analyst who specialized
in Middle Eastern and African affairs with a particular eye on
Soviet subversion.

After retiring, he served with various public policy foundations, was a visiting professor at the National War College and
set up an intelligence assessment group at the Justice Department to aid drug law enforcement. In 1975 he became a consultant at the Defense Intelligence Agency and was hired full-time
a few months later. Equipped with a giant ego, he also fancied
himself as something of a lover, and in 1977, despite his advanced age, he was maintaining two households, one with his
wife and the other with his girl friend, a youngish blonde of
heroic proportions from East Germany who worked at the
Iranian embassy.

Wilson first met Dubberstein in the halls of Langley and had him out to Mount Airy several times, often when Shackley and Clines were there, and he used to see him again after Clines became CIA liaison with the Pentagon. Wilson was aware of the financial burdens of Dubberstein's secret life, and he got him to sell out relatively cheap—$36,000 plus plane tickets for a little relaxation in places like Rome, Paris and Monte Carlo. It wasn't that cut-and-dried, though. Playing on Dubberstein's vainglorious nature, Wilson first spoke of the divisions he'd seen among Libyan intelligence officers, of a pro-American faction ranged against a pro-Soviet one, and of the opportunity, the need, to cultivate friendly Libyans. The old CIA estimate that the Qaddafi regime could be brought into the Western fold was yet viable, and whoever pulled it off would be a big man.

The best way to gain influence was to give the Libyans some information. What difference did it make, anyway? "We could hand them everything we've got," Wilson said, "and the Egyptians would still beat the hell out of them." No thought was given to whether the classified material would stop in Tripoli; all Wilson cared about was staying in Libya's good graces.

Once the hook was set, the money kept Dubberstein on the line. For the next two years—until a mob stormed and sacked the American embassy in Tripoli in December 1979—he periodically provided highly classified data that included, besides U.S. troop readiness, an inside look at the evolving relationship between Israel and Egypt; Egyptian military deployment by unit as well as missile strength and placement; and, most sensitive of all, a detailed rundown on Egyptian invasion plans in case of war. Doug Schlachter was the courier for many of these papers, although Dubberstein himself was once taken into Libya to brief Hajazzi, Senussi and other Libyan intelligence people on current U.S. thinking on the Middle East.

Afterward Wilson said, "Waldo, you're a real patriot."

3

When Barcella first reviewed the FBI's investigative report covering the activities of Edwin P. Wilson and Frank Terpil, Dubberstein's role, the recruitment of the Green Berets and the two shipments of Composition C-4 all remained unknown.

Still, the report was chilling enough, and Barcella was struck by the paradox, between the Wilson and Terpil case on the one hand and the bomb murder of Orlando Letelier on the other. In Letelier, the crime was clear; the problem was to find the perpetrators. In Wilson, it was exactly the opposite; the perpetrators were evident, but what, legally, was the crime?

Wilson had adroitly protected himself; federal law enforcement, on the face of it, was ill-equipped to deal with him. The FBI report, nearly fourteen months in the making, relied heavily on the leads and documents provided by Kevin Mulcahy. It described the contract between Inter-Technology and el-Kanuni and Company for explosives and timers allegedly to clear mine fields, as well as the secret proposal, which showed that the true purpose of the contract was to support Libyan-backed terrorism and subversion.

It contained interviews with William Weisenburger about the timers he had obtained, noting that he was an employee of the CIA; other interviews with the Harpers and with John Ward and Edward Gainor about how Wilson had approached the former agency "render safe" men to teach Libyans to construct and disarm explosive devices; interviews with Edward Walsh, the other ex–CIA technician, who had manufactured timers for Wilson; more interviews with Jerome Brower and with Rafael Quintero and the Villaverde brothers about their trip to Geneva; and an interview with the president of Scientific Communications about the thousand timers he had supplied to Wilson.

Finally, there was no doubt that the secret proposal originated in the offices of Inter-Technology; Terpil's fingerprints were lifted from the copy of it that Mulcahy had stolen.

From every angle it appeared to be a monstrous conspiracy on behalf of the world's preeminent terrorist state, except that legally it wasn't. The Foreign Agents Registration Act had been designed to protect the United States against persons acting politically and directly for other nations. But the contract Inter-Technology entered into with el-Kanuni was between two private companies, and there was no evidence of any political activity by Wilson or Terpil on Libya's behalf. Mulcahy claimed that Terpil had an office in the Libyan embassy in London, which turned out not to be so.

As for the secret proposal, the FBI report said that even granting it could be "interpreted" as the outline for a terrorist training program, none of the booby-trap bombs had been manufactured or assembled within U.S. jurisdiction. And it could easily be argued in court that the time-delay detonators were for commercial use, and therefore not subject to any export restrictions imposed by the Office of Munitions Control.

The same went for the explosive materials that Brower had acknowledged sending to Libya in August 1976. By themselves, when they left Los Angeles, they were not explosives, but rather the component parts for explosive devices. Brower possessed a valid license that had been issued by the Bureau of Alcohol, Tobacco and Firearms and he never budged in his insistence that all the materials which he had provided were for mine-clearing operations. John Harper, still afraid of what Wilson might do to him, backed up Brower. In two separate interviews, Harper declared that none of his work in Libya had involved anything other than mine-clearing.

So the FBI concluded, with Justice Department approval, "We believe there are no prosecutable violations of Federal laws pertaining to explosives, destructive devices, and registration of foreign agents."

That left the solicitation-to-murder statute that had been used against Herbert Springer. And now Barcella decided to use the statute again, in the assassination plot against the Libyan defector Umar Abdullah Muhayshi, as a wedge to look further into Wilson. It was thin, but Barcella, his sense of justice and the law assaulted by what Wilson was getting away with, didn't care. At least the special grand juries that sat for the Major Crimes Unit were accustomed to strange cases and to being part of an investigative process in which all evidence for possible indictments had not yet been gathered. They were in session for eighteen months at a stretch, usually meeting twice a week.

At home that evening, Barcella said, "Guess what? An old ghost has reappeared."

"Really?" Mary Barcella said. "Who?"

"Edwin P. Wilson. Remember that story Woodward wrote about the Letelier bombing?"

She did, of course, and she would come to know the name only too well, and detest it passionately, as Wilson began first to intrude into their life together and then insidiously to dominate it month after month, year after year, until she feared he would hover over them forever.

In studying the FBI report, with its frequent mentions of the CIA, Barcella was sensitive to a possible agency connection in all of this. For more than twenty years there had been a secret understanding between the CIA and the Justice Department that gave the agency wide latitude in concealing crimes that its agents committed. But that had been abrogated almost a year ago by President Ford.

Maybe some people in the clandestine directorate hadn't adjusted yet. The CIA was denying any official link with Wilson and Libya, although it had not been notably forthcoming with information about him. No matter what, though, solicitation to commit murder was a felony. Just ask Herbert Springer. The thing to do was start with that and pick and nibble away and see how it developed.

So at long last, on January 24, 1978, Kevin Mulcahy was quietly sworn in as a grand jury witness to set the stage for an investigation of what Wilson and Terpil had been up to. The initial step in a possible indictment had been taken.

He was followed by Quintero and the Villaverde brothers. Barcella was especially impressed by Quintero. It was obviously very difficult for him to say anything to outsiders that might reflect badly on the CIA or on someone as close to Clines as Wilson was. But he was doing it. If Quintero was disturbed by what was going on, so should everybody else be.

Then Barcella found out about Luke Thompson. When the FBI was interviewing Mulcahy, he'd been drinking steadily, floating in and out of reality, his memory of events often blurred and fragmented. But now, in talking to Barcella before his grand jury appearance, he suddenly recalled hearing something about Wilson trying to enlist ex–Green Berets to go to Libya. That was all he knew.

Barcella spoke to the agent in charge of the original fourteen-month-long FBI investigation, William Hart, and asked him to go over the files for any possible violations of the Neutrality Act, which prohibited American citizens from serving in foreign military forces. And Hart turned up Thompson's report about being in Libya, which he'd given to the FBI's Fayetteville office.

The way Wilson had set it up, Thompson's recruitment by itself didn't violate existing laws. But Barcella hadn't given up also going after Wilson as a foreign agent for Libya, and Luke Thompson's testimony could be another building block toward that end.

Thompson went to Langley to make sure it was all right to be a witness, and when Wilson learned this, he got edgy. But Ken Conklin brought reassuring news. Conklin had telephoned Thompson after he'd been before the grand jury and Thompson said that most of the questions had been about whether the "A" team was an assassination team, which he had denied. He had been asked who Edwin Wilson was, and he had replied that Wilson, to the best of his knowledge, was the boss of a company doing business in Libya. According to Conklin, Thompson portrayed the grand jury as a bunch of "fat, black females" and said he had refused to answer many of the queries because the jurors didn't look to him like good security risks.

Then Wilson got momentarily lucky.

A break had occurred in the Letelier case. One of the key figures in the former ambassador's murder was now known to be hiding in Chile. Other suspects were being sought. There were delicate negotiations not only with Chile but with the State Department. Nearly every day the press was reporting new developments leaked by political factions on both the left and the right. Attorney General Griffin Bell considered Letelier his biggest headache, and Barcella was ordered into the case full-time and Ed Wilson was all but forgotten.

But then something else happened that Wilson could never have counted on.

TWELVE

The teletype query came into the Washington district office of the Bureau of Alcohol, Tobacco and Firearms from Boston on May 23, 1978.

A confidential source had reported that a phone call had been made to an arms dealer in Springfield, Massachusetts, about purchasing fifty Remington .308 rifles with sniper scopes. If the order could be filled promptly, more rifles, hundreds of them, possibly thousands, might be required. The name of the caller, according to the teletype, was not known, but he had left a District of Columbia number. Boston asked for a "subscriber information" check. Of particular concern was that the rifles were for delivery to Libya, and there was a total embargo on any Libyan arms sales. The caller had added that he was speaking on behalf of a former general, whose name also was not known.

Rick Wadsworth, a young BATF agent who had completed his training some six months before, got the assignment. Wadsworth discovered that the subscriber was J. J. Cappucci and Associates. Cappucci, he learned, was a retired Air Force brigadier general who had been chief of its Office of Special Investigations. Cappucci and Associates shared space with another firm called Consultants International, the president of which was somebody named Edwin P. Wilson.

Then Boston reported that a second contact had been made, and now the caller's name was known—Peter Goulding. One morning in the middle of July, while Wadsworth was still in the process of trying to get a fix on Goulding, he started talking to another man in the office, Dick Pedersen, about what he was doing.

A ten-year BATF veteran, Pedersen had returned to Washington as a senior special agent after a tour supervising a small BATF office in northwestern Virginia. Pedersen had missed the big-city street action. He was thirty-five, tall and blond, and had the kind of ageless preppie face and easy manner that made it seem as though he had stepped right off a prestigious campus, an impression further enhanced by his customary dress of loafers, gray flannel slacks and single-breasted blue blazer. Lulled by his appearance and demeanor, somebody being interrogated by Pedersen tended to fall apart when he suddenly got tough.

Wadsworth had just finished telling Pedersen that he hadn't yet been able to establish whether Cappucci or Wilson was running this rifle deal when Gene Reagan, the BATF agent who had talked to Kevin Mulcahy two years before, popped up from his adjoining cubicle and said, "Wilson? Did I hear you say Edwin Wilson?"

"Yeah, why?" Wadsworth said, and then Reagan told them about his on-again, off-again encounters with Mulcahy in the spring and fall of 1976. "Wait a minute, I think I have his number somewhere," he said, and rummaged around and found it. "You can't miss him. He's flaky as hell and he only has one leg."

Wadsworth met Mulcahy in a Washington bar and was immediately taken by his engaging manner. Wadsworth had arrived early. About twenty minutes later, a black-haired man rushed in and said, "You Wadsworth?" The agent, taken aback, said, "I thought you had one leg," and Mulcahy laughed and said, "Well, sometimes I do." During his sessions with Reagan, he'd been on crutches, without his artificial limb.

Pedersen was on another case, and a week or so passed before Wadsworth caught up with him. "Let me run this by you," he said, and related what Mulcahy had told him about Ed Wilson and Frank Terpil. "What should we do?" he asked. "What do we have here?"

"Well, okay, something's fishy," Pedersen said. "At least we know they went over the line on the Remingtons. It's worth a look."

"You want to get into this? I'd like your help."

"Sure, why not?"

As soon as he heard Kevin talk, Pedersen understood how Wadsworth had become so intrigued. Mulcahy was on the wagon. He was as hyper as hell, Pedersen thought, but he spelled out a good, logical story. He came off like someone who knew what he was saying. Pedersen noticed that he landed hardest on Terpil. Terpil, he said, was now in Uganda, selling all kinds of stuff to Idi Amin. He seemed scared of Wilson. He spoke about how Wilson loved to pick fights, of how he had seen him "coldcock guys" in bars. "You don't mess with Ed," Mulcahy said. "He's ex-CIA. He knows his way around. He's very dangerous."

Mulcahy revealed that he had scores of documents he had stolen from the Inter-Technology files. "Hey, we've got to see them," Pedersen said, and Mulcahy retorted, "Why the hell should you? All I've gotten is a runaround—from Justice, from the FBI, from the U.S. Attorney's Office. Why should I waste my fucking time?"

This was some sort of test, Pedersen thought. "Look, Kevin," he said, "stop playing games. You want help, help us. Or, you know, good-bye."

The papers were squirreled away at a place in the Shenandoah Valley, Mulcahy said. He'd been hiding out there. He had to. Right after he'd gone to the FBI, Wilson had found out about it. There wasn't anybody he could trust anymore.

The plaintive note in Mulcahy's voice seemed genuine, but Pedersen ignored it. "When you get the papers," he said, "call us." Afterward, Wadsworth said, "Weren't you a little hard on him?" and Pedersen said, "Yes. But who's on whose team?"

A week later Mulcahy arrived with a suitcaseful of documents. There were records of arms sales, mostly Terpil's and mostly small, to places like Zambia, Ethiopia, Venezuela. Mulcahy had a copy of the manifest that the FBI had gotten for Brower's original explosives delivery in August 1976. Pedersen immediately saw that none of the explosive material, as listed, was illegal. Mulcahy insisted that Brower had sent other explosives as well, but he couldn't remember what. And Pedersen thought that there really was an excessive amount of Triex and

Quadrex—not exactly what your everyday terrorist yearned for —and he wondered if something else might have been in those drums. But how did you prove it?

Then, when he and Rick Wadsworth saw the secret proposal, they experienced the same wave of indignation that had swept over Barcella. Some law had to have been broken. Pedersen remembered an obscure subsection of the U.S. Criminal Code which said that shipping any substance "with a knowledge or intent" that it could be used to kill, injure or intimidate any individual was felonious. If they could link up the Brower shipment with the secret proposal, that might do it. Okay, it wasn't great, but at least it would enable them to get a go-ahead from the BATF hierarchy. In real life, though, they both knew, the only solid lead they had at the moment was a lousy fifty Remington rifles.

They went to see Barcella and Gene Propper, who were practically joined at the hip working on the Letelier case, and got everything that had come in from the FBI investigation. Barcella knew Pedersen from the phony fencing operation that had netted so many Washington burglars a couple of years before, and he said, "I'm glad you're in this. I really think there's something there. But we're up to our ass in Letelier, and we don't have the time right now. You need subpoena powers, anything, just holler."

The first step was to get some sense of the action and the players at Wilson's townhouse headquarters at 1016 22nd Street. Toll-call records from all the phones in it were collected. Surveillances were set up. From a nearby roof, Wadsworth began snapping pictures of everyone entering and leaving the townhouse.

And the two agents kept querying Mulcahy, trying to dredge up every scrap of information about Wilson's operation, and about Wilson himself, how *he* operated, how he might react in a given situation. J. J. Cappucci was just a figurehead for Wilson, according to Mulcahy. Wilson had decided to "buy a general." Cappucci was being used mostly for security contracts in Korea, the Philippines and Egypt. "Look, he knows what's going on, but he doesn't know," Mulcahy said. As for Peter Goulding, Mulcahy wasn't much help. Goulding was after his time.

Pedersen reflected on Goulding. If Goulding had been

dumb enough to mention Libya out loud on the call to Springfield about the rifles, maybe there was a shortcut to all of this.
The alternative was a long, painstaking investigation that might
require months, even years. Seeing Barcella again reminded
Pedersen of the fencing sting. Maybe they could suck Wilson
and this Goulding into a phony—and illegal—arms buy and
wrap up the whole thing right off the bat.

2

Companies all over America are dotted with eager-to-
please junior executives like Peter R. Goulding trying to climb
the corporate ladder. He was twenty-eight. Conventionally
good-looking, with a pretty wife four years younger, he was
raised near Boston and had graduated from Northeastern University. After service as an infantry captain in the Army, he went
to work as a production manager for a Massachusetts parachute
manufacturer. In early 1978 one of the former Green Berets in
Wilson's employ approached Goulding about a special order for
black air-foil parachutes, the kind used for commando free-fall
drops with the chute opening at the last minute for controlled,
glide landings.

The Green Beret took Goulding to see Wilson in Washington, where, after some chitchat, Wilson suggested forming a
company, in which Goulding would be a minority partner, to
supply the parachutes. It would be, said Wilson, a "clean front."
While the CIA was never actually mentioned, there was, as
Goulding later put it, "a lot of winking and nodding."

Goulding was immediately impressed by his surroundings.
Along with J. J. Cappucci, there was another retired Air Force
general, Robert C. Richardson, who was busy acquiring C-130
airplane parts. A parade of government and political figures also
passed in and out of the office; the one he remembered the most,
because of his name, was Congressman Charles Wilson of
Texas. He soon discovered that besides parachutes there was a
whole shopping list of other items he was expected to procure,
among them compasses, trench tools, jump gear, oxygen bail-
out bottles—and Remington .308 rifles and scopes. Using one
of Cappucci's phones, he called a source in Springfield about
them. Goulding had been on the job for only about two months,
and when he made the call, he had no idea that Libya was on any
arms embargo list.

Another newcomer who had joined Wilson's expanding organization was a striking auburn-haired thirty-year-old bookkeeper named Roberta Barnes. An army brat, she first started working as a stewardess for Northeast Airlines. She married an accountant, found she had a knack for accounting herself and when she got divorced, the mother now of a son, she got a business degree from a community college in northern Virginia.

What she liked about accounting, she was fond of saying, was that it was all black and white, and everything had to balance out. Still, something was missing. She recalled her adventurous childhood, being in places like Germany and Turkey with her parents, and regretted her present humdrum life. She was doing the books for several firms in the Washington area, including a blueprint reproduction house and an auto-leasing outfit, when she saw a classified ad for a bookkeeper in the Washington *Post*. The company name alone had an exciting ring to it—Consultants International. In her application, she wrote that her reason for wanting a job change was the desire for a "more challenging and rewarding position."

She succeeded beyond her wildest dreams. She not only was hired but also displaced Joanne Loomis as Wilson's girl friend and then became his mistress. Not noted for his largesse in these affairs, he even bought her a mink coat and installed her in a townhouse in Alexandria, Virginia, although he purchased the residence and held it in the name of one of his corporations.

When Loomis realized what was happening, she showed Barnes a copy of the Woodward article linking Wilson to the Letelier murder. If this was designed to frighten her off, its effect was exactly the opposite. Gee! the new bookkeeper thought. The CIA, bombings, foreign intrigue! "Life with Ed," she confided to a friend, "is like being in a movie." Her code name on telexes and in phone communications was "Wonder Woman." And before it was over, she would know more about what Wilson was doing than anyone else.

Early one morning, a couple of weeks after she started her new job, she found a strange man in the office. "Who are you?" she asked.

"My name's Pierre," said Thomas Clines.

She checked right away with the office manager, who said that it was okay. Later, Wilson told her that Clines had come in for some money; he always needed money. "Give him what he wants," Wilson said, "so long as it's not more than two thousand at a clip."

Clines had been very helpful. Wilson had learned that a grand jury was in session from Clines, who was told about it by Rafael Quintero. So he asked Clines for a list of Soviet weaponry in Libya that might be of interest to the agency and the Pentagon. That way, if the U.S. Attorney's Office kept nosing around, Wilson figured, he could claim that his Libyan activities were really serving U.S. intelligence. Clines had come up with about twenty items, including a new surface-to-air missile, an electronic mine, a MiG-25 fighter and a T-72 Russian tank. Schlachter got the list directly from Clines on one of his courier runs to carry back the classified data Waldo Dubberstein was passing to the Libyans.

In July 1978, just as Pedersen and Wadsworth were interviewing Kevin Mulcahy, Clines decided to make preparations to quit the CIA. He was nearing thirty years of service, more than enough for a full pension, and with Admiral Stansfield Turner as the CIA director, any hope for advancement was, to put it mildly, bleak.

Turner was anathema not only to Clines and Shackley but also to Wilson. He had come to believe Turner was behind the leaks to the Washington *Post* and he regaled Roberta Barnes and Peter Goulding about how he was going to fix Turner's ass. It would be right out of the agency book. He'd set up a deal with a publishing house to offer Turner $500,000 for his memoirs, payable at $100,000 annually, and after Turner accepted the first payment and resigned, Wilson would cut off the rest of the money.

It was worth a few chuckles, but he never followed through. What he did do was help Clines launch a business of his own that would broker the sale of U.S. oil-drilling equipment to various countries. Clines had it all figured. He'd start with Mexico, where the faithful Quintero and Ricardo Chavez, another Cuban exile who had been a daredevil boat skipper for the CIA's Miami station, had inside connections with the Mexican petroleum monopoly, Pemex.

In the fall of 1978, Joanne Loomis was called before the grand jury. She acknowledged arranging for the flight that Luke Thompson and the other Green Berets had taken to Libya, but so what? She maintained that she was just a dutiful secretary obeying her boss's instructions. As a matter of fact, she said, she was so uninterested in her job that she had left it, and Barcella, preoccupied with the Letelier case, simply didn't have enough information to box her in, to make her think twice about perjuring herself.

Wilson wasn't worried that she'd say anything. She was in a little too deep herself, and besides, she was afraid of him. But the fact that Barcella was still poking around was a disturbing sign. Wilson had already gotten rid of William Bittman, the Watergate defense lawyer he first hired, and, taking a totally different tack, had retained a Watergate prosecutor, Seymour Glanzer, who had worked closely in the U.S. Attorney's Office with Barcella's immediate superior, Don Campbell.

Glanzer had advised Wilson that on paper his scheme to train Libyan troops with ex–Green Berets was not subject to any registration or licensing as long as the instruction was limited to the "mere operation of weapons or simple tactical matters." The trick now was to convince Barcella of that and get Barcella off his back.

Except for the annoyance of the grand jury, 1978 had been as rewarding as Wilson could wish, and he decided to treat himself to a year-end bonus by purchasing one more spectacular piece of property in the northern Virginia hunt country, the thousand-acre Apple Manor estate, about five miles from Mount Airy Farms, for $1.2 million.

All of a sudden, though, he had a problem infinitely more pressing and vexing than Barcella. In December, in Geneva, Douglas Schlachter, sitting on top of a sizable fortune himself, told Wilson that he was fed up with Libya. And there was more to it. Schlachter, during his trips back and forth to Washington, had fallen in love with a lusty secretary named Tina Simons, who worked for Texas congressman Charles Wilson, and she wasn't about to bed down in Tripoli.

Edwin P. Wilson was dependent on Schlachter's being in Libya on a daily basis and tried to argue him out of leaving. If Schlachter would only stay on for another year, he'd raise the ante. But Schlachter was adamant. He wanted to be with Tina and he wanted to go into business for himself. So Wilson had no choice. To keep him happy and quiet, he let Schlachter take over one of his companies, Delex International, which specialized in the sale of surveillance and security equipment. Part of the deal was that Schlachter would also look after Wilson's new Apple Manor acquisition.

Wilson wasn't about to move to Libya either. He thought that some of the slack caused by Schlachter's departure could be handled by a former Army master sergeant and explosives expert, John Heath, who had been in the original team recruited by Brower to work in the bomb factory. Heath had remained after his year's contract was up; he epitomized the good soldier who did what he was told, and he seemed to get along pretty well with the Libyans.

Still, it was clear to Wilson that he would have to spend much more time in Libya. Perhaps the best solution was to set up a base in London; from there it would be easier to fly in and out of Tripoli.

As Wilson was brooding over all of this after the first of the year in his townhouse at 1016 22nd Street, he received a call from a man who, after identifying himself, said, "You remember me, don't you?" and Wilson said, "No. Well, yeah, maybe. What do you want? I'm busy as hell."

"It's about some hardware," the man said. "This guy contacted me. He's got good references. He's a Jew, I think, from New York, fronting for one of those crazy Jew outfits. They want to make a significant buy, ah, for over there. I thought you'd be interested."

"Okay," Wilson said, "bring him in. I'll have a look."

3

All through December Pedersen and Wadsworth had hashed over the scam. An undercover BATF agent would be brought down from New York. The idea was that the agent would pose as a representative of a radical Zionist organization, like the Jewish Defense League, who wanted to purchase a quantity of small arms for "protection" overseas.

The timing was perfect. The newspapers were running stories about Israeli settlers moving into the West Bank on their own. But he wouldn't spell this out. He'd simply say that he was acting on behalf of some concerned citizens in New York. It was vital to force Wilson into faking an end-user's certificate that attested to the ultimate destination of weaponry and equipment restricted by U.S. export controls.

The problem was getting in the front door, and Kevin Mulcahy came up with the answer. There was a fellow, a consultant in the security field, who had hung around the Inter-Technology office trying to promote some action, and Wilson had met him once or twice. Mulcahy would go to the man and say he had run across this hot deal, but he and Wilson were temporarily on the outs. Once the deal went through, they'd split the finder's fee, everything would be cool with Wilson and afterward who knew what might be next.

It worked. The BATF undercover agent pretending to be an arms buyer was Gerard H. Rudden. He said his name was "Jerry Riddick." Rudden was wired when he and his unwitting intermediary went to the townhouse. Pedersen and Wadsworth listened in a car parked down the block.

The first thing Wilson said was, "You with CBS, NBC?" After more than two years of investigation and headlines, the Orlando Letelier murder trial had finally gotten under way and when Rudden snapped, "Sure, and *The New York Times*," Wilson said, "Look, sorry, forget it. You won't believe how my ass was burned once on the Letelier thing."

Wilson seemed distracted. "Pete Goulding here handles all the stuff you want," he said. He told Goulding he had to leave, to meet "Tom."

Rudden gave Goulding a list of the desired arms. It was on the stationery of "Can-Do Associates," with a Manhattan address. The telephone number had an answering service. The list included Remington .308 rifles with night scopes, MAC-10 submachine guns, Smith & Wesson nine-millimeter pistols with silencers, shotguns, grenade launchers and ammunition.

"I don't see any problems with this," said Goulding. "None at all. What would be the destination?"

"Let's just say the southern Mediterranean area," Rudden said. "I don't want to get into it geographically that much more."

"I see, of course."

"Maybe the desert, like the Sinai, say."

"I understand," Goulding said. "We don't have to have a firm destination. If you prefer, just give us the map coordinates and we can have it parachuted in anywhere in the world."

"That's good to know. Right now, delivery could be by ship, by air. I got to check with my people."

"I just want to make it clear," Goulding said, "that while

we're happy to service this small order, we can make rapid delivery on more sophisticated material—surface-to-air, planes, artillery, tanks, whatever. So please keep us in mind."

"I'll be in touch," Rudden said.

"I'll work up some quotes," Goulding replied.

Oh, boy, Pedersen thought.

There were more meetings and discussions with Goulding, about delivery dates, cost estimates, the availability of certain guns. The list had been devised so that most of the weapons had to be American-made. Goulding's total price was around $650,-000. He had to have ten percent down "for the paperwork," which meant the payoffs for a spurious end-user certificate. "We have a number of options here," he assured Rudden. "Nigeria, Portugal, Spain, Belgium."

Pedersen already had gotten a $25,000 commitment from the BATF. Barcella went to the FBI for the rest of the money. He was told that more information would be needed, and Pedersen couldn't wait. He tried U.S. Customs and got a no thanks. Then Barcella called the Justice Department, which said it would look into it and never got back to him. The fact was that Ed Wilson no longer rated as a high-priority item.

Then, suddenly, it didn't matter. Wilson packed up most of his operation in the townhouse and, complete with Roberta Barnes, moved to London. Pedersen wondered if Wilson had been tipped off. He had no idea of the complications caused by Doug Schlachter's decision to leave Libya, or of some other projects Wilson had cooking.

Pedersen sensed it all slipping away. After a series of overseas phone calls with Rudden, Goulding said that Rudden's people would have to come to England, or to Belgium, if they wanted the transaction to go through. It wasn't as if they had been doing business regularly together, and to execute the sale in the United States at this time was too perilous. "Ed," Goulding said, "has decided that the risk is just not worth it for an order of this size."

Rudden made a last-ditch effort to turn Goulding around. All through his conversations with him, without actually saying so, Rudden had painted his group's benefactor as a cantankerous but wealthy Jewish clothing manufacturer. "My money guy," he said, "is an old guy. He's used to hanging garments on people. He won't fly. He told me, 'Why can't we look at the stuff here, if it's made here?' You know, Peter, how can I answer that?"

"I appreciate what you're saying," Goulding said. "But Ed's mind is made up. Perhaps we'll be in contact on something in the future." And Pedersen and Wadsworth, watching the tape reels spin as Rudden spoke on the phone, knew that they would have to start all over again. Go back to the beginning. Interview everybody. Unravel this the hard way.

THIRTEEN

It was eerie, Barcella thought, how Wilson kept impinging on Letelier. Under great pressure exerted by Barcella and Propper through various government agencies, an American named Michael Townley was extradited from Chile. He had been working for the Chilean secret police and had constructed the device that killed Letelier.

To hide its hand, the Chilean regime also had used a number of ultra-right Cuban exiles in the conspiracy, but the case against them was so tenuous that Barcella and Propper needed Townley's testimony and had to let him plea-bargain a ten-year sentence in return for becoming a federal witness. Even the charges against Townley were weak, lacking key testimony from high Chilean officials, and Barcella figured they were lucky to have outfoxed Townley's attorney enough to get the plea. Worse yet, two Cubans, who actually had triggered the bomb by remote control, had fled the United States once they knew they were going to be fingered by Townley.

Which was how Barcella learned that Seymour Glanzer was now representing Wilson. Washington was such a revolving-door town. Glanzer was Townley's lawyer as well, and when he asked for a meeting, Barcella and Propper assumed it was to iron out some details about Townley's sentencing.

But instead it was Ed Wilson that Glanzer had come to talk about. How interested was Barcella in Wilson? Would Barcella drop whatever charges he was contemplating against him if Wilson was able to produce the Letelier fugitives? Wilson had all kinds of lines into the Cuban community. It wasn't that Wilson was so worried, but it was bad for business to have this cloud hanging over him. "That's tough," Barcella said. Something might be possible, but under no circumstances would he give Wilson a free ride.

Well, what about reducing the charges to a misdemeanor? The government, Glanzer argued, would have a horrendous time making a case that would stand up in court. Barcella said, "We'll see."

The Letelier trial, which resulted in life-term murder convictions not only for the two Cuban fugitives but for others involved in the conspiracy, had exactly paralleled the six-week undercover arms-buy Pedersen and Wadsworth tried to engineer. Barcella wished he had been able to give them more support, but he really didn't have a choice.

During the trial, Barcella had lost fifteen pounds. Fighting off the flu, he had taken to using a nasal spray and after doing so for more than a month, had suddenly lost his sense of smell and taste. His doctor told him to take a look at the directions the next time—do not exceed a week's usage—and just managed to save the nerve endings in Barcella's nose after nearly a year of treatment. His doctor also was the Washington coroner. When a friend observed that at least the price was right, Barcella said, "Yeah, but there's a down side to it. He's used to attaching his bill to your toe."

Now Barcella began spending hours with Kevin Mulcahy, trying to get insights into Wilson, and at the CIA headquarters in Langley. The agency continued to deny that it had the slightest connection with Wilson's Libyan activities. It also was less than open about his career as an agent. Barcella had to bargain with the CIA's legal office, which then took his requests to the clandestine side, and the information would come, at best, in maddening dribs and drabs. "You know," he said, "talking to me isn't exactly like talking to a reporter." The Navy, on the other hand, had been pretty straight about Wilson's years in Task Force 157.

2

Pedersen and Wadsworth went back to square one—the fifty Remington rifles that had been sought in Springfield—and dropped by to see General J. J. Cappucci. A short, bald man with a pompous air, he had vacated Wilson's townhouse and set up offices of his own. According to Cappucci, he had teamed up with Wilson for only a brief period. He hadn't cared one bit for Wilson's Libyan venture, especially since he had a contract to train security personnel for Qaddafi's bitter enemy, Egyptian president Anwar Sadat. Later, when Sadat was assassinated, Pedersen would wonder if Cappucci still included the contract in his résumé.

"Tell us about Libya," Wadsworth said, and Cappucci insisted that he knew none of the details. "You have to understand," he said. "Wilson had his things, and I had mine."

Pedersen brought up the rifles. He was sorry, Cappucci said. He didn't have any idea of what they were for, or where they were going.

As evasive as Cappucci was, he had said something of interest. If they wanted to know about Libya, they should talk to Doug Schlachter. That was the second time the two BATF agents had heard his name.

Mulcahy had mentioned him, although all he knew about Schlachter was that he had accompanied John Harper and his son when they first went to Tripoli. Mulcahy also continued to push the idea that Jerome Brower had sent more explosives than were specified in the lading bills the FBI had retrieved. Pedersen returned to his original thought. Maybe the declared cargo had disguised what really was shipped out. Either way, it was worth another crack at Brower.

An FBI interview in 1977 had simply recorded Brower's answers without challenging them. Pedersen could picture the scene. Washington had sent out a memo and some guy in the Los Angeles office had caught it. Go see Brower about the shipment. It was probably one of twenty such requests he had on his desk that day and in the FBI it was important to keep your desk clean. That was a big advantage BATF agents had. If a case was important, they could follow it in person.

On Thursday afternoon before Memorial Day weekend, 1979, Pedersen and Wadsworth went to see Barcella and Propper about authorizing a grand jury subpoena for Brower. But

Barcella had taken the week off, his first vacation in three years, so they told Propper what they wanted and were floored to hear him say that if anything was to be done regarding Wilson, it would be on solicitation to commit murder and possibly failing to register as a foreign agent.

My God, Pedersen thought, this was a polite way of telling them that their services were no longer needed, that the investigation was over. "Gene," he pleaded, "it's clear what happened. Brower could be the key."

"I appreciate your efforts," Propper said. "We're going with the case the way it is."

The two agents had picked up rumors that Propper intended to leave the U.S. Attorney's Office to go into private practice and write a book about the Letelier affair. In a bar over beers, Wadsworth said, "That's all he's thinking about, his goddamn book! How can he close it off so fast? What do we have to show for our time? Is that how it is?"

Yes, sometimes it was, Pedersen wanted to say, but didn't. "Look," he said, trying to calm down Wadsworth, "we'll ask for a formal write-up. Make them decline on paper."

The next day, still steaming, Rick Wadsworth went on his own to the U.S. Attorney's Office to poke through the file on Wilson and Terpil. Because of the holiday weekend, he knew that only a skeleton staff would be on duty. He told one of the secretaries that he had to look up something on the investigation, so she opened Propper's safe and got the file and he started reading through it page by page. Around three o'clock, he phoned Pedersen and said, "Jesus, Dick, I've found something. Get right down here."

What Wadsworth had discovered was the original Libyan explosives list typed up by Eula Harper, then Wilson's secretary, for the meeting in Washington nearly three years ago, the one attended by Wilson, Terpil, John Harper, Mulcahy and Walter Doerr, the Lufthansa representative.

The Harpers had been served with a subpoena requiring them to produce all documents that related to Wilson and Terpil. Faced with obstruction-of-justice charges, they had finally complied with a packet of papers that included the list Wadsworth had in his hands. But the papers arrived in the middle of the Letelier trial and nobody had the time then to look at them.

On it were all the explosives Brower had acknowledged sending—*plus* quantities of Composition C-4 in both bulk and sheet form. Alongside each item were handwritten notations concerning price quotes and an occasional correction in terminology. When Pedersen saw the list, he couldn't believe it. "Where'd you get this?" he asked.

"It was there in the safe all the time. Want to bet whose handwriting that is?"

"Hey, no contest," Pedersen said. "It's got to be Jerry Brower."

First thing the following Tuesday, when Barcella got back, Pedersen and Wadsworth saw him alone. They showed him the list and said they needed a subpoena for Brower. This could be a big break, but Propper had told them that the case was dead. "Well, it isn't a corpse yet," Barcella said, promising the subpoena. "Maybe you can breathe some life into it."

They had another problem, Pedersen said. Their own boss was questioning where the investigation was going, so Barcella agreed to call him. The two agents, he said, had developed a significant new lead in California and he trusted that they would be permitted to pursue it. The U.S. Attorney's Office was committed to the case. It was, he would realize, the first time he had actually said this out loud.

Brower played the put-upon citizen when Pedersen telephoned and said he wanted to discuss an explosives shipment to Libya that J. S. Brower and Associates had made for Edwin P. Wilson and Frank Terpil in August 1976. He'd gone through all this before with the FBI. "I've been inconvenienced enough," he said. How so? Pedersen asked, and Brower said, "I told you. The FBI." The explosives were for a mine-clearing operation. He'd even advised Wilson and Terpil that some of the explosives they desired were not suitable for such a project.

Why, Pedersen persisted, hadn't he gotten an export license for the Primacord, the detonating cord that had a C-4 core? "I didn't think I needed it," Brower said. "You're drawing a pretty fine line there, fellow." The indignation in his voice mounted. Listen, he said, he'd been called in again and again for his counsel on legislation by the Bureau of Alcohol, Tobacco and Firearms. Was this his reward?

"I'd like to set up an appointment to see you," Pedersen replied mildly. Well, that was too bad, Brower snapped. He was leaving on an extended business trip overseas that very day. Wouldn't be back till August. "I'll wait," Pedersen said.

A few days later, Barcella read in the Washington *Post* that there was going to be a Green Beret reunion in one of the city's hotels. It might be just the time to round up some of the men Luke Thompson had recruited for Wilson. Wadsworth went over with a batch of subpoenas and found three of them. The reunion dress was as bizarre as anything he had ever seen. Most of the participants were in black tie, but the usual satin lapels and trouser piping had been replaced with camouflage uniform material. Wadsworth asked if anyone knew Douglas Schlachter and was told, "He was here, left his card." The next day Pedersen served Schlachter in his Delex International office. "He was real shook up," Pedersen said.

All three ex-Berets were represented by Ken Conklin and each parroted the same tale before the grand jury. The program they conducted in Libya was strictly low-level, very basic instruction. A little parachuting. A little medical training. A little small-arms indoctrination. Nothing sophisticated. Nothing remotely related to terrorism. And each emphasized that he had been hired by a private commercial enterprise based in Geneva, Switzerland. They weren't mercenaries. They had broken no laws. As they individually testified they employed almost the same words. It was too pat, Barcella thought. Conklin must have rehearsed them for hours.

Schlachter never showed up. Conklin was his lawyer also. He informed Barcella that his client was off on an emergency trip to Egypt and had fallen ill there. And then, according to Conklin, he really didn't know where Schlachter was. He'd be in touch when he got some news. In fact, Conklin did know. Schlachter had panicked and fled the country. First he tried to rejoin Wilson, but Wilson was regretful; he had no further use for him. Next he looked up Frank Terpil in London. By now, Idi Amin, to whom Terpil had been supplying explosives, guns and torture equipment, had been overthrown in Uganda. Terpil was on the hunt for more action and thought maybe through Schlachter's connections he could worm back into the mother lode, Libya.

3

When the two BATF agents finally met with Brower in his Pomona office on August 15, Pedersen did the interrogating while Wadsworth was off to one side taking notes. Brower's attorney, Edward Bloom, who had flown from Houston with the twenty-one-ton C-4 delivery, sat next to him.

Brower repeated his story. Wilson and Terpil had a contract to clear mines in Libya. It was that simple. No, C-4 was never discussed, he said.

Pedersen wanted to know about the Triex and Quadrex binary explosives. Were they the kinds of substances you used for mine-clearing? *He* didn't have to be told about Triex, Brower said. *He* had patented it. All you had to do was pour it around a mine, and good-bye mine. Quadrex, he admitted, deteriorated when exposed to moisture, but in case they didn't know it, Libya had a quite dry climate.

What about the ammonium nitrate? By itself, it was a fertilizer, but if mixed with diesel oil and set off by a stick of dynamite, it became a powerful blasting agent that had been used, for example, by a radical student group in 1970 to blow up a research center at the University of Wisconsin.

"Look," said Brower, "let me tell you the bottom line on that. I told them that personally I would recommend other stuff, but they wanted it. What can I tell you? The customer's always right."

Bloom, a chubby man, jowls quivering, broke in. "What the hell's going on here!" he exclaimed, and launched into a harangue about Brower. He was a patriot, a war hero, a man of courage, he said, pointing at Brower's hand with the missing fingers, a man always available to aid law-enforcement agencies, a man whose counsel the U.S. Senate held in the highest esteem. Why was he being subjected to this?

"Mr. Brower," Pedersen said, "who was at the meeting in Washington besides Wilson and Terpil?"

"John Harper. I'd met him once before. He's a Mason, like me. And Harper's wife. Someone from Lufthansa. And a kid, Kevin something. Wilson's errand boy, I think. Sort of wacky, if you ask me."

"Did you make any other shipments for Wilson or Terpil to Libya besides the one in August 1976?"

"No," Brower said. "That was it."

After a lunch break, Pedersen dropped the "Mr. Brower." He handed him a copy of the explosives list Wadsworth had found in the safe and said, "Hey, Jerry, I thought you told us you didn't discuss any C-4. That's your handwriting there, isn't it?"

The two agents watched him sag back as he stared at the list. Almost a minute passed before he pulled himself together. "Oh, yes, you're right. I guess I forgot. Seeing this refreshes my recollection. But what difference does it make? I didn't ship it."

"Didn't you call your office to find out how much C-4 you had and give instructions about how to package it?"

"No, I just asked about availability. I told Wilson I wasn't shipping it unless he got the licenses, and he didn't."

"How come you didn't tell the FBI Wilson wanted you to ship prohibited explosives?"

"Because they didn't ask."

Pedersen took a flyer. "You know what I think, Jerry. You didn't ship the nitrate and half that other stuff. You packed C-4 in those drums." But Brower was vehement in his denials.

"Okay," Pedersen said, "see you in Washington," and presented him with a subpoena, answerable in a week, to appear before the grand jury.

When they left Brower's office, Wadsworth said, "You know, I'll bet you anything there were other shipments."

"Yeah," Pedersen said, "but how are we going to find out? Jerry's got a lot of balls."

Under oath, Brower stayed with his story. He insisted that the bomb factory with Americans working in it that Luke Thompson had described was news to him. Finally he admitted that one of his men, Doug Smith, had gone over to check on the shipment, but that was all. At first, though, he couldn't even remember Smith's name. Some other Americans were also around. He couldn't recall their names either, or what they were doing. They were Wilson's people. Brower was very cool on the stand. Defense lawyers are not allowed in grand jury sessions but in the corridor outside, pacing to and fro, Bloom looked as if he might keel over any second. That was funny, Pedersen thought. Normally, you'd expect the lawyer to be the cool one.

Right after his testimony, Brower flew to London to fill in Wilson on what he'd been asked, and what he had said. But he was worried. Just as he was stepping into an elevator in the courthouse to leave, he had seen Barcella and asked him, "Are you finally satisfied I'm telling the truth?" and Barcella had said, "No, I'm not." Then Barcella heard his muffled yelling on the other side of the door after it closed.

Take it easy, Wilson told Brower. His lawyer in Washington had good lines into the U.S. Attorney's Office. It was all smoke and no fire. All they had to do was hang tough, and sooner or later, it would blow away.

4

In London Wilson had leased a fashionable mews house for himself and Roberta Barnes and maintained offices for another company he had created, Brilhurst, Ltd., across the way from Harrods department store. He bought a country home in West Sussex called Staplefield Grange and was extensively refurbishing another estate, Broxmead Farm.

In Geneva he had still another office. And in Tripoli, because of the time he now had to spend there following Schlachter's departure, he purchased a two-story villa by the sea, with adjoining twin apartments on the second floor and a work area below.

Even with Schlachter no longer on the scene, everything was going swimmingly, so in the spring of 1979 he was more than eager to oblige Major Hajazzi's request for some American handguns.

Wilson placed an overseas call to Wally Klink, one of the many former Green Berets recruited for Libya. He had found Klink exceptionally stable, and after his contract was up and he wanted to return to the States, Wilson gave him a job caring for all his farm machinery at Mount Airy. Wilson told him he needed four used pistols, and not to go to any dealers where the sales would be recorded. The lady of the house, Barbara Wilson, would provide the money. Then Wilson phoned his wife and instructed her to advance $1,500 in cash to Klink.

The only place Klink knew of to acquire the handguns was his old stamping grounds in Fayetteville, North Carolina, around Fort Bragg. He contacted a Special Forces friend, explained what he wanted and said that the guns were for his boss, who was "ex-CIA." His friend squired him to the Bonnie Doone Volunteer Fire Department in Fayetteville. One of the firemen, whose wife was a deputy sheriff, had two guns for sale, a Smith & Wesson .38 and a Magnum .357. Klink bought them for $300. At another stop, he got two more pistols, also for $300.

Klink gave them to Reginald Slocombe, Wilson's Mormon freight forwarder. Slocombe bought a portable toolbox at his local hardware store in Purcellville, Virginia, collected some hammers, wrenches and pieces of pipe to confuse X-ray detection, and wrapping them in sponge rubber along with the pistols, put everything in the box and bound it with metal straps.

At Heathrow Airport in London, Slocombe left the toolbox in transit storage, telephoned Wilson in Geneva and told him, "Mission accomplished." The delivery had to be made that night at eleven o'clock in Bonn, Wilson said. Essadine Monseur, a Libyan intelligence officer whom Slocombe had once met in Tripoli, would be waiting in front of the train station. Wilson then gave Slocombe a Rotterdam number for Peter Goulding, who was in Holland on another assignment. Goulding would meet him, and they were to drive together to the West German capital.

Declaring that he was carrying tools, Slocombe got through Dutch customs without incident. He removed the weapons from the box and hid them under the rear seat of Goulding's car. The two crossed the German border after a cursory inspection and sped in the night toward Bonn.

Slocombe recognized Monseur at the station and followed his car through the city's streets on a circuitous route that ended near the Libyan embassy, where he finally handed over the four guns.

5

In Libya Colonel Qaddafi had issued an ultimatum directed to certain Libyans living abroad. "Either you return to the masses of the People's Republic when called, or you are condemned to death wherever you are." And in the ensuing months at least ten Libyan expatriates were slain on the European continent and in England. One of those who had failed to heed the colonel's summons to return to Tripoli was forty-two-year-old Omran el-Mehdawi, a former attaché for economic affairs and an intelligence officer in Libya's embassy in Bonn. He had started a successful export-import business, married a German woman and was now the father of a baby girl.

About a year after Slocombe delivered the handguns, Mehdawi was on his way to his office. Vehicular traffic was banned in Bonn's inner city. The train station was on the edge of the restricted area, and as usual, Mehdawi parked his Mercedes on the far side of the station to walk through an underpass. Munching an apple, he entered the underpass and had just reached the end of it when Bashiv Emimida, twenty-five, fired four bullets into his back. A German attorney turned upon hearing the shots, saw Emimida holding a revolver and grabbed him before he could escape. A vagrant passing by also joined in, biting Emimida's ear to further subdue him.

Emimida first claimed that he had shot Mehdawi because of an unpaid debt. But soon afterward, he admitted that he was acting on behalf of the "Community of the Masses," that the people of Libya had sentenced Mehdawi to death and he had been sent as a legitimate executioner. After his conviction for murder, he was deported to Libya in exchange for three West German geologists who had been conveniently imprisoned by the Qaddafi regime on vague espionage charges.

The weapon used in the murder was the same .357 Magnum that Wally Klink had acquired at the Bonnie Doone Volunteer Fire Department in Fayetteville.

flu, say, and something was needed, the prospect of locating it was not dazzling.

He asked Bruce to pull together the many disparate elements of the case—the FBI interviews, the BATF interviews, interviews conducted by the U.S. Attorney's Office, grand jury testimony, whatever information had been derived from the CIA —all the leads thus far developed.

Barcella wanted the magnitude of the case put down on paper. There was a sense that the investigation was a waste of time, that it wasn't ever going to go anywhere, and this feeling might suddenly mushroom irretrievably. Carl Rauh, number two in the office, had needled him mildly, "Listen, Larry, aren't you going a little overboard on a couple of exploding ashtrays?" Rauh could have taken him off the case, but he was one of Barcella's closest friends, and he didn't.

At the end of September Brower's man Doug Smith went before the grand jury. Nobody then knew that Smith had personally trucked a shipment of Composition C-4 to Los Angeles International Airport in April 1977, and had supervised the packing of twenty-one tons of C-4 in hundreds of cans labeled oil-drilling mud six months later, so he was asked only about the one shipment that was known—the first planeload of explosives ordered by Wilson and Terpil that had gone out in August 1976.

Now a Brower vice president, Smith echoed his boss exactly. The shipment had been legal. Yes, he'd gone to Libya to make sure everything was all right and afterward had just sat around for a while. No, he couldn't remember the names of any other Americans he had been with.

But Smith's grand jury appearance opened up a new avenue of investigation. His passport was subpoenaed and in it was an entry visa for Idi Amin's Uganda dated September 22, 1977. Frank Terpil had moved to Uganda when he and Wilson split. What was Smith doing there?

Well, he had accompanied still another cargo, like the one for Libya, nothing illegal. Terpil wanted him to teach the Ugandans scuba-diving for underwater demolition work. Barcella was incredulous. In crocodile-filled Lake Victoria in the middle of Africa? Idi Amin himself, Smith insisted, had bestowed diplomas when the instruction course was completed. As a matter of fact, said Smith, he had his students playing basketball to build up their wind.

Barcella kept thinking about the Americans Luke Thompson had seen making terrorist explosive devices. Brower, like Smith, had danced all around their identities. First he couldn't recall their names. Next he allowed that he might have helped Wilson get them, but was unable to remember any specifics. Finally he had taken the Fifth.

Brower had to have recruited them. Nothing in Wilson's background indicated any knowledgeability about explosives. That's why he had approached Brower in the first place. Dick Pedersen and Rick Wadsworth were returning to California to see if they could dredge up more on Brower's Libyan shipment and now the one to Uganda, and Barcella had an idea. If Brower had hired the unknown Americans, it was just possible that he had arranged for their transportation as well. With his world-wide business, Brower surely must have a travel agency.

Pedersen fell back on an old gimmick. He telephoned Brower's office, got his secretary on the line, said that he was with a new travel service in Pomona, and if Brower didn't already have an agency, would he like one?

"Well, he does," she said.

"Could I send over some brochures anyway?" Pedersen said.

"If you wish, but I should tell you, young man, that Mr. Brower is very happy with the agency he has."

"Darn! Which one is it?"

"Jones Travel Associates, down on Foothills Boulevard. Mr. Brower has used it for years."

Pedersen and Wadsworth arrived at Jones Travel with a subpoena for the travel records of J. S. Brower and Associates and for Brower himself during the past five years. As soon as he could, Pedersen phoned Barcella, "You were right, Larry. We've got them."

The first name, Doug Smith, was no surprise. But the others were stunners. Two of them were Dennis J. Wilson and Robert Earl Swallow, security-cleared civilian employees of a top secret Navy weapons-testing facility at China Lake, California, in the Mojave Desert, both of whom had been granted leaves of absence to go to Libya. A fourth was John Heath, a former Army master sergeant and expert in explosives and bomb disposal who had often been called upon by the Secret Service for his help on presidential protection details. Heath had retired from the Army immediately prior to his departure for Libya.

All four left the United States together on the same date, October 3, 1976. A fifth man, George Doritty, also a retired Army explosives sergeant, who replaced Smith, had gone to Libya on January 4, 1977. He was now back in the United States at the Redstone Arsenal in Huntsville, Alabama, conducting seminars for law-enforcement officers about the vagaries of terrorist bomb devices, how they were built and how to dismantle them.

Once again the specter rose that this was somehow an agency-sanctioned operation, or that at least some cabal in the Langley labyrinth knew about it. How else could men in positions of such obvious trust have permitted themselves to become involved in a conspiracy like this? Could they have been that venal?

Through U.S. Customs declarations, Pedersen and Wadsworth got their addresses, dates of birth and signatures. Heath's listed domicile was in Seattle, but when Wadsworth tried to find him, he was told that Heath hadn't been seen in a couple of years, that he was working somewhere out of the country.

Swallow and Dennis Wilson were still living in a Mojave Desert town. The two agents first visited Swallow, who remained a China Lake employee. Although he seemed nervous, he appeared to have been forewarned. He excused himself to make a sandwich and chomped at it throughout the interview. A slick way, Dick Pedersen thought, to hide his stress.

Swallow admitted going to Libya for Brower. It was a mine-clearing project, he said. But to tell the truth, he'd had a drinking problem then and it was all very fuzzy. Mostly he hadn't done much more than sit around. Listen, Pedersen said, they weren't zeroing in on him. They just wanted information. Why not explain what happened in Libya, and something could be worked out. "I don't know what you're talking about," Swallow said.

They found Dennis Wilson in a trailer park. He had left China Lake and was selling real estate. Pedersen noticed a copy of the Koran on a table and a palm-branch cross on the wall from a Palm Sunday service. Hey, wow, Pedersen thought, this guy is into everything.

Hostile and unyielding, he told the same story about

Brower hiring him for mine-clearing. On the basis of this, he said, he had no trouble getting a leave from China Lake. He'd done some demolition teaching in Libya, but it was sporadic. He, too, had plenty of spare time. The boiler broke where he had been quartered, and he busied himself repairing it. He had picked oranges in a nearby grove and he started mowing the grass on an expanse of lawn that was going to seed. Like Swallow, Dennis Wilson was given a grand jury subpoena.

Pedersen reached George Doritty in Huntsville, Alabama, by phone. Even long distance, he could hear the quaver in Doritty's voice when he told him why he was calling. Doritty would be contacted in Huntsville or brought to the U.S. Attorney's Office in Washington. In any event, he was to make himself available, and Doritty had whispered, "Yes, sir."

Next Pedersen and Wadsworth turned their attention to an airport in Ontario, California, not far from Brower's Fontana bunkers, where Doug Smith said he had taken off for Uganda. They discovered that the shipment, two years before, had been the talk of the town. It wasn't every day that a Ugandan airliner with an Egyptian captain, a Ugandan copilot and a Lebanese flight engineer flew in. The airport's assistant manager told Pedersen and Wadsworth that the 707 had arrived out of nowhere. Then a man named Frank Terpil had showed up with an explosives export declaration from Brower and Associates that had passed muster with the State Department munitions control office.

How much C-4 might have been in the drums loaded on the 707 couldn't be determined. "I wouldn't know it if I saw it," one of the customs agents said. What everyone at the airport most recalled was that the tab for food, fuel and services for the plane and its crew was paid by the pilot out of a suitcase bulging with cash.

2

While Terpil was occupying Pedersen and Wadsworth in California, he had also come on center stage for Barcella. And again it was the Letelier case that triggered it. The FBI case agent on Letelier told Barcella that he had gotten a tip out of New York that might lead them to the two fugitive Cuban killers. A defense lawyer had advised a convicted narcotics dealer that he was in for a heavy sentence and nothing could be done about it, and he ought to think about skipping the country. The lawyer knew just the place, a kind of halfway house for fugitives, a hotel called Hunters Lodge in Crewe, England. Among others who had stayed there, he said, were two Cubans wanted in the Letelier murder.

Major U.S. embassies have FBI agents, who are called legal attachés, stationed in them, and Barcella had a cable sent to the one in London requesting information about the Crewe hotel. A week later he learned that while title to the hotel was held by a corporation, the local constabulary believed that it actually had been purchased for $500,000 by an American named Frank, last name unknown.

Crewe was near the city of Manchester, headquarters for Samuel Cummings, one of the world's biggest arms merchants, and it took Barcella about five seconds to decide that "Frank" was Frank Terpil. Now he wanted to see the lawyer, but word came back from New York that he had mysteriously disappeared. The rumor was that he was in the custody of the Manhattan district attorney, Robert Morgenthau, but nobody knew why.

Barcella, who wasn't acquainted with anyone in Morgenthau's office, asked the Justice Department to intervene. The response, he was told, was distinctly chilly, and it wasn't unexpected. There was an enormous rivalry between federal and local law enforcement in New York.

Finally Barcella flew to New York to meet with members of Morgenthau's staff. He saw at once that there was an uncommon concern about Terpil, and he laid it all out, explaining Terpil's connection with Wilson, everything he had found out about him. "Look," he said, "I only want him nailed. I don't care who gets the credit." His listeners remained noncommittal. "We'll think about it."

The next day Morgenthau asked Barcella to return. It was unusual for someone from Washington to be so open, he said, but his interest in Terpil involved an unrelated case. Terpil had been around New York hustling arms deals. Two undercover cops, posing as Latin Americans seeking weapons to support revolutionary activity, approached him and began negotiating a $2 million sale that included thousands of machine guns. At that very moment, one of the undercover cops was in England meeting with Terpil to inspect the merchandise.

Morgenthau told Barcella that his men had recorded Terpil as he laughingly described life in Uganda with Idi Amin: how one of Amin's political prisoners had been tied down and a rat placed on his stomach which was then covered by a heavy iron pot, so that the only way the rat could escape was by gnawing through the man's body, and how, on another occasion at a banquet a covered dish was brought in which contained the severed head of a cabinet minister Amin suspected of plotting against him. "Our friend Frank sounds like quite a fellow," Morgenthau observed in his customary low-key fashion, puffing on a cigar.

They were going to have to close out the case fairly soon, he added. Terpil was insisting on a cash down payment. A couple of weeks later, on December 22, 1979, Barcella and Carol Bruce were invited to be on hand for the arrest. Right afterward Barcella was allowed an opportunity to interview Terpil, on the chance that this might be the moment he'd be ready to talk. It was the first time they had met and Terpil turned on the charm. He'd like to help on Libya, but he couldn't. "Ed aced me out after two or three months," he said. "We haven't been together in I don't know how many years. Anyway, everything you're after was Wilson's, it wasn't really mine. I know what that crazy fuck Mulcahy is saying. But he's a fucking drunk. He doesn't know which way is up."

"What about the hotel in Crewe?" Barcella said. "I heard you were running an underground railroad for fugitives."

"Listen, pal, you get to know me better, you'll find out I embroider things a little bit. I might have said something to somebody, but it wasn't so. That hotel was just an investment."

There was no evidence to the contrary when Scotland Yard raided the hotel and also a London residence Terpil had. Barcella, Bruce and Rick Wadsworth made a quick trip over to examine the documents that had been seized. Papers at the London address showed that Doug Schlachter, in evading his grand jury subpoena, had spent a good deal of time there throughout the fall. Among the items were telephone messages from Schlachter's Washington lawyer, Ken Conklin. Schlachter had been trying to get back into business in Libya with Terpil, but Wilson had them thrown out.

Over Morgenthau's bitter protests, Terpil was released after posting a $100,000 bond. In Washington a CIA spokesman refused comment on whether Terpil had ever been an agency employee.

3

About the time of Terpil's arrest, Carol Bruce finally finished her "Summary of the Facts" in the Wilson/Terpil case. It had taken more than two months and was worth the wait.

She began with all the known background information on both men. The typed summary, running forty-four pages, was divided into six categories: the August 1976 meeting to ship explosives to Libya; an account of efforts to obtain and then to manufacture time-delay detonators; the secret proposal entered into between Inter-Technology and Libya to train terrorists and the recruitment of Americans for the bomb factory, with a subsection devoted to Frank Terpil's activities in Uganda; the solicitation of the three Cubans for an assassination plot; the shipment of long-range surveillance vans with day/night-vision cameras to Libya via Canada; and the recruitment of former U.S. Special Forces personnel to instruct a cadre of Libyan military officers in "commando and terrorist-type activities."

The summary was written in narrative, nonlegalese form. Even though it did not mention the C-4 shipments, nobody who read it made any more wisecracks about exploding ashtrays. Also included was a section suggesting possible violations of U.S. criminal statutes. And that was the rub. A great deal of the evidence was circumstantial, many of the violations technically grounded in legal quicksand that defense lawyers could have a field day with.

Someone had to crack, and nobody had yet. Barcella and Bruce decided to grant immunity to John Harper, his wife and son. To get indictments, they had to have their testimony, and with immunity the Harpers would have to cooperate or face either perjury or contempt charges. The former CIA explosives man then admitted drawing up the original requisition list, including C-4, on the orders of Wilson and Terpil.

Wayne Harper acknowledged that he had constructed at least twenty-five booby-trap bombs after Wilson had taken his father out of Libya, although he claimed to have rendered some of them inoperable; he had stayed on, he said, because of the money.

Eula Harper said that she had really paid William Weisenburger, the CIA technical man, $8,000 in cash for the first batch of timers, not the $1,800 billed by the manufacturer.

Toward the end of January, George Doritty was brought to Washington. Pedersen had told Barcella that of all the people he had spoken to, he had a hunch that Doritty was the one who might cave in. Interviewing him in Barcella's office, away from his home turf in Alabama, might pressure him some more.

Doritty, accompanied by a lawyer, appeared nervous, but at first he stuck to a familiar story. He had gone over to Libya for mine-clearing. He, too, had sat around a lot. Even mowed the lawn, like Dennis Wilson.

Pedersen suddenly snapped, "How long are you going to keep up this I-was-only-cutting-the-grass routine? We know what you were doing. You know what you can get for perjury?" Doritty looked panic-stricken and Barcella said, "Will you excuse yourself for a moment?" Then he told the lawyer just how much trouble his client was in.

After a brief recess, Doritty's lawyer asked the first question. "Did you ever make or have a contract to make camouflaged explosive devices?"

"Yes," Doritty whispered.

"Did you ever see any C-4?" Barcella asked.

"Uh, I think so."

"Yes or no?"

"Yes."

"Where?"

"In Tripoli. At the airport. In some cans."

"When?"

"I can't remember. It was warm. Around the spring, I think."

"What happened to it?"

"Well, I'm not sure."

"Did you make any devices using C-4?"

Now Doritty was ashen. "Yes," he said.

"What kind of devices?"

"Things, uh, to look like lamps, ashtrays, radios, you know."

Silent tears ran down Doritty's cheeks. Once with the other men—Robert Swallow, Dennis Wilson and John Heath—he had helped rig some car bombs. A Libyan intelligence officer, a Major Hajazzi, he said, also came out to watch a demonstration for a book bomb that Doritty had constructed. When the book was opened, it exploded on schedule, and Hajazzi had pumped his hand in delight.

In the late spring of 1977, he said more former Army ordnance men arrived, and he named them. Around June or July of that year, Doritty couldn't recall exactly, they got a hurry-up order to pack the devices on hand—hidden in transistor radios, flashlights, attaché cases, calculators and so forth, and still others that could be connected to doors and windows—and were flown to the city of Tobruk in northeast Libya. Some sort of trouble, he said, was brewing with Egypt, and the Libyans were all steamed up.

He watched as Libyan soldiers loaded the devices on a truck. They were handling the stuff pretty casually, and Doritty already had begun moving away when the truck went up in a ball of fire. At least three Libyans were killed. One of the new Army ordnance arrivals was badly burned and a second was in severe shock. Doritty himself narrowly escaped death when a piece of flying metal grazed his skull, leaving an ugly gash. His next assignment, he said, was to run a class for uniformed Libyans in demolition safety.

Doritty continued to weep. He didn't know why he had done what he had. He guessed it was for the money.

Pedersen remembered that you could have heard a pin drop when Doritty had finished. If he continued to tell the truth, Barcella told him, he would not face prosecution, and Doritty appeared very grateful.

4

Larry Barcella and Carol Bruce began to draft an analysis of the evidence and applicable law to support indictments against Wilson, Terpil and Brower. It was laborious, tedious research, just what Barcella most hated and Bruce seemed to take to. But it had to be done. Permission to proceed had to be gotten from the U.S. Attorney and, because violation of the Foreign Agents Registration Act was being included, from the Justice Department as well.

Bruce concentrated on the registration side and the extremely complex laws governing the shipment of hazardous materials; Barcella worked on the solicitation-to-murder count and Jerome Brower's apparent perjury.

There were two sets of statutes concerning the registration of foreign agents. One was at the Justice Department, but it was only regulatory and had a commercial exclusion clause that Wilson was betting on. The other was with the Department of State. At first glance, it looked good. It had a section that covered the activities of *any* entity or person operating "at the order, request, or under the direction or control" of a foreign government.

The bad part, however, was that the statute had a murky court history. It had rarely been invoked, and when it was, the reason was usually espionage, which was the use originally intended when it was passed by Congress. A gun-running case had once been thrown out because the State Department admittedly kept such sloppy registration records. That raised the argument that there really was no point in registering at all. But for all its faults, Barcella needed the act as a sort of umbrella so that the secret proposal for terrorist training, the shipping of explosives and related equipment and the recruitment of the Green Berets would be admissible in a trial.

As for the shipping of explosives and related material, there were myriad and often contradictory statutes, at the Munitions Control Board, the Federal Aviation Commission and the Department of Transportation, about what was or was not a violation, and Bruce fell back on the subsection in the U.S. Criminal Code that Dick Pedersen had first thought of—that the "intent" regarding their use was paramount.

The solicitation-to-commit-murder aspect of the indictment presented jurisdictional problems. The original approach to Rafael Quintero about assassinating a Libyan defector had taken place across the Potomac, in Virginia. But Barcella argued that a second meeting with the Cuban occurred in the District of Columbia and constituted a "continuing or renewed solicitation" in the conspiracy.

When you got down to it, though, the strongest elements of the case legally were not against Wilson or Terpil but against Brower for perjury: for lying about the mine-clearing operation and explosives, despite ample opportunity to reflect on it; and also for swearing that he could not recall the names of the men he had sent to Libya or what they were doing there. In the end, Barcella thought, Brower would be the key to breaking open the case.

Bruce prepared extradition papers for Wilson. Barcella wasn't worried about Brower going anywhere. Terpil at the time was hanging around Washington. He had acquired a townhouse at 2020 Connecticut Avenue for his business and lived in an expensive Japanese-style home in McLean, Virginia, across the road from Hickory Hill, the Robert F. Kennedy estate. While the indictment draft was being prepared, Terpil came to see Barcella. But his tune was the same. He'd like to be of assistance, but what was being dubbed Wilson and Terpil was a misnomer. It was pure Wilson.

Wilson's whereabouts was another matter. As the indictments neared completion, Barcella sent inquiries to the legal attachés in London and Bern to try to locate him. But he hadn't been seen in England since early February. And the Bern legal attaché said that Wilson had left Switzerland on April 6. Obviously, he had been warned to lie low. Out at Langley, for instance, it was no secret that an indictment was imminent. And Wilson's attorney, Seymour Glanzer, knew about it. Glanzer had even come in to tell Barcella it was ridiculous to think that the charge of failing to register as a foreign agent would hold up.

The charges against Wilson, Terpil and Brower were returned on April 23, 1980. They were kept sealed from public view briefly, in the vain hope that Wilson might surface and to make sure Terpil did not skip. Dick Pedersen and Rick Wadsworth found Terpil drumming up sales at a "law-enforcement trade show" on the grounds of the U.S. Secret Service training academy in Beltsville, Maryland. The Bureau of Alcohol, Tobacco and Firearms and the Secret Service were sister agencies of the Treasury Department, and the response from on high was heated and swift. Couldn't the two agents have displayed some discretion regarding the site of the arrest?

Wilson, meanwhile, was on the island of Malta, in a lovely villa with a swimming pool. Three years before in the States he had purchased a Beech Baron airplane outfitted for executive use, and after his move to Europe, he had it brought over. With the Beech Baron, it was an easy hop from Tripoli. He could only take Libya for so long and the Maltese retreat offered an ideal respite. Best of all, Barcella didn't know a thing about it.

FIFTEEN

In January 1979 as Dick Pedersen and Rick Wadsworth were launching their undercover scam to buy guns from Edwin P. Wilson and his hired hand, Peter Goulding, the world waited for the final outcome of the Camp David peace meetings between Menachem Begin and Anwar Sadat.

But insiders already knew that President Carter had sweetened the pot for Cairo. Once the accords were signed, Egypt was going to get boatloads of U.S. military aid worth more than $4 billion. The sales would be financed by long-range American loans. And in a move unparalleled in sales of similar size to Israel, Iran and Saudi Arabia, the United States agreed to advance the money to ship these armaments. For anybody in the freight-forwarding business who could get a lock on the contract, the bonanza was mind-bending.

The deputy director of the Pentagon's Defense Security Assistance Agency, Erich von Marbod—"Redhead" in Wilson's codebook—had the job of making sure that the arms sales to Egypt got off to a fast, smooth start. And who better? Von Marbod was fresh from Teheran, where he had supervised the salvage operation after the fall of the shah, just as he had done in Saigon. Nobody personified the American frontier spirit more. Joseph Kraft, the syndicated columnist, recalled that von

Marbod used to begin phone conversations with the exhorta-
tion, "What have you done for your country today?"

A key item in the arms sales, F-16 Phantom fighters, would
be flown directly to Egypt, but all the support equipment for
them was to go commercially. "The General," Richard Secord,
worked closely with von Marbod on the shipments. He'd become the Air Force's director of international programs. Ed
Wilson had done a couple of favors for Secord. Tom Clines had
sold Secord a house as an investment, but it turned out to be a
bummer. So Wilson had taken it off his hands, rescuing him
from a mortgage cash drain. Wilson also let him use his Beech
Baron for personal trips whenever he wished. Secord's lawyer
would later claim that Secord had done Wilson a favor by keeping the plane in tiptop flying condition.

Clines, meanwhile, was all over the lot. After Wilson helped
him set up his oil-drilling equipment company, he formed another small firm, Systems Services International, that specialized
in security. Even before he left the CIA, he was promoting a deal
with the Nicaraguan tyrant, Anastasio Somoza, to create a
search-and-destroy apparatus against Somoza's enemies. They
were still haggling over the price when Somoza was forced into
exile by the Sandinista rebels.

And now, in January 1979, Clines was talking to Wilson
about still another company, to be incorporated offshore in
Bermuda, called International Research and Trade. This time
his vision was anything but small.

Within six months Theodore Shackley—"Ted" in the codebook—would give up any hope of making a comeback in the
CIA. He resigned and became a consultant in both the companies Clines had formed.

2

Roberta Barnes first heard about the loan to Clines in Geneva in mid-January. "Five hundred thousand dollars!" she said.
"You must have lost your mind."

"It's my fucking money," Wilson snarled. "I can do what I
want with it."

Toward the end of the month she dined with Wilson, von
Marbod and Secord in London. She'd never seen Ed in better
spirits.

He later told her what the deal was. He was in with Clines,

Shackley, von Marbod and Secord. They were setting up a company that would make millions shipping U.S. arms to Egypt. The $500,000 was the seed money. Each of them had a twenty-percent share. But his name wouldn't be on any of the papers. That's where he had been smart, Wilson said. He had told Clines that he didn't have that much cash himself, but he could raise it from some Arab partners in a Liberian corporation called Arcadia, Ltd. Wilson was, in fact, Arcadia. But if there were any double crosses, he could hold up the prospect of murderous Moslem vengeance.

Ed Coughlin, Wilson's lawyer in Geneva, handled the details. Clines arrived on January 11 with a handwritten summary of the loan proposal he had prepared on a single sheet of legal-size notepaper. Among its five points was that a Liberian corporation *"not identified with Wilson"* would transfer money to a custodial account in Bermuda. Once International Research and Trade was in business, it would open a "sales and purchasing office in the U.S.A."

"If I understand correctly," Coughlin wrote Wilson in a memo on January 18, "it is proposed that an offshore corporation be organized with, eventually, five equal shareholders. Four of these 20% shareholders are individual U.S. citizens, and the fifth would be a foreign corporation, not controlled by U.S. persons."

The money was transferred to a Bermuda bank in late February in two chunks, first $200,000, then $300,000 more. Over the next months there was considerable wrangling in person between Clines and Coughlin, and by letter, phone and telex between Coughlin and a Washington lawyer representing Clines, about whether the $500,000 was to be convertible into Wilson's one-fifth corporate share, or whether it was a loan to be repaid in full, giving Wilson the right to acquire his stock for the same measly $600 that each of the other partners was to put up. "This is 'seed money,' Barbara," Coughlin querulously wrote to Barbara Rossotti, Clines's lawyer, "not a Christmas present."

While all this was going on, a former Egyptian intelligence officer, Hussein K. Salem, unexpectedly showed up in von Marbod's Pentagon office with a letter signed by the defense minister of Egypt authorizing *him* to handle the arms shipments. Von Marbod refused to consider it. Salem had no visible track record

as a freight forwarder, didn't even know that American vessels
had to be used and drew a blank on Pentagon billing procedures.

But Salem wouldn't go away. And he did have the defense
minister's letter. Finally he was informed by the military attaché
in Egypt's Washington embassy, General Mohammed Abu
Ghazala, who would subsequently return to Cairo to become
defense minister himself, that to get the contract, Salem would
have to have an American partner. Who turned out to be Tom
Clines.

In August, Salem and Clines, funneling money from International Research and Trade to his security firm, Systems Services International, formed an entirely new enterprise called
Egyptian American Transport Services, Inc., or EATSCO for
short. Salem held fifty-one percent of the stock and Systems
Services the rest. If Salem's background as a shipper was unknown, Clines's experience was nonexistent, and an established
freight forwarder, R. G. Hobelmann, Inc., of Baltimore, was
retained.

Like magic, von Marbod then approved the exclusive contract to EATSCO. What's more, he authorized an advance payment of $13.5 million to EATSCO for shipping costs, which was
promptly put in an interest deposit in a Swiss bank at the expense of U.S. taxpayers. It was followed by a series of additional
advances of $7.5 million each, totaling in the end some $71
million, with no accounting required until after the money was
spent.

Along the way, General Ghazala got at least one check for
$10,070.94, sent directly to him by the Defense Security Assist-
ance Agency. According to J. E. Hartsock, the agency's chief
financial officer, it was issued on "oral instructions" from von
Marbod. Hartsock would confide to the Washington *Post*'s Scott
Armstrong that he couldn't recall another instance of aid funds
being forwarded to a foreign official.

Throughout 1979 and into early 1980 Edward Coughlin
vainly tried to settle the contractual status of Wilson's "loan."
Clines kept flying to Geneva with draft proposals to resolve it.
When they proved unacceptable, he insisted on keeping the only
copies. In the correspondence between Coughlin and Clines's
attorney in Washington, no names were ever mentioned; on
both sides, it was always "my clients" and "your clients."

Then, after Wilson's April 23, 1980, indictment became

public knowledge, recorded communications from Clines came to a dead halt.

3

In Malta, when Wilson learned of the charges against him, Terpil and Brower, he jumped back and forth from angry arrogance to bitter complaints. It was Terpil's fault, he ranted to Roberta Barnes. If Terpil hadn't been so dumb getting picked up for gun-running in New York and stirred up the press, none of this would have happened.

But she noticed that Wilson began to focus more and more on Barcella. Who was this fucking Barcella? Why was he doing this after so long? What did he want? Suddenly, though, Wilson would brighten up. Barcella wasn't going to get anywhere. Terpil was in too deep to make a deal, and Brower would stand firm. "Jerry, they don't have anything," Wilson had told him. Barcella was just after headlines. When he discovered that he was butting his head against a stone wall, he'd walk away. Time, Wilson said, was on his side. Pip-squeak prosecutors like Barcella came and went.

Hubris took hold. He'd return to answer these charges when the time was ripe. At *his* choosing, after the heat had settled down, and without Terpil sitting next to him in court as a codefendant. Shackley and Clines would testify about the valuable information he had been sending back from Libya. He'd have Rafael Quintero get to work on finding out where those missing Cubans in the Letelier case were.

Not once, Roberta Barnes remembered, did he blame himself for anything.

Throughout all of this, Wilson's wife, Barbara, remained at Mount Airy, essentially alone. Her troubled older son, whom Kevin Mulcahy had once counseled, was in a treatment center. The younger one, Eric, seemed to have fallen under the spell of his father, had spent time with him in Libya and in Geneva, and when he was in Washington, preferred to stay at the now unused townhouse on 22nd Street, further embittering her.

Her marriage had been so acrimonious for so long that no vestige of nostalgia nor even the slightest wistfulness was left. She knew all about Barnes. She had not seen or spoken to Wilson in more than a year. Money to run their properties was forwarded by his accountant.

Seymour Glanzer advised her that to the best of his knowledge Wilson was in Tripoli. Her husband had been told of the charges against him and also of the consequences should he elect not to submit to U.S. court jurisdiction. Glanzer added that he was prepared to mount a vigorous defense. The decision, however, was Wilson's. "After all," Glanzer said, "this is his life."

4

At convocations of the Mount Airy Gun Club, where members of the intelligence community and generals and admirals—most of them retired—gathered to hunt on Wilson's property, the conventional wisdom was that it was an agency operation, something Ted Shackley might have thought up. It sounded just like one of Shackley's free-lance ventures. Things like this happened all the time in the clandestine directorate—unofficially, of course. The indictments were probably another element in an elaborate cover. One heard that C-130 parts were involved, and that was pure agency. If you controlled the parts, you controlled the operation.

Paul Cyr, the alcoholic ex–World War II intelligence operative whom Wilson had put on the Consultants International payroll back in 1969 to tip him about Army shipping needs, pushed this line of reasoning. Cyr, who had organized the club, had gotten permission from Wilson to hunt at both his Mount Airy and Apple Manor estates, and now Cyr had done Wilson a huge service, earning $10,000 for his trouble.

In Wilson's package deal to equip the mobile strike force that Colonel Qaddafi desired, he had contracted to deliver 5,000 M-16 automatic rifles. Peter Goulding had gotten a price quote of $300 per M-16 from an arms merchant in Belgium that Wilson often used, so he decided to charge the Libyans $350, for an easy profit of a quarter of a million dollars, and there would be additional money for getting the ammunition.

The contract stipulated that the rifles had to be American-made. Then everything started going haywire. First, the Belgian arms merchant was unable to come up with the rifles. Next, Wilson had Goulding contact Interarms, the huge Samuel Cummings arms organization; it had the rifles, but with inflation worldwide, the price had gone to $400 each. The idea of absorbing a loss was too much for Wilson to bear. He'd find a better deal. Word, however, began to spread about his increasingly frantic shopping around. The price for an M-16 immediately ballooned to $600.

Taiwan had a license from Colt Industries to manufacture the rifle, but the Libyans considered it an inferior version and stuck to the letter of the contract. Tripoli grew restive, demanding to see at least a sample rifle. But the way the shadowy arms bazaar worked, obtaining one rifle was as difficult as purchasing thousands of them. Then Wilson remembered that Cyr had hanging on his wall an M-16 that had been presented by Colt to the Army general in charge of its procurement program. Reginald Slocombe brought over Cyr's M-16, this time in a foot locker filled with steel axles.

Wilson himself was waiting at the Amsterdam airport with Peter Goulding for Slocombe's arrival. A chartered jet was standing by to fly him and the rifle to Tripoli. A few hours later Wilson telephoned Goulding, laughing uproariously. The contract had been saved. Sayed Qaddafadam, Qaddafi's cousin, who would command the strike force, had taken the M-16, shoved in a thirty-round clip and delightedly sprayed bullets out of his office window.

5

In June, after the indictments, Barcella and Carol Bruce flew to England to try to locate Roberta Barnes. But the sole occupant in Wilson's London office was a waiflike Welsh woman named Diane Byrne. She acted as a general secretary for Wilson, she said, and as a sort of communications link for his various enterprises. No, she didn't know where Roberta Barnes was. Perhaps in Geneva. She believed Wilson was in Tripoli.

She had first met him there. Her husband had worked in the Libyan oil fields, and as a lark she started brewing homemade beer. Wilson and some of his associates began dropping by, and then, when her husband left her and she returned to Britain with two small children to care for, she had asked him for a job and about a year and a half ago he had hired her. Ed Wilson was a wonderful man, she said. Whenever he came into England, he brought her children presents. And he would remember their birthdays with cards and more presents. Sometimes he would even call from Geneva or Tripoli just to speak to them, to see how they were.

Her main responsibility was a company called Western Recruitment. All she did was place advertisements for mechanics and pilots to go to Libya, arrange to get them there and make sure their salary checks were properly processed. "Am I violating the law?" she asked, and Barcella replied, "No, probably not."

She appeared thunderstruck when Barcella explained the indictment counts, the shipping of explosives, conspiracy to solicit and commit murder. "I can't believe it," she said. "That's not the Ed Wilson I know."

Barcella didn't doubt her sincerity. She'd given him new insights into Wilson. He was more complex than Barcella had thought. In manipulating people, Wilson went beyond just calculating their greed or simply steamrollering them. He probed weaknesses. Diane Byrne's main concern was the welfare of her children, and he had spotted it instantly and worked it to his own advantage. Barcella was under no illusion that she would ever reveal anything about Wilson's operation that she didn't absolutely have to.

In England, Barcella visited a widow, Christina McKenzie, whose husband, Bruce, had been murdered with Terpil's help. McKenzie had been a member of the cabinet in Kenya. When Israeli troops stormed the Entebbe airport in Uganda to rescue passengers in a plane hijacked by Palestinian terrorists, they used Kenya as a staging area. McKenzie provided vital assistance. He'd been associated with the engineering firm that built the airport and gave the Israelis a detailed picture of its layout.

Although he had been counseled not to, McKenzie went to Uganda as part of a Kenya trade mission to patch up relations with Idi Amin. The warnings seemed unnecessary. Amin himself was on hand to bid McKenzie good-bye, presenting him with the traditional Ugandan friendship gift, an African antelope's head. Soon after McKenzie's plane took off, it blew up. Inside the antelope head was a bomb, placed there by Frank Terpil.

There was another guest at the McKenzie home, a short, thin man with close-cropped hair named Civil Zamir, the former chief of Mossad, the Israeli intelligence service. Barcella walked with him in the garden after lunch. "Hasn't your CIA helped you on this case?" Zamir asked.

"To some extent, yes," Barcella said.

"Well, I'm not suggesting the CIA was involved with Wilson and Terpil, but I'm confident it was aware of what they were doing. *We* were."

6

When Barcella returned to Washington, he got the break he'd been waiting for. Jerome Brower appeared ready to talk.

It was the fault of Brower's new attorney, Seymour Glanzer complained in a letter to Roberta Barnes. Brower would "rue the day he decided to plead guilty and cooperate." If he hadn't waived his right to a speedy trial, the indictment against him would have "foundered."

The lawyer Glanzer was talking about was William G. Hundley, one of the country's ranking defense attorneys. He took a look at the spot Brower was in and went for a plea bargain. Brower's mistake was going before the grand jury in the first place. Barcella had him dead on perjury. And the perjury would color everything else. He was facing a long haul in prison —at his age, possibly for the rest of his life.

Among judges, prosecutors and reporters in Washington, Hundley was a class act. He'd been a prosecutor himself, famous for his deadpan style. Once, as chief of the Organized Crime Section under Bobby Kennedy, he was assigned to prosecute the brother of one of JFK's earliest and most important political supporters. An influential columnist wrote that the fix was in. When the jury returned a guilty verdict, Hundley said, "What did I do right?"

Nevertheless, there was still a poker game to play. While Barcella had more than enough to put Brower away, he didn't have that much of a case against Wilson without Brower's help. At last a deal was worked out. Brower agreed to plead guilty to a single five-year count of conspiracy to ship explosives. How much time he would have to serve was up to the judge.

But all this depended on Brower's telling the truth. And it didn't come easily. Brower was a basket case. It wasn't that he was unwilling to talk, Barcella thought. The problem was his inability to admit that the patriotic persona he had so carefully cultivated was a lie. As if it made a difference, he claimed that he hadn't realized what Wilson and Terpil were up to until he actually got to Libya and saw what the men Wilson had asked him to recruit were doing.

Barcella kept hammering at him. Finally Brower confessed

that he had helped construct some of the devices. And he admitted discussing with Wilson the feasibility of building plants in Libya to manufacture napalm and C-4. But he ferociously denied delivering any C-4 himself.

"I swear on my dead mother's grave," he shouted. "Tie me to a chair. Shoot me full of truth serum. Why should I lie? I'm pleading, aren't I? What more do you want, for Christ's sake?"

Brower's performance was impressive. Listening to it, Dick Pedersen remembered thinking maybe they were wrong about the C-4. But Rick Wadsworth reminded everyone what George Doritty had said. In the spring of 1977 Doritty had seen C-4 being unloaded in Tripoli. There had to have been other shipments that Brower made besides the one in August of 1976.

In mid-July, after Brower once again denied that he had shipped any C-4 for Wilson, Barcella took Hundley aside and said, "Bill, we've got a problem. Jerry's blowing the deal. He isn't leveling. There was a big shipment of C-4 in 1977 and he just hasn't told us about it."

"You're pretty sure on that?"

"We're sure."

"Let me go to talk to him then."

About an hour later Hundley came into the basement cafeteria of the U.S. courthouse where Barcella was having lunch with Pedersen and Wadsworth. "Can I see you privately?" he said. They moved to another table, and Hundley said, "Well, you've got him."

"What do you mean?"

"He was positive nobody knew about the forty thousand pounds of C-4."

Jesus, Barcella said to himself, keep a straight face. When he had spoken about a "big" shipment, he had been thinking of something on the order of a couple of hundred pounds, and here Hundley was talking about *forty thousand pounds*.

He remembered gripping the sides of the table, suddenly lightheaded. He recalled the wisecracks about this being an "exploding ashtray" case. Forty thousand pounds of C-4! He thought of all the terrorist bombings during the past three years in Europe and the Middle East.

From that second on, whenever a bomb went off—in a West Berlin discotheque, on a TWA plane over Greece, on a train in Italy—he would wonder if it had come from that huge cache sitting in Qaddafi's Libya. C-4 was practically indestructible. It could be used in every climate, from arctic to tropical. Under the most minimal care, it had a life expectancy of at least twenty years.

Barcella's mouth had gone so dry that he was afraid to speak.

"Jerry realizes there's no point in hiding anything anymore," Hundley said. "He figures if you know about the C-4, you know it all. How it got over, the DC-8 from Houston, everything."

Barcella finessed it. "Bill, as I told you," he said, "we know a lot more than people give us credit for."

"The problem was Bloom," Hundley said. "Bloom's been his lawyer and buddy for years and he was involved in the shipment. He really doesn't want to talk about Bloom. Don't ask me why. If Bloom hadn't let him go before the grand jury, he wouldn't be where he is now. He'll talk about the shipment, but not Bloom. You'll have to talk to Bloom yourself."

In Barcella's office, all the bombast was gone from Brower. A burly man, he seemed oddly shrunken. Dick Pedersen remembered how his hand with the missing fingers kept twitching.

"Okay, Jerry," Barcella said, "let's talk about the C-4. Exactly how much was it?"

"Around forty thousand pounds. Maybe a little more."

"Where did it go?"

"Libya."

"How did it get there?"

"Chartered jet."

"Where did you get it?"

"Some from Canada. And a couple of places in the States. Goex in Texas and some place down around the Gulf, in Louisiana."

"Where was it shipped from?"

"Houston."

"Houston?"

"Yeah, we trucked it there."

"In crates?"

"No, in five-gallon cans."

Pedersen, as he heard this, fought the impulse to laugh and scream. He noticed that Barcella was chain-smoking to cover his excitement.

"Where did you get the jet?"

"I don't know the details. A friend of mine handled that."
Like Doritty, Brower had tears in his eyes. He paused to brush
them away. "And a shipping guy Wilson had. Slocombe I think
his name was. I forget. I wasn't there."

On July 18, Brower underwent a polygraph examination at
the district office of the Bureau of Alcohol, Tobacco and Firearms. Afterward, Pedersen phoned Barcella. "Larry, he's still
not coming clean on all the C-4. There has to be more of it. He
flunked on whether he was being completely truthful."

Hundley said, "I'll talk to him again," and then Hundley
reported that, well, yes, there had been another C-4 shipment,
a relatively small one, around March or April in 1977. If they
wanted to know more about it, they would have to talk to Doug
Smith. "Jerry's pretty well shot," Hundley said. "You're not
going to get much more out of him."

They would need corroboration on Houston. So Barcella
issued a grand jury subpoena for Reginald Slocombe. The Mormon churchman had first been connected with Wilson during
the surveillance Pedersen and Wadsworth had conducted outside the townhouse at 1016 22nd Street, but little was known
about him except that he seemed to be a legitimate freight
forwarder.

Slocombe came in with a lawyer, who said his client wasn't
saying a word without immunity. Granting it was a decision
Barcella would regret. At the time, though, nobody was aware
of how deeply enmeshed Slocombe was in Wilson's schemes.
But since Brower had not been present for either the chartering
of the DC-8 or the flight from Houston, his testimony on that
was inadmissible hearsay.

With only perjury to worry about, Slocombe appeared to
talk freely. In the fall of 1976, he had been working for Behring
International, a major freight forwarder in Houston, when he
got a call from Douglas Schlachter. He went to Mount Airy and
met Wilson, who offered to finance a new firm called Aroundworld Shipping and Chartering. Wilson wanted a freight-
forwarding outfit of his own. That way he could keep all the
shipping fees. Slocombe's salary was $36,000 a year plus com-
missions, medical and pension benefits and a car. He also got
a one-third interest in Aroundworld.

He confessed to smuggling Remington .308 rifles from the

United States to Libya. Most of the weapons and ammunition that he had handled for Libyan delivery, however, had originated in Europe, from an arms merchant in Belgium named Armand Donnay.

He admitted his part in the C-4 shipment. Wilson had phoned him from Tripoli about negotiating the transport of a large amount of explosives, instructing him not to jeopardize Aroundworld by involving it directly. The C-4, Wilson said, would be disguised as oil-drilling mud. He would get everything else he had to know from Jerome Brower, although it had been Brower's attorney, Ed Bloom, that he ended up dealing with.

Bloom had arranged the trucking of the C-4 from California. Bloom had gone with him to Miami to contract for the DC-8 charter. Bloom had been on the scene when the C-4 was placed on board and then flew overseas with it. Slocombe described it all with breezy matter-of-factness; he might just as well have been talking about a rush order of bananas.

Afterward, at his home in Palm Springs, California, Edward Bloom received Pedersen and Wadsworth and said without much enthusiasm, "Nice to see you fellows again." He said he was talking to them only because Brower wanted him to. Then he confirmed everything that Slocombe had said, along with his trip to Switzerland to pick up the money to pay for the C-4. "I was simply working for my client," he first said. Then Bloom would claim that he thought it was all part of an intelligence operation. He wasn't going to plead guilty to any criminal acts.

Doug Smith, however, now made no effort to use an intelligence dodge. For Smith, it had been very simple. He revered Jerry Brower. Did whatever Brower ordered. He showed Pedersen and Wadsworth the excess C-4 stored in the Fontana bunkers—the C-4 that Brower had billed Wilson for but had not delivered. He had been in charge of transferring the twenty-one tons of the explosives from cases to cans. It had been a hell of a job, he said, taking a month almost around the clock. He had fashioned a jackhammer with a round steel dish at the end to tamp the C-4 into the cans before covering it with oil-drilling mud. A lot of extra manpower had to be hired, including an out-of-work screenwriter.

For the other shipment in the spring of 1977, he alone had packed the C-4 in cans of DAP and driven it to the Lufthansa cargo facility in Los Angeles. He couldn't recall the names of the personnel at the airlines. There also had been four pistols. Pedersen had always wondered why Brower had come clean on the twenty-one tons and was so reluctant to talk about the spring shipment; he decided that it must have been Brower's embarrassment about the guns. There was a certain abstract quality about explosives. Handguns, though, were very personal.

Smith had said that the whole package was around eleven hundred pounds or so, but Pedersen and Wadsworth could find nobody in Los Angeles at Lufthansa who remembered a shipment of that size during the time frame specified by Smith. Pedersen was sure that the local Lufthansa officials were lying, but there wasn't anything he could do about it.

In Houston, Pedersen and Wadsworth interviewed several participants who recalled the storing and then the difficulty in loading hundreds of five-gallon cans aboard a DC-8, but to a man they claimed that as far as they knew, the cans had contained drilling mud. But one of them, a freight forwarder who'd been in Slocombe's employ, struck Pedersen as being especially apprehensive, his eyes darting this way and that. So he paid him a return visit later.

"Hey, look," Pedersen said, as if he were a friendly career-guidance counselor, "you're probably going to get indicted. We know what was in those cans. Why not tell us the story and maybe we can work something out. Why should you take the fall? Think about it."

"I don't have to," the freight forwarder suddenly said. "I'll tell you right now. I want to get it off my chest. Everybody knew it was explosives." He gazed miserably at Pedersen. "It was all, you know, cash."

"Yeah, I understand," Pedersen said.

At Miami International Airport, the two BATF agents located the DC-8 parked in an area called cockroach corner. They had intended to seize the plane, but it had been cannibalized; two engines were completely gone. They stared at it for a long time, thinking about what it had carried.

The shipment out of Los Angeles continued to rankle Pedersen. There had to be some trace of it. Weren't Germans renowned for keeping meticulous records? He went to Jamaica, New York, to Lufthansa's North American headquarters, and asked for a computer printout of every cargo that had been moved in March and April 1977. He had only the approximate weight and date to go on, and it took him most of the day, but there it was. April 3. From Los Angeles to Tripoli via Frankfurt. "Machine parts."

Now all that was missing was Wilson.

SIXTEEN

The CIA said that Wilson was in Tripoli, but that was all. Barcella thought about the National Security Agency and its fabled worldwide communications monitoring capability. Any phone calls in English originating in Tripoli shouldn't be that difficult to pick up. But when he made the request, he was informed that law enforcement was not in the agency's charter.

Then on August 13, while Pedersen and Wadsworth were still on the road chasing down the C-4 shipments, Carol Bruce got a call from the International Affairs office at the Justice Department. A tip had come in that Wilson might be in Malta for a meeting of some sort in a few days, around the eighteenth.

As vague as it was, Barcella asked the Department of State to notify the American embassy in Malta to advise local officials that he was a fugitive, that his passport had been revoked, and to hold him for extradition if he showed up. The FBI agent at the embassy in Rome also covered Malta and Barcella wanted him on the scene. But the State Department refused. The matter would be handled through diplomatic channels. Barcella started preparing extradition papers based on the murder conspiracy counts against Wilson.

By August 20, it appeared to have been a false alarm after all. According to the Maltese police, no trace of Wilson could be found. But the next day another cable arrived saying a "source" had heard that he was in fact there and had been arrested the day before while attempting to depart for Libya in a private Beech Baron aircraft.

Barcella started getting edgy. Why was the information coming from a so-called source rather than directly from the Maltese government? He tried once more to have the legal attaché at the Rome embassy sent to Malta and was rebuffed. Still another cable came in, this time confirming that Wilson was in custody. There were complications, though. Questions about whether the murder conspiracy counts as drawn up constituted a crime under Maltese law.

Then Barcella learned that Wilson had listed his permanent residence as London. That gave him an idea. Instead of hassling with Malta over the fine points of extraditable offenses, couldn't the State Department use some clout simply to have him expelled back to Britain as an undesirable? As more cables arrived from Malta, Bruce, Dick Pedersen and Rick Wadsworth gathered in Barcella's office, hovering over the messages like stockbrokers watching price fluctuations on a ticker tape.

Finally, on August 24, word arrived that Malta might agree to the plan. In England, Scotland Yard had assigned an inspector, Roger Bendle, to act as liaison on Wilson and Terpil. Barcella called him to explain what was in the works. Malta would provide ample notice of Wilson's departure and flight number if it chose the option Barcella had suggested. What he didn't know, however, was that a lawyer Wilson retained had gotten him out of jail on a habeas corpus writ.

At home around eight o'clock on the morning of August 28, Barcella made his favorite breakfast—a glass of orange juice and peanut butter on an English muffin—and turned to the sports section of the *Post* to catch up on training-camp news about the Washington Redskins. He was an ardent Redskins fan and the headline wasn't good; John Riggins, the star running back, had yet to report and it was becoming alarmingly clear that he was determined to sit out the season because of a salary dispute.

Then the phone rang and Barcella forgot all about Riggins. Roger Bendle was on the line. "Larry," he said, "Wilson's come through and now we don't know where he is."

"What do you mean?" Barcella said. "We haven't gotten any notification from the State Department about anything."

Well, said Bendle, Scotland Yard hadn't been notified either. In the middle of the night, London time, an airliner from Malta had landed, with Wilson as just another passenger. At that lazy hour, he had passed an immigration checkpoint.

About twenty minutes later, the officer manning the checkpoint took a tea break and happened to spot a photograph that Scotland Yard had sent out for identification purposes. Wilson's entry form said he'd be staying at the London Hilton, but, of course, he wasn't there, nor had he turned up at any other hotel. He had, said Bendle, vanished.

Barcella phoned the State Department in a rage. The response from the Malta desk was icy. "Listen, Barcella," he was told, "we've had about enough of this from you. Mr. Wilson, as a matter of fact, is in Malta. We've been advised that our people will be meeting with police officials regarding his deportation within the next hour."

The next call was from the State Department's legal office. "Uh, guess who just canceled the meeting about Wilson?"

"Yeah, the Maltese," Barcella said. "It's a little tough to have a meeting about him when he isn't there." He demanded that a formal protest be lodged, but the Malta desk officer demurred. "You don't understand how important Malta is in the larger scheme of things," he said.

"You guys are all alike," Barcella said. "Sometimes I wonder who you're representing."

Bendle reported no luck in the search. Diane Byrne, despite stiff questioning, maintained that she had no idea of his present whereabouts.

2

Some September, Barcella thought.

Wilson had slipped through his fingers. Then Frank Terpil, who had remained free on bail, fled the country on the eve of his New York trial for gun-running.

And to top everything off, not only were the two key defendants in the Letelier case still fugitives, but a federal appeals court reversed the convictions of those who had not skipped. The decision was based on a Supreme Court ruling, handed down in another case after the trial, that said a government informant could not be used in a "situation likely to induce" incriminating statements by a defendant.

While a jailhouse informant had been used, it was clear on the record that he hadn't even known about Letelier's murder until one of the defendants started talking about it. So how could anything have been induced? Barcella argued for an appeal, and for a while it seemed likely, but finally the solicitor general decided that it was too soon to go back to the Supreme Court on an issue that had any resemblance to the one cited in the reversal. The Letelier case had to be retried, or forget it.

He knew he was supposed to be professional about such things. But the anguish, and the frustration, on this one cut deeply in his gut. He would have quit on the spot if it hadn't been for the vision of Edwin P. Wilson out there somewhere, thumbing his nose. Barcella wondered if he'd ever get another crack at him.

3

In Malta, before his arrest there, Wilson had been busy. Seymour Glanzer was still his attorney for the indictment. But he kept Ken Conklin on the payroll for assignments he didn't want Glanzer to know about.

And in Malta in June, after Wilson's indictment, the ex–Green Beret turned lawyer flew in to give him an update on the identity of witnesses that Barcella was bringing before the grand jury. He reviewed the various countries Wilson could go to where extradition would be difficult or impossible. Wilson wanted to know if Barcella could subpoena witnesses abroad. Conklin said it couldn't be done. A witness had to return to the States voluntarily.

That was comforting. He'd been concerned about Peter Goulding. Goulding was a wimp. Worse yet, he was the one who had so blithely accepted the quote for the M-16 rifles from Armand Donnay, the Belgian arms dealer, which was causing so much grief, and Wilson had laced into him. All of a sudden, Goulding started asking questions about their hasty exodus from Washington and rumors of a federal probe. Wilson had taken him to a London pizza parlor for a little talk. Everything was under control, he said. He controlled all his people in Libya, for instance, because they would be in deep shit with the Internal Revenue Service if they ever talked. He also controlled Goulding, and when Goulding looked perplexed, Wilson slashed at the pizza with his knife. If Goulding ever caused him any problems, his pretty young wife would get the same treatment. He watched Goulding turn ashen. Goulding, he was certain, wouldn't be running off to Barcella on his own.

In Malta, Conklin said that Barcella showed no signs of letting up. Wilson ought to convert his real estate holdings into cash and bury it in Switzerland or Liechtenstein. But that was unthinkable. Mount Airy was his monument to himself. He'd sooner cut off an arm or a leg than lose it, he said. Besides, his bitch wife had joint ownership of most of his property, and she'd stir up all kinds of trouble. He'd return to defend himself at the right time. He wanted to see what happened to Terpil first.

In July he brought Barbara Wilson and her lawyer over to Malta to discuss a divorce. "I'll give you two million bucks to get out of my life," he said. "Take it or leave it."

Afterward he and Roberta Barnes flew to Taiwan, where Wilson contracted for a planeload of M-16 ammunition. The delivery date for the rifles was about to run out, but ammunition had been part of the package, and he hoped that a few million rounds would satisfy the Libyans for a while. It was Roberta's first trip to the Far East and it brought back the excitement that life with Ed had promised. Larry Barcella seemed so remote then.

In August they both were in Malta again for another meeting with Conklin, the one that Barcella had been tipped off about. Besides the M-16s, a second deal was going sour. Wilson had contracted to provide uniforms to the Libyan armed forces and through Reginald Slocombe had hooked up with a clothing supplier in Oklahoma named Francis Heydt, who did business with the Army. He thought it was one of his slickest moves. While he was charging the Libyans $8 million, he was paying Heydt only half that much. What's more, Heydt had to post an $800,000 performance bond in an American bank.

Based on a Libyan letter of credit, Wilson started advancing money to Heydt against the bond. Cost controls were sloppy, however, and Wilson had paid out more than a million dollars before the first shipments arrived. They were a disaster. Although the contract had specified that the uniforms were to be American-made, they had been fashioned on the cheap in South Korea and were practically falling apart. The Libyans cut off further credit on the clothing contract.

And now Wilson was screaming at Conklin to threaten

Heydt with all sorts of mayhem, and if that didn't work, to sue him on the bond. Roberta Barnes marveled that Ed could even think of suing someone, considering the position he was in.

She flew to Belgium to see if Donnay had been able to do anything about the M-16s, but the arms dealer said he was sorry. The price was double his original quote. Everyone around, he told her, knew how much Wilson wanted them. It took her the better part of a day to put through a call to him in Tripoli, only to learn that he wasn't there.

She went to Geneva, where she could dial directly. Still no Ed. She discovered that Qaddafi's cousin Sayed Qaddafadam, who had ordered the M-16s for the new Libyan strike force, also was in town. Outside Libya, Qaddafadam was something of a playboy, so she joined him at a local discotheque and with the music pounding got him to sign a six-month extension on the contract.

Then she tried phoning a businessman in Malta whom Wilson had become friendly with. That was when she learned he was in jail. The businessman said he had gotten Wilson a lawyer. He thought something might be worked out.

4

Wilson had been picked up the day after she left, just as he was preparing to depart himself. At first he thought that it was a mistake of some kind. He was about to pull out a card, signed by Major Hajazzi, which said he was affiliated with Libyan military intelligence—that would make the Maltese think twice—but then he found out that the American embassy was behind his arrest. Wilson had been telling the Libyans that his indictment really was a political charade, aimed more at Qaddafi than anything else. The last thing he needed now was for them to know about this latest development.

It cost him $29,000 to get released. Expulsion to Libya was impossible. The government, he was told, already had committed itself to England. But there was a way out. Although the U.S. embassy was to be informed of his departure ahead of time, there could be a bureaucratic communications breakdown. The bribe included the lawyer's retainer. If anybody ever asked, the money was for various fees and taxes associated with the Beech Baron.

When he landed in London, Heathrow Airport was nearly

deserted. A half-dozen immigration officers were on duty. Wilson chose the one who seemed to be the most bleary-eyed, observed how nice it was to be back in Britain and passed through without incident.

He immediately telephoned Roberta Barnes in Geneva and instructed her to fly in and register at the Portman Hotel, where he would meet her. She also was to contact Wilson's personal pilot in Tripoli, Mike Lucker, and relay the message that "Angus" was in England. Lucker was to hop on the first available commercial flight to London and contact "Winky"—Diane Byrne.

While he waited for Lucker, Wilson told Byrne to step up her recruiting of American, British and Canadian pilots and mechanics. Qaddafi had to have them to ferry in bombs, fuel, weapons and troops, and carry out the wounded, to support his invasion of Libya's southern neighbor Chad. But mostly he railed on about Larry Barcella. No longer were there any lofty predictions that Barcella would vanish from the scene. Barcella was the root of all his problems. He'd have to take care of him one way or another.

Then he and Barnes hid out at Staplefield Grange, one of the two English estates he had purchased through his string of Swiss corporations. Along with a pool, tennis court, pond and gardens, the five-bedroom country house about thirty-five miles south of London had been equipped with a telex so he could keep in constant touch with Tripoli and Geneva. He had bought the Grange, as it was called, for investment purposes and as a temporary residence while restorations, already in excess of $250,000, proceeded in the seventeenth-century manor of his much grander and more isolated acquisition nearby, Broxmead Farm.

When Lucker arrived, he leased a twin-engine Piper Aztec at Stanstead Airport, a facility used mainly for cargo and charters, which was an easy drive from the Grange. With Wilson, Barnes and a British copilot on board, Lucker put down in Liège, Belgium, where Barnes disembarked to keep after Donnay and the M-16s. The copilot, when he learned that Libya was their ultimate destination, also left, and Lucker and Wilson continued puddle-jumping through France to Sardinia and across the Mediterranean into Tripoli.

Celebrating his escape, Wilson got falling-down drunk with

Lucker at his seaside house. In the middle of the night he was crawling barefoot on the floor when he heard Lucker giggle, "Gee, Ed, you've sure got pretty toes." He lurched up, grabbed Lucker by the shirt and smashed his huge fist into Lucker's jaw, breaking it in two places. He hit Lucker again, crushing his nose.

"The fucking fag made a pass at me," he would explain.

SEVENTEEN

A four-lane highway leads into Tripoli from the airport. The landscape is barren. Cars haphazardly dot the sides of the highway. Some, like a Volkswagen wrapped around an olive tree, are the obvious result of accidents. Others, though, sit abandoned, as if they had suffered malfunctions beyond comprehension and their drivers had just got out and walked away.

Near the outskirts of the city banners wave, giving the impression that a festival or parade is in the works, but they are always there, bearing portraits and the maxims of Colonel Qaddafi. The city itself, flat and about a mile square, has blocks of monotonous Soviet-style apartment houses.

A funereal feeling hangs in the air, like that in Communist-bloc cities in Eastern Europe, and there is none of the lively bazaar life, the shops and the persistent cry of street vendors so characteristic of other Arab capitals. The old, walled part of town, by the port, where gold and silver markets once flourished and goods were traded, is as subdued as everything else. All enterprise is run by the state, concentrated in four or five new, unexpectedly modern, highly organized buildings—the Libyan version of a supermarket on the ground floor, escalators to appliances on the next floor, clothing on still another floor. The interiors are uniformly painted green, Qaddafi's favorite color.

There's a pervasive smell of lamb cooking—the people, most of them only recently removed from the desert, still prefer outdoor fires—and the odor of garbage from open dumps. Except for a handful of restaurants and coffee houses, there is no night life. Soldiers are everywhere.

The Beach Hotel, Tripoli's best, east of the port, is a drab brick building. A cavernous hall serves as a dining room for visitors from Japan, China and Korea, from both sides of the Iron Curtain, all anxious to do business. No one can remember the last time the pool was usable.

Wilson's two-story villa was a couple of hundred yards down the way, on the sea side of a blacktopped road, surrounded by a concrete wall. Actually it was composed of twin connected stucco houses. Below on the left were offices, with Wilson's apartment above; on the right was a small apartment for his English secretary, Barbara Thompson, and bedrooms for key employees, and on the second floor, an exercise room and another apartment for important guests.

Wilson hated being there.

Once the euphoria of evading Barcella wore off, all he could do was glower out of his windows at the littered, rocky beach, at the sea, and in his mind's eye, at Malta just over the horizon, only two hundred miles away. Even Malta, which in comparison with Libya seemed the most elegant of resorts, was denied to him now.

By now, he knew there was an Interpol "red notice" on him since he sneaked out of England. Of course, there was always the chance that a lazy immigration officer wouldn't spot him again, or that he could buy a passport from one of the oil-field workers in Libya and have him report it stolen, and razor in his own picture for a one-shot trip, but it was too risky with all the heat.

While his contracts for Libyan army uniforms and the M-16 rifles were in trouble, instructors, principally Green Berets, were busy training Qaddafi's strike force at Bengazi, to the east of Tripoli on the far side of the Gulf of Sidra. Dozens of pilots and mechanics were answering ads placed by Diane Byrne, including more than thirty former Air Force, Marine and Navy fliers from America alone. Arms and night-vision gear were streaming in, and so were the critical C-130 and Chinook helicopter parts.

Reginald Slocombe had come up with a European staging

area, a bonded warehouse in Rotterdam owned by a German named Wolfgang Steiniger, built to store drilling equipment from Houston for the North Sea oil fields. The parts would arrive and be relabeled for Libyan delivery. It was an ideal setup. Now and then there was a cursory inspection of the warehouse. But the Dutch couldn't have cared less as long as the same crates and their contents moved in and out of the country under bond, technically never having been in the Netherlands at all.

He depended on Byrne to run the London office under the supervision of Roberta Barnes, who was based in Geneva alongside his lawyer, Ed Coughlin. And he sent John Heath to Liège to be near Donnay and the Steiniger warehouse. Since the departure of Douglas Schlachter, Wilson had picked the best of a succession of ex–Green Berets to manage the day-to-day routine in Tripoli, but as his closest aide, his Libyan eyes and ears, he had relied on Heath.

The former Army explosives expert had been in Libya longer than anyone else working for Wilson. Lean and conventionally handsome with black-flecked gray hair, he was given the code name "Silver Fox." Wilson told him, "Hey, you look like a U.S. senator," but his character was bland and obedient. At first, Heath, who was divorced and without any real roots, rationalized that he was involved in an intelligence mission, but that didn't wash for long. In the end, it simply got down to the tax-free money, and then more money. Just to be on the safe side, as Heath was leaving for Belgium, Wilson warned him that he also had been indicted. It had been kept sealed, though, in case Heath showed up in the States. If he did, Wilson said, he was staring at thirty-five years in prison.

About then, more anxious than ever to ingratiate himself with the Libyans, Wilson responded at once to a request from Major Hajazzi. Colonel Qaddafi, Hajazzi said, was still suffering great personal pain from the activities of counterrevolutionary Libyan dissidents living abroad. Two married students at Colorado State University, Faisal Zagallai and his wife, Farida, were real troublemakers. After the Qaddafi regime had sent them to the United States, paying for their education, they refused to return to help the masses. Instead they had spearheaded the formation of the Free Libyan Students Union, had organized rallies in the United States against Qaddafi that had been given considerable television coverage and now were

smuggling in inflammatory leaflets and posters denouncing
the colonel. They had to be eliminated as an object lesson.

Wilson had just the man for it, forty-six-year-old Eugene
Tafoya, one of the Green Berets at the Bengazi instruction
camp. While retired Berets were not your normal run of citi-
zenry, and now and again one of them, unable to cope with life
in Libya, had to be replaced, they were by and large professional in their behavior, glad to get the money, to be back in
action and away from the boredom of backyard cookouts in
Fayetteville. Tafoya, however, was different. He was a beefy,
acne-scarred thug, widely disliked by his comrades, who after a
few glasses of "flash," the Libyan equivalent of bathtub gin,
would boast about all the people he'd blown away behind
enemy lines in Vietnam. Wilson immediately spotted him as a
born killer.

He had already used Tafoya for a couple of special assignments the previous spring. One involved Robert Manina, a Canadian whom Wilson had taken on as a partner in delivering
surveillance vans equipped with night-vision gear. He suspected
Manina of shipping vans behind his back. "The son of a bitch
screwed me out of a million dollars," Wilson told Tafoya.

He wanted a message sent to him to pay up or else, and in
the middle of the night on May 26, 1980, Tafoya firebombed a
Jaguar parked in the driveway of Manina's home in Kitchner,
Ontario, by stuffing a roll of toilet paper in the gas tank and
lighting a match to it. Terrified, Manina went into hiding, but
he never gave Wilson the money. Tafoya had neglected to con-
vey any word about why the bombing had occurred.

Next, Tafoya went to the lavish headquarters of EATSCO
in Falls Church, Virginia, to see Thomas Clines. After his indictment had been made public, Wilson, in a rare moment of realism, concluded that he was going to be cut out of the profits
from the arms shipments to Egypt, but he was determined to get
back the $500,000 he had advanced to Clines. Although Clines
had made three payments totaling $92,500 the year before, Ed
Coughlin never was able to pin down whether it was part of the
principal or interest.

Wilson, however, chose to regard it as interest; now he
wanted all the money back. This time Tafoya got the message
across. To make certain Clines knew where Tafoya was coming
from, Wilson had dictated some pertinent data, like the name of

Clines's Egyptian majority stockholder, Hussein Salem, and of General Ghazala, Egypt's military attaché in Washington. Shortly afterward, Clines showed up in Coughlin's Geneva office and assured him that Wilson had nothing to worry about; as soon as the paperwork was completed, he'd have every penny.

In late September, Tafoya left Libya, heading for Fort Collins, Colorado, and the Zagallais. Both Faisal and Farida, in their early thirties, were working on doctorates in sociology. They had been ardent supporters of Qaddafi until he issued a series of decrees abrogating a free press and all of Libya's laws regarding individual liberty. Since then, financial aid from Libya had been halted, so Faisal could hardly believe his luck when a woman called on October 13, saying that she represented a number of companies looking for people to translate technical manuals into Arabic at a salary of $2,000 a month. An interviewer would drop by the next evening.

Farida, however, was apprehensive—the offer sounded too grand—but Faisal shrugged her off. Her nervousness increased when Tafoya arrived around seven P.M. She smelt liquor on his breath and some of the questions he was asking weren't like those for any job interview she'd ever heard. She was coming in from the kitchen with a glass of orange juice for Tafoya when she saw him attacking her husband and ran out of their ground-floor apartment screaming for help.

Faisal, a slight man, lunged for a gun he had bought for protection. The much stronger Tafoya grappled with him, drawing a .22-caliber automatic and firing three shots. One of them completely missed Faisal. Another entered his temple, coursing downward and lodging near his palate. A third passed through the front of his skull, severing an optic nerve. He fell bleeding to the floor. As neighbors gathered in some confusion, Tafoya rushed out and sped away in a waiting car.

Four days later, the official Libyan press agency, believing Faisal to be on his hospital deathbed, issued a taunting release that said, "Zagallai studied at the expense of the community for ten years. But instead of returning to serve his country and people, he became an agent and spy for American intelligence." However, while blinded permanently in his right eye, he did not die.

2

In Belgium one of John Heath's jobs was to get visas for anyone Wilson wanted in Tripoli. All Heath knew about Tafoya was that he was one of the Green Berets Wilson had recruited, and on the afternoon of November 2 Heath was surprised to find him sidling up to him at the bar of the Holiday Inn in Liège. He needed a visa, Tafoya said, and then added, "I guess you heard what happened."

Heath didn't have the slightest notion of what he meant. "Oh, yeah," he replied noncommittally.

"Well, I blew it."

"Really?" Heath said. "How so?"

"I got the fucker in the head twice and he's alive. You believe it?"

Heath still didn't know what Tafoya was talking about. There had been no mention of the Zagallai shooting in the *International Herald Tribune.* "What did you use, a .38 Special or a .357?"

"No, just a Magnum .22. You get anybody in the head twice, regardless what you use, he should be dead, right?" Tafoya appeared to be bemused by the vagaries of fate. Then he excused himself for a moment and returned with a sexy brunette, whom he introduced as Betty Jo, his wife, in fact his fourth wife. She also needed a visa. Ordering a round of drinks, Tafoya kept harping on the failed killing. "It wasn't my fault," he said. "Nobody told me he had a gun."

Heath rolled his eyes. But Tafoya just grinned and said, "Don't worry about her. She knows all about it. She was driving the car."

Heath checked with the office in Tripoli to make sure the visas were authorized, and after the Tafoyas left, he turned to another assignment. Major Hajazzi had told Wilson that he wanted some of the C-4 from the Houston shipment moved to a place of easy access in Europe, and three drums of it, still labeled "drilling mud," were airlifted to the Steiniger warehouse in Rotterdam.

Now Heath was to take fifty pounds of C-4 from one of the drums and repackage it in a commercially acceptable manner so that it could be brought into England. How he did it was up to him. He bought cans of white paint, emptied the cans into other

containers and put in the C-4, covering each batch with a few
inches of paint.

In early December, he was told to proceed to London. He
checked in at the Ladbrooke Hotel, where Steiniger, who
brought the paint cans through customs, contacted him. Heath
loaded the cans into a rented car. When he signaled Tripoli that
he had the "merchandise," he got instructions to be at the end
of the hotel bar the next afternoon. Someone who had his description would contact him. As Heath sat there with a drink, a
swarthy man approached him and said, "John?" He followed the
man in his car to the Libyan embassy and watched the cans being
carried inside.

About three years later, in the spring of 1984, a rash of
bombings rocked houses in Manchester where anti-Qaddafi
Libyans lived, injuring more than two dozen of them. The timer
on one of these devices malfunctioned. The explosive was
American-made C-4, although this was not publicized. Demon-
strations were held by groups of jeering exiles, many of them
masked to hide their identities, outside the Libyan embassy on
St. James's Square. Suddenly a fusillade of shots came from the
embassy, hitting a young female British constable on security
duty, mortally wounding her.

Relations with Libya were broken off. Unable to enter the
embassy or to seize its occupants because of the laws governing
diplomatic immunity, the police ringed the building for a week
while the Qaddafi loyalists inside packed up and were escorted
out of England. Afterward a search turned up several handguns.
They were, I learned, from a shipment of fifty revolvers delivered in 1976 in the company of Frank Terpil by Joseph McElroy,
the Pennsylvania entrepreneur who first started Wilson and Terpil on their road to riches in Libya.

In Tripoli, British diplomats were held hostage by Qaddafi's troops until his London staff had returned. Afterward,
Qaddafi trumpeted that the British had a gun hidden in their
embassy as well. The serial number was given to Interpol with
a demand that it be traced. But the Libyans quickly dropped this
line.

It was a bit embarrassing. The last sale of the pistol they
claimed to have found took place in Bailey's Crossroads, Virginia, at the Texaco station owned by Douglas Schlachter's
brother.

EIGHTEEN

By December 1980, Wilson was in his fourth month of being penned up in Libya. Since the Woodward article in 1977, he had received relatively little press. There had been his indictment, of course, along with those of Terpil and Brower, and he had appeared in some of the stories after Terpil fled the country.

In October there had also been four columns by the Washington muckracker Jack Anderson about how Wilson and Terpil had run a terrorist school in Libya, but Terpil got most of the play. One column tried to tie them in with Billy Carter, the president's brother, who visited Libya after Qaddafi gave him $300,000 in a vain effort to obtain the release of the C-130 planes still being held in Georgia. Terpil, however, was long gone, and while Wilson knew about Carter's visit, he neither met him nor even saw him.

It was that fucking Qaddafi, he thought. Washington was shipping arms all over the place, for God's sake. If Qaddafi had only played his cards right, Edwin P. Wilson would be a hero instead of a fugitive. Another Anderson column, though, caught his fancy. It implied that the CIA had at least known about, and perhaps had actually condoned, his activities in Libya. That was more like it.

Then on December 6 a four-paragraph story appeared in

the Washington *Post* reporting that Brower had pleaded guilty
to a conspiracy charge in connection with an alleged shipment
of munitions and weapons to Libya and that he faced up to five
years in jail and a $10,000 fine. Wilson and Terpil were cited as
having been indicted with Brower earlier in the year. E. Lawrence Barcella was quoted as telling the presiding judge that
Brower's role in the conspiracy was to help Wilson and Terpil
fulfill a contract to supply the government of Libya with explosive devices.

Roberta Barnes flew in with the clipping. Wilson read it
over and over again. It wasn't much of a story. Obviously,
Brower was talking. But what was he saying? How far had he
gone? Wilson went crazy trying to figure it out.

Roberta Barnes had gotten the clipping from Seymour
Glanzer. Wilson questioned her as if she had been in court. Had
she talked to Glanzer? What had he said? Many of the grand jury
witnesses called by Barcella had contacted Wilson and he had
sent them to Glanzer, who then picked lawyers for them. So
Glanzer had been able to provide a pretty good reading on what
was happening, but now everything had dried up about Brower.
What good was Glanzer? He was supposed to take care of Barcella, and Glanzer had failed. He'd have to find himself another
lawyer, someone who could do the fucking job right.

Listening to these tirades, Barnes began to think that the
isolation of Libya was affecting his judgment. She would come
down every month or so and stay for two or three days, despis-
ing the country, the grime, the joylessness, the hostility everywhere. Xenophobia was a constant, like the desert wind.

Magazines and newspapers mailed into Libya were cen-
sored, and overseas phone service, except to Geneva, was a
maddening experience. Sometimes a call would get through
immediately. The next one would require hours or days. Wilson's main link with the outside world was his telex machine.
He would hover over it for hours on end. He had started
drinking heavily. Occasionally he would manage to get a bottle
of Scotch, but mostly he consumed flash, which was distilled
from potatoes and was so raw that it was bearable only when
mixed with orange or grapefruit juice. Often by midafternoon
he was incoherent.

He found himself saddled with irritants that he would have
ignored in the old days, when he moved about as he pleased, or

would have turned over to somebody else to resolve. Chief among these irritants were the Tafoyas. He had allowed Tafoya to bring in his wife because he feared that one or both might have been identified by Zagallai. Now the wife was complaining bitterly about living conditions in an unheated cottage they were occupying by the sea. She wanted to go home and Tafoya himself was getting unpleasant. The Libyans had reneged on the $50,000 he was supposed to have gotten for the kill, and Tafoya kept saying it wasn't his fault that the guy had not died.

At last Wilson brought Heath in from Belgium. "Babysit them," he said. "You're good at that. Try to calm them down. See if you think she'll crack if I let her go."

Heath by then had learned the details of the Fort Collins shooting and thought Wilson's reasoning was nutty. Why would Betty Jo Tafoya volunteer information about her complicity in an attempted assassination? After a week, he said that if she was going to crack, it would be because she couldn't leave Libya. Give her some money and send her on her way. Wilson finally agreed to a $10,000 settlement. But Heath would have to accompany her to London, take her to the country and observe how she behaved. If she showed the slightest instability, he was to terminate her and bury her body.

"Right, Ed," Heath said. He flew up with Betty Jo, who gratefully gulped down one Scotch after another, spent two nights in bed with her and saw her off to the States at Heathrow Airport.

In Libya, when Tafoya's belligerence kept on, Heath suggested letting him go, too. "He's a problem you don't need and it's going to get worse," he said. "Yeah, well, how do we know he'll stand up?" Wilson shouted, waving a glass of flash and grapefruit juice. "How do we know how that investigation's going?" He had a better idea. He'd tell Tafoya that he was sending him with Heath to England for a well-deserved holiday, and then at Broxmead Farm Heath would murder him at his earliest opportunity. "Get him drunk first," Wilson said.

Heath had no intention of taking on Tafoya, and four days after their arrival, he reached Wilson by phone. "It's just not possible," he said. "But don't worry, he'll stand up."

"Good, send him back to the States," said Wilson, as if it were of no consequence. "By the way," he offhandedly added, "tell Gene to keep in touch. I might need him for some other jobs." Heath had braced himself for an argument. Wilson's abrupt personality switch was truly scary, he thought.

In early February, Wilson learned that Brower had been sentenced to only four months in prison with three years probation, and a $3,000 fine.

Even Barcella had expected a stiffer sentence. But Hundley had been eloquent in court. He skipped all the nonsense about Brower believing he was involved in a covert intelligence operation. His client, Hundley argued, was just a patriotic fool who had fallen on hard financial times and got sucked in deeper and deeper by Wilson. Something that could happen to anybody.

In Tripoli, though, what shook Wilson the most was Barcella's first open reference in court to the Houston deal. "The largest nonmilitary shipment of plastic explosives out of the United States now known to federal officials," Barcella had said. If Brower was talking about the C-4, he had spilled everything.

Swigs of flash bucked him up. So what, he said to Heath. Let Brower say anything he wanted to. He saw himself on the stand declaring that whatever went on with Brower and the Libyans was strictly between them. Sure, he had known something about it, but none of the details. He'd slyly observe that Brower, being an experienced explosives man, should have known enough to get the right permits. He had no idea about the drilling-mud caper. Only Slocombe could connect him to the shipment, and he hadn't heard a peep from him about any of this. The thought of Reginald Slocombe got him all worked up again. He had told Slocombe not to get involved personally, and that Mormon asshole had gone to Miami with Bloom to charter the fucking DC-8!

As he brooded about Slocombe, his mercurial mind-jumps led him back to Francis Heydt in Oklahoma and the Libyan army uniforms contract. Slocombe had been the intermediary with Heydt on the uniform contracts, and Heydt had walked off with hundreds of thousands of dollars, and he wondered if Slocombe had been in cahoots with Heydt.

He had to get that money from Heydt. Cash flow was an increasing worry. It wasn't just the uniforms, but the M-16 rifles, and because of this the Libyans were delaying their payments on other contracts. In return he had held out on the delivery of C-130 plane parts. But he was playing a losing game. The Libyans had him where it hurt. He ranted to Heath and Roberta

Barnes that he wouldn't be in this spot if he weren't surrounded by a bunch of drunks, flakes, incompetents, con artists and weaklings.

Look how Tom Clines was screwing him, he said. He'd advanced the funding to set up the Egyptian arms shipments, and now he was out in the cold and out the $500,000 he'd given Clines. Clines still hadn't come through with the money. He decided to call Clines himself, but he had to be cagey about it. There might be a time when he would need Clines to testify for him. So he told Clines that he wasn't contacting him on his own; it was just that his partners in Arcadia wanted the $500,000. "Listen," he said, "these aren't people you fuck with. It's my ass or yours, and I'm not taking the fall," and Clines once again said be patient, it was just a matter of time.

He stalked the beach, cursing Clines. If only he had some mobility, Wilson thought, the attitude of ingrates like Clines and Heydt would change pretty quick. Well, he'd taken steps in that direction. Through his lawyer in Malta, he had reached into Malta's underworld, to a fixer named Hollywood Charlie, who said he could get Wilson a Maltese passport for $9,000, and in the middle of February word came that it was ready.

He sent John Dutcher for it. A tough-guy ex-Marine who had been running a karate school in Washington, he was recruited to instruct Libyan commando teams in the martial arts. Now Dutcher was his personal bodyguard. In the shadow play inside Wilson's head, a new scenario had emerged. Suddenly he felt vulnerable living on the coast. A sub could surface offshore in the night, sending frogmen stealthily paddling in on a rubber raft to kidnap him—or worse. Who knew what Barcella would conjure up next?

The Maltese passport was issued in the name of Giovanni Zammit, allegedly a businessman and native of Malta born August 2, 1929. It had a photograph of Wilson wearing round steel-rimmed spectacles that gave him a benign, somewhat quizzical look. Once he had tried dying his hair, but the result was a terrible, attention-getting orange hue. He had also considered plastic surgery, had even thought of flying in a Swiss specialist to do the job. However, both Barnes and Heath pointed out there wasn't much that could be done about his height, short of chopping him off at the knees, and finally he abandoned the idea. At least he had a way out now with the Maltese passport.

And he was expecting an Irish one as well. An Irishman, an oil-field worker named "Mac" McCormick who bootlegged flash, told him that for $10,000 there was nothing to it. He'd have his dear brother Philip, back in Eire, apply for a passport by post. All Wilson had to do was come up with the cash and a picture.

Then Wilson's capacity to instill fear collapsed on another front. On March 2, his wife rejected his $2 million take-it-or-leave-it offer to get out of his life. "To protect my equity," Barbara Wilson informed him, she was instituting divorce proceedings. "I am going to terminate the impossible situation in which I find myself," she wrote. Well, what about *his* situation? he yelled at Heath, who did not respond. To say anything, Heath had learned, just sent Edwin P. Wilson off on another rampage.

2

All through the fall of 1980, and into '81, the tension kept mounting in Barcella's office. The excitement of finally cracking the enormous C-4 shipment out of Houston was instantly deflated when Wilson made his escape from Malta.

Inaction left everyone's nerves ragged.

In October, while Barcella brought witnesses before the grand jury to buttress the Houston case, Dick Pedersen and Rick Wadsworth were detached to help the Secret Service during the Carter/Reagan presidential campaign. After better than two years of putting something together on Wilson, the new assignment was a dreary letdown, and when they returned, they both complained that nothing was being done. Like what? Barcella asked, and they said, How about indicting Wilson and Bloom on the C-4 shipment and how about this guy Heath? They had enough on him, didn't they? "You know, let's bang a few heads," Pedersen said. "Let's get on with it."

But Barcella argued that with Wilson still on the loose, to say nothing of Terpil, what good would it do? All the specifics on the C-4 shipment, and Wilson's role in it, hadn't been released yet. Conceivably, he could be lulled into leaving his Libyan sanctuary and they'd have another pop at him.

Then Carol Bruce accused Barcella of being preoccupied with the Orlando Letelier retrial. He resisted pointing out that she also was engaged full-time in prosecuting a judge up on corruption charges. Still, it was true that he cared profoundly about the Letelier killing, although not to the exclusion of Wilson.

Barcella could recall crying only three times in his adult life —when his father died, when Harold Sullivan died, and then, two years ago, when he sat in the jury box of an empty courtroom while Gene Propper led Letelier's widow, Isabel, through a practice run of her testimony. He recalled as if it were yesterday her wide, tremulous eyes, her fingers clutching a medallion at her neck, carved by Letelier out of lava with a spoon to maintain his sanity after the ruling junta had jailed him on a desolate island in the Tierra del Fuego. He had listened as she spoke of how her husband had fought for a democratic Chile. How in America he continued his fiery orations against the junta until it stripped him of his Chilean citizenship. And how one day, in September 1976, she received a phone call summoning her to the hospital her husband had been taken to, where, upon her arrival, she learned that he was dead, and the doctors and the FBI agents present pleaded with her not to view his mangled body.

"You cannot deny me," she had told them. "He was my husband, my friend and my lover for twenty years." She spoke of kissing what remained of him, and then she looked dazedly out into the courtroom, at Barcella, her hands lifted in helpless supplication, and softly said, "And now I am here."

He understood the frustration around him about Wilson. *He* was frustrated too, not knowing what Wilson was doing, what he was planning. Since the U.S. embassy had been burned down nearly a year before, there was no American presence in Libya that Barcella had access to. If the CIA knew anything, it wasn't telling. And the CIA seemed to be saying, What's the point, who needs all this anyway? It was as though the agency would just as soon have the whole matter fade away.

The FBI certainly didn't care. The agent that the bureau had acting as liaison on the case, William Hart, was loaded down with what the bureau deemed a far more pressing assignment— doing background checks on job applicants for the Reagan administration.

Kevin Mulcahy had fallen off the wagon. From the beginning he'd been angry at Barcella's refusal to let him be part of the investigation, and after his return from several weeks in a rehabilitation center, he was still angrier. "Look, Kevin," Barcella said. "You're a witness. You can't know everything that's going on."

Mulcahy had shouted back, "You're a fucking fraud, Larry. You're like all the rest. Nothing's going to happen. It's the big fix."

3

On March 1, 1981, Barcella himself exploded. The Wilson case remained at a standstill, and all his efforts to get the Justice Department to appeal the Letelier reversal had failed. Then Secretary of State Alexander Haig lifted sanctions against Chile that had been imposed after Letelier's assassination. When a reporter asked for his comments, Barcella said that only a month ago Haig had called for an all-out war against terrorists around the world. Now he had "in effect condoned an act of international terrorism."

"You know, you're basically calling the secretary of state a hypocrite," the reporter said. "I don't usually do this, but I'm going to give you a chance to think about it. You sure you want to say that?"

"I'll get back to you in a few minutes," Barcella said. He phoned his wife, Mary. She said, "You're right, aren't you?" and after he said yes, she said, "Well, don't worry about it."

"Hey," he said, "did I ever tell you how much I love you?" and she said, "Don't worry about that either."

The story made page one of the Washington *Post*. A call came in from the Chilean desk officer at the State Department. "That wasn't a very politic remark," he said, and Barcella said, "You remind me of the guy on the Malta desk." When his caller responded, "Pardon me, I don't quite understand," Barcella said, "Forget it. You never will."

Still seething in his office, Barcella got a call from Scotland Yard's Inspector Bendle. For once the news was good. Bendle said that he believed two rural retreats Wilson had in England had been discovered. There was a jeep parked at one of them with Virginia license plates. Barcella put him on hold while he checked. "Bingo!" he was saying a couple of minutes later. "They're registered to Edwin P. Wilson, Box 176, in Upperville."

The search had taken months. A couple who had once rented Wilson his mews house in London thought he might have

a place somewhere in West Sussex. Next, Bendle confronted
Diane Byrne, who said that well, now that Bendle mentioned it,
she too had heard talk of a country home, but where it was she
couldn't say. "Mr. Wilson," she observed, "was a very close-
mouthed man."

"Yes, I'm sure," Bendle said. The only available photograph of Wilson was his passport picture, which Barcella had
blown up and distributed to the press and to Interpol, and
Bendle and his men had gone up and down one obscure country
lane after another with it until a neighbor of Wilson's finally
recognized him.

According to the neighbor, the properties had remained
unoccupied for some time, except for two recent stays by a
silver-headed fellow, once with a woman and then with a rough-
looking man. At that point, Barcella had no idea who the Tafoyas were or how they fitted in, but the description of the man
with silver hair matched up with John Heath. Bendle said that
he would have the local constabulary keep a quiet watch on both
places. Perhaps Wilson himself might show up.

And just maybe, Barcella thought, this all was an omen of
better things ahead.

NINETEEN

In Tripoli, Wilson was sure that he had finally found a way to neutralize Barcella. It began when Armand Donnay sent a message from Belgium that he would be able to deliver fissionable material and testing equipment that would put an A-bomb in Qaddafi's hands. At first, tens of millions of dollars danced in Wilson's head. There was nothing the colonel wanted more than an A-bomb.

In mid-February 1981, Donnay arrived in Libya with uranium samples and a packet two inches thick of blueprints, drawings and equations to show a Libyan nuclear commission. Wilson brought Heath along as his technical adviser; Heath's explosives ordnance training in disarming nuclear devices in case of a mishap had also included what went into them.

But it turned out that the uranium lacked purity and the papers, so impressive to the untrained eye, were incomplete. Wilson couldn't believe it. What did these Arabs know? Then Heath told him that they were right; Donnay's stuff didn't add up to much. Wilson berated Donnay, who professed innocence. He was, he said, just a middleman, and in a second meeting he promised to supply designs that would answer everyone's reservations.

In his heart, though, Wilson knew that it wasn't going to

come off. He started hitting a couple of cases of Cutty Sark that had been smuggled in with a shipment of C-130 parts, his thoughts scampering around like rats in a laboratory maze. Maybe he could turn this to his advantage. What difference did it make whether Donnay's packet of papers was any good? Wasn't the bottom line that Qaddafi had tried to get hold of an A-bomb and he, Edwin P. Wilson, had foiled him? The more he thought about it, the better it played.

Almost as if he had convinced himself, he summoned Roberta Barnes to Tripoli, drove her to a remote spot along the beach and showed her the material that Donnay had brought. "These are plans for an A-bomb that Qaddafi wants," he said. "I've got to get them to Washington. Tell Cyr to get his ass over to London right away."

But when Paul Cyr arrived, he wanted no part of it. It was too hazardous. Suppose the Libyans searched him? Barnes put him on the phone with Wilson, but he wouldn't change his mind. The talk turned to Wilson's legal problems. "I'm getting a bum rap," Wilson said. Seymour Glanzer was supposed to negotiate a deal with Barcella and he had failed. Now his wife had filed for divorce and he could end up losing Mount Airy and Apple Manor.

Cyr said he knew a terrific lawyer in Washington named John Keats. He was not only a member of the Mount Airy Gun Club but a pal of Barcella's besides. Wilson perked up at that. A personal approach might be just the thing. "Okay, sound him out," Wilson said. "Tell him I want him."

Iconoclastic by nature, an avid outdoorsman who rode and hunted, Keats had tangled in court with Barcella many times. But they had developed a special relationship on one case. Keats had a client, a prominent lobbyist, who was up on two counts of sodomy and a rape.

The lobbyist waived a jury trial and was found guilty. But Keats, using a battery of psychological evaluations, got the judge to impose a sentence of only two years, despite Barcella's objections. Then, after the lobbyist was released, the detective on the case called Barcella and said, "We got him again. Same thing." But a subsequent investigation convinced Barcella that this time the man was innocent. "Look," the detective said, "he goes on the stand with his record and he gets what he should have before." Barcella said, "Yeah, but we can't do it that way,"

and afterward Keats said to him, "I appreciate what you did. I
know it wasn't easy."

Barcella said, "You're wrong. It was easy. I didn't like it, but
it was the only choice I had."

Keats left for Tripoli on March 11. Wilson drove him directly to his villa. Keats was a little surprised that Wilson made
no effort to suggest that he was a covert agent—he had heard
all those retired intelligence types in the gun club gossip about
how Ed Wilson had to be part of a CIA front. On the other hand,
when Keats reflected on it, that was exactly the way Wilson
should be acting if he were an agent. Who knew what sort of
pretzel-bending the CIA was capable of? Keats had read somewhere that the agency had a section devoted to reading spy
thrillers to get ideas from them.

Wilson said he was just trying to do normal business in
Libya. He had bent over backwards to stay within the law. If
there had been any transgressions, his former partner Frank
Terpil was to blame. As soon as he discovered what Terpil was
like, he had split with him. All Keats had to do was to look at
what Terpil did on his own, getting mixed up with that fucking
nigger Idi Amin. And selling machine guns to undercover cops
in New York. *Jesus!*

The same went for this guy Jerry Brower. God knows what
he was saying, Wilson told Keats. Terpil had found Brower.
Wilson insisted that the original idea was completely legitimate,
to ship in explosives to clear mine fields. If Terpil and Brower
had engineered other deals on the side, he wasn't aware of them
at the time.

He also claimed that Brower had contracted directly with
Libya for some C-4, but none of it was his doing. And a goddamn drunk named Kevin Mulcahy was behind his indictment,
an ex–agency kid he tried to help straighten out but finally had
to fire. "You should have seen him," Wilson said, "running
around bare-ass in a hotel in London pounding on doors."
The minute any of them—Terpil, Brower, Mulcahy and the
rest—got into trouble, the next thing they did was to lay it on
Ed Wilson.

"It's all bullshit," he said. "We've got to work this out. You
know, negotiate some probationary time if I have to. And pay
a fine and get it over with. Glanzer isn't moving on anything."
Keats remembered him pouring out glasses of Cutty Sark.

"What's Barcella like? Isn't there somebody higher up we can deal with?"

"Barcella's your best bet," he said. "You ought to sit down with him in some neutral spot, so you can hear it from the horse's mouth."

"Look, I'm not crazy," Wilson said. "I'd have to have a guarantee in writing."

That was the point, Keats told him. If they wanted to grab him, a piece of paper wouldn't help. What counted was Barcella's word, and you could trust him.

"I'll think about it," Wilson said.

In the morning Wilson still insisted on something in writing. "What if I gave him the Letelier fugitives? I passed the word back once. They were in South America someplace, Ecuador, I think, but the feds blew it. I have people on them right now. I expect news any day."

Then Wilson turned over his hole card, the A-bomb plans. That was even better, Keats said, but he wasn't going to chance taking them out. If they were delivered to him in Washington, he'd see that Barcella got them.

Keats was in Libya for three days. Except for one tour around Tripoli, he had spent all of his time in Wilson's combined residence and office. It wasn't the ultimate in luxury, but it wasn't shabby either. A cook prepared food in a kitchen on the ground floor and a servant brought it up.

Most of their conversations were private, but John Dutcher and Wilson's secretary Barbara Thompson joined them for dinner. In the absence of Roberta Barnes, Wilson had taken up with her. The only entertainment in the evening was black market videocassette movies. On the night before Keats left, the end was missing from a film they had been watching. Wilson stared at the blank screen and then at Keats. "I can't stand it here," he said.

2

In Washington the first thing Monday morning, March 16, Keats telephoned Barcella for an appointment.

"John, it's been a while."

"Ask me where I've been."

"Okay, where?"

"Tripoli, Libya."

Barcella let that percolate for a second. "Ed Wilson?"

"You've got it."

"Come right over."

Barcella wondered what was up. He hadn't heard anything from Glanzer to indicate that he was off the case, but Keats said, "I have authority to represent Ed Wilson in all matters," and Barcella said, "Okay, that's good enough for me."

"How would you like to have a meeting with Wilson?"

"To what end?"

"Who knows? Maybe he can convince you that you're wrong about him, although he probably won't be able to. I know you better than that. But maybe you can work something out. It's worth a try."

"Why?"

"Well, there's a couple of things that might be of interest to you. He may be able to get the Letelier fugitives back."

"John, I've heard that one before. About two years ago. It didn't pan out."

"I'm telling you, Larry. He thinks he can do it."

"Yeah, he's read that I've got the Letelier retrial coming up. Look, I'd love to have them back. I don't have to tell you what those two big empty seats will mean. You know what a retrial's like. It's a bitch of a case right now. With those two seats filled, I'd be in a hell of lot better shape. But you also know I'm not going to give up the courthouse to get those guys. What else?"

"Ed can probably give you some information—Larry, this is really very sensitive—on Libya's attempt to get the A-bomb."

Barcella gazed at him in disbelief. "*What?*"

"I'm not kidding. I mean, I'm no expert, but he has something. I've seen it myself."

"All right, that could make a difference," Barcella said. "Let me get back to you." He met with Charles Ruff, then the U.S. attorney for the District of Columbia, and filled him in. He pointed out that while a meeting like this was unusual, it wasn't unheard-of. Federal prosecutors, for instance, had met secretly with the fugitive financier Robert Vesco when he was in Costa Rica. As for Wilson, they already had one indictment against him and a second one on the Houston C-4 shipment was nearing completion. "I don't see what we have to lose," Barcella said, and Ruff agreed.

"We have to have something up front," Barcella told Keats.

"The A-bomb stuff." If Wilson arranged to get the plans to London and deliver them to the U.S. embassy's legal attaché, Barcella would see to it that they were forwarded to Washington. The next day, Keats said that it was all set.

The Justice Department had to be brought in because of the new ramifications, and Mark Richard, the deputy chief of the Criminal Division, sent a letter to the CIA's assistant general counsel, Edmund Cohen, alerting him to what was about to drop in the agency's lap. ". . . the possible benefit of the proffered information," he wrote, "is such that we feel it is necessary to objectively evaluate it before making any decisions in the case."

John Dutcher flew with the plans to London. Then, with Keats present, Barcella turned them over to a CIA emissary. A few days later, Barcella called Keats and said, "Langley says they're worthless. They don't go boom. That's a quote."

"Shit," Keats said, "let me see what I can do."

Almost at once Keats was back on the phone to Barcella. "Ed tells me he's gotten a lot more from Donnay, the guy in Belgium, and the Libyans haven't seen it."

The new material was considerably heftier, about a foot high. Although Barcella couldn't make heads or tails of it, he could see there was much more detail, more diagrams and formulas. It looked like the real thing, he thought.

A week passed without a word from the CIA. Keats started calling, sometimes two or three times a day. "Come on, Larry, what's happening? Ed says that the test equipment is sitting in a railroad yard in Liège. If it moves out, we're dead."

Barcella kept hounding Langley. Where was their analysis? Why couldn't someone check those freight cars in Liège? They were working on the documents as fast as possible, he was told. Stop worrying, they knew how to handle this.

Then, after another nerve-racking week, he was informed that the documents had "no intelligence value."

"What's that mean?" he asked.

"Between us," his CIA contact said, "it's a mishmash. Some of it's highly technical, the rest is rudimentary. But it doesn't go anywhere. Somebody's scamming somebody. Either Wilson's scamming the Libyans, or us, or Donnay's scamming Wilson. It's hard to say."

All he told Keats, though, was that the new stuff still didn't add up to anything.

Keats said, "Do you believe the agency?"

"Sure, why not? They don't have any reason to lie on this."

Keats suggested that they call Tripoli together. It was the first time he heard Wilson's voice. Even with the overseas line distortion, it was deep and fast-talking—and etched now in apparent astonishment. How could the agency possibly have arrived at such a conclusion? And how about those boxcars in Liège? "Hell, I'll stop them myself," he said.

"Be my guest," Barcella said.

"What about the Letelier fugitives, can't we get together on them?" Wilson said, and Barcella remembered thinking that he'd listened to this kind of switch dozens of times from defendants. If one thing didn't fly, forget it. Try the next.

By then it was near the end of April, and the Letelier retrial was a week or so away. "That'd be fine," Barcella said, "but I can't spare three or four days to meet you somewhere. How about giving them to me up front? John Keats knows I'm fair. It obviously isn't going to hurt you if you come up with those two guys."

Well, said Wilson, he was working on it, but he didn't know whether he could pull it off that fast.

"Okay, Ed," Barcella said. "All I care about right now is Letelier." After hanging up, he thought that Wilson had sounded a little panicky. He was certain they'd be talking again.

3

Barcella had told Carol Bruce, Dick Pedersen and Rick Wadsworth and the FBI's Bill Hart about the proposed meeting. Nobody had to be reminded to keep it from Kevin Mulcahy. He'd caused enough headaches.

Barcella was torn about Mulcahy. Barcella appreciated his disappointment at not being part of the investigative team, but it couldn't be. Mulcahy was a witness. And the cruel truth now was that Barcella needed him only to get into evidence the secret proposal to train terrorists in Libya, the one Mulcahy had taken over Labor Day weekend in 1976 from the offices of Inter-Technology, Inc.

But in February, just as Wilson's A-bomb scheme was being hatched, Barcella learned that Mulcahy was cooperating on a story about Wilson and Terpil with two reporters on the Boston

Globe's "Spotlight" investigative team, Steve Kurkjian and Ben Bradlee, Jr. "Look, Larry, I only want to help you," Mulcahy said. "You're not getting any support, from Justice or the FBI or the agency. I'm going to light a fire under them."

Sure, he'd like more support, Barcella said, but the approach Mulcahy was taking wasn't the right one. "You start drumming up headlines," he told Kevin, "and I'll have nothing but chiefs running in here, fucking everything up," and Mulcahy replied that Barcella didn't know what he was talking about.

The lengthy article appeared in the *Globe*'s Sunday magazine. Barcella was surprised and relieved that it didn't create more of an uproar. Part of the reason was that Mulcahy had insisted on anonymity as a source, and while Bradlee on his own had tracked Luke Thompson to Newfoundland, where he was working on an oil rig, much of what he said had to be attributed to nameless Green Berets.

But the biggest factor was that a story like this required follow-ups, and there weren't any. It might have been different if there had been a continuing front-page series. But an internal editorial dispute had erupted at the *Globe:* the "Spotlight" team was supposed to concentrate on local stories, not national ones, which was why the exposé wound up as a single piece in the magazine.

Disappointed at the response, Mulcahy seemed to change. He told Bradlee he had some hot material for another article, but now he wanted to be paid, and Bradlee said he would see what he could do. Next, Mulcahy went to the CBS news magazine *60 Minutes* and also to ABC's *20/20* and was rebuffed, again because of money demands. Then he told Bradlee to forget it. He had acquired a New York literary agent, Sterling Lord, and was going to write a book. He was sorry, but to create interest in the book, he would need *The New York Times.*

Barcella's first inkling of this, on the eve of the Letelier retrial, was when Mulcahy said he wanted him to speak to Seymour Hersh, a former reporter for the *Times* who had left the paper to write a book about Henry Kissinger.

"What have you been talking to Hersh about?"

"Well, just my feelings on this whole thing, Larry. You got to talk to him. You'll like him. He's a solid guy."

"Kevin, number one, I don't have time to talk to Seymour

Hersh. And number two, you know my position on reporters. I'm not going to tell him things I can't discuss, give him any great insights, especially with an indictment."

"Listen, Larry, he's a Pulitzer Prize winner. Do you know what this can do for the case? We can get all the visibility we need."

"I've already been through this with you," Barcella said.

"You better talk to Hersh, or I'll dump on you."

"That's cute, real cute. You know what I think about that. I don't give a damn."

"Hey, babe, you'll be sorry," Mulcahy said. "I mean, this is my story I'm telling Hersh. You don't talk to him, I'll light a fire under you one way or another."

"Kevin, you don't have to light any fires. I'm going to get back on this as soon as Letelier is over. We *are* doing things that are none of your business."

"What do you mean, they're none of my business?"

"Just that. Please, I've never forgotten what you've done. But you're a witness."

"Yeah, well, maybe I won't testify. You're going to regret this!" Mulcahy shouted and stormed out.

TWENTY

As Barcella was preparing the Letelier retrial, FBI agents, accompanied by Ray Martinez, a Fort Collins detective, surrounded the residence of Eugene Tafoya in Truth or Consequences, New Mexico.

Earlier, in Colorado, two teenage boys had found a .22-caliber pistol in a drainage ditch not far from where Faisal Zagallai had been shot. The last recorded sale was traced to a pawnshop in Fayetteville, North Carolina, where the pistol had been purchased by a former Green Beret, then living in Florida.

The ex-Beret said that he had sold it to another retired Special Forces man, Gene Tafoya, and supplied his address. A check of outbound flights on the night of the shooting revealed that Eugene Tafoya had left Fort Collins for El Paso, Texas, about an hour's drive from Truth or Consequences.

After he was taken into custody, a search of Tafoya's house turned up a recording he had taped of a phone conversation with another Green Beret veteran named Jimmy Dean, who had acted as Wilson's straw boss for the instructors who were brought in to train the Libyans. In the conversation Dean said that he had just come back from "over there," and Tafoya then described how he had carried out his firebomb warning to the Canadian, Robert Manina. Tafoya asked if there was anybody "that should quit breathing permanently," and Dean said, "While I was over there, I talked to that man and he said that he had some possibilities."

Among other items in Tafoya's possession was an address book that included the phone numbers for Wilson, for Roberta Barnes, for Wilson's Geneva attorney and for Ken Conklin in Washington. There was a list of the names, addresses and physical descriptions of past Wilson associates with whom he had fallen out and the names of anti-Qaddafi Libyans living in America.

And there also were the notes that Tafoya had written when Wilson sent him to see Tom Clines about the money he had advanced for what eventually became EATSCO.

In the meantime, the Letelier retrial confirmed Barcella's worst misgivings. Trying a case again, he liked to say, was tantamount to kissing a rattlesnake, "never pleasant and usually fatal."

Since his prosecution was based on what he believed to be the truth, there wasn't much he could change. But the defense lawyers, poring over what had and hadn't worked the first time around, could switch their strategy drastically, and they did. In the first trial, they had tried to paint the CIA, with its allegedly close ties to the ruthless Chilean military dictatorship, as the villain of the piece. This had failed, so now the new hidden hand behind Letelier's murder was the Chilean secret police. Michael Townley, Barcella's key witness, who confessed to placing the bomb under Letelier's car, was still loyal to his old bosses and on their orders had made scapegoats out of some innocent Cuban freedom fighters.

Without the presence of the two Cuban fugitives who had actually detonated the bomb by remote control, all this produced enough of a reasonable doubt, and on a Saturday at the end of May, after three weeks of testimony, the jury returned a "not guilty" verdict on conspiracy to murder for the remaining defendants.

That afternoon Barcella sat in a favorite saloon and downed five Jack Danielses. When he got home, he told Mary, "Hell, I can't even get drunk. I never should have had to try this one, and I wouldn't have if the goddamn solicitor general wasn't more worried about his Supreme Court batting average than he is in justice."

The next day he stomped around the house, snapping at everyone in sight, until Mary finally said, "Larry, you did the best you could. How long is this going to keep up?" He looked at her and said, "You're right. Tell you what I'm going to do. I'm taking you out to dinner tonight. I'm going to build that playhouse I've been promising Laura. And Monday morning I'm getting back to Edwin P. Wilson et al."

2

During the trial, Keats had called again about meeting Wilson. He really wants it, Keats said, and he has a hot new lead on the Cubans. Couldn't Larry do it over a weekend? "No," Barcella replied. "John, I'm spending damn near twenty hours a day on Letelier and it's not going well. I haven't even seen my wife and daughter since it started."

On Monday, June 1, he contacted Keats and said, "Okay, John, let's talk about it."

"Ed's going to want something in writing," Keats said.

Dick Pedersen was the most resistant to the idea of a meeting. "What's the point? He's just going to try to lie his way out."

They were stuck on a dime, Barcella said. Wilson could stay in Libya for the rest of his life, and the indictments weren't going anywhere unless they got him back. Sure, there were some other defendants in the C-4 shipment, but Wilson was the main guy. The thing was to break the ice and at least get some feel of him.

And there was another consideration, the nagging thought that the CIA was somehow involved. Personally, Barcella didn't buy it. But there'd been all the agency foot-dragging whenever information had been sought, and he remembered the former chief of Mossad telling him in Christina McKenzie's garden in England that the Israelis had known about Wilson from the beginning, that it was inconceivable the CIA didn't know, too.

"Where's the meeting going to be?" Pedersen asked, and Barcella said that he was thinking about Rome, and Pedersen grinned and said, "Hey, Larry, that's the best reason yet."

Actually, he had picked Rome because it was the closest big western city with direct flights out of Tripoli—in case Wilson entertained any thoughts of using the free ride he was getting to detour elsewhere on the way.

During the sessions Carol Bruce and Barcella had with Keats, Barcella spoke by phone to Wilson and said he would

attempt to obtain the consent of Italian authorities to lift the
Interpol warrant for a minimum period of three days. If it
worked out, Wilson was to enter Italy on his revoked U.S. passport, which he then would have to surrender.

"I'm assuming," Barcella said, "that this isn't going to be
a wild-goose chase for either of us."

"No, no!" Wilson exclaimed. "Don't worry. It's going to be
profitable. Very, very profitable!"

In a letter addressed to Keats, Barcella promised that, "assuming there are no problems independent of this case, no
efforts will be made to arrest, detain, deport or extradite Mr.
Wilson from Italy to the United States."

First on the agenda would be "Mr. Wilson providing us with
all knowledge of the past, present and future whereabouts" of
the two Cuban fugitives wanted in the Letelier murder conspiracy. If this information was accurate, it would "constitute a
demonstration of good faith." Then Wilson was to submit to a
debriefing "on topics of our choosing and additional topics of
Mr. Wilson's choosing."

No promises were being made, except that his statements
would not be used directly against him. There were a number
of other charges pending against Wilson, and they would not be
cast aside "simply because of this meeting." But, Keats was
advised, "You should also understand that the degree of Mr.
Wilson's candor would most certainly be a significant factor in
any future decision to negotiate with him."

That, Barcella thought, put the ball right in Wilson's court.
If he had anything to offer, he'd never have a better chance.

3

During the Letelier trial Barcella finally met Seymour Hersh
for a brief interview after the reporter charged that he was trying
to duck him. Hersh wanted to know about Mulcahy's credibility.
Barcella was in an awkward position. He had no idea of how
Kevin might be embroidering his story; on the other hand, there
was no way he would go on record casting any doubt on a
witness he intended to put on the stand. He wouldn't, he said,
vouch for, confirm or deny whatever Kevin may have said, but
yes, generally speaking, he was reliable.

Hersh's articles appeared in two successive installments in
The New York Times Magazine, the first on Sunday, June 14, 1981,

featuring a photograph of Wilson on the cover—the passport picture that Barcella had distributed—and one of Terpil. Although they contained basically the same substantive material as had been in the *Globe* story, they created an instant uproar. The difference was that Hersh's version was dramatically personal. Mulcahy was portrayed as a sort of lonely David battling one Goliath after another, all the while living in dire fear of the unknown.

"He's tired of waiting for this segment of his life to end," Hersh wrote. "He wants to be listed again in the telephone directory, to hold a driver's license in his own name, to vote, to own property, to stop living as if he—and not Wilson and Terpil —had been indicted for wrongdoing."

Unnamed sources said that Wilson had a "warm, personal friendship" with Qaddafi, whom he had in fact never met; that six months after he became a fugitive, at a time when he was holed up in Libya, he was seen openly dining with old employees in a Washington restaurant; that he had been a CIA "paymaster" during the Bay of Pigs invasion, when in reality he was a graduate student at Cornell University.

The articles nonetheless reported on a sinister-sounding "old-boy network of former CIA operatives and military men," and Theodore Shackley and Tom Clines were identified in print for the first time as close friends and associates of Wilson's.

And for anyone who wanted to see darker implications, they were right there. In an interview with Hersh, Shackley acknowledged being present at a meeting in which Wilson said that he was on his way to Libya, but he denied knowing anything about a terrorist training program. He had met with Wilson on that occasion and others only to obtain "stray bits of intelligence." Wilson, Hersh quoted Shackley as saying, "was a guy who knew about a lot of things. He was a good contact."

But the drumbeat of the articles was monumental federal indifference, if not a cover-up, regarding the activities of Wilson and Terpil. The problem with the U.S. Attorney's Office, according to Mulcahy, was a "simple lack of commitment." Carol Bruce had been "a breath of fresh air" until she also had turned against him, threatening to indict him as a conspirator unless he agreed to testify publicly.

Even the one grudging bouquet Mulcahy handed to federal officials—that in a late-night visit to Wilson's Upperville estate,

they had warned him that if anything happened to Mulcahy,
"they would come looking for him"—was melodramatic fantasy,
but it made for vivid reading. There was an ominous note that
Mulcahy had begun "research for a book on his experiences."

Wilson and Terpil—and Mulcahy—were the talk of the
town. On the Saturday before the second installment was to
appear, advance copies of it already in circulation, Barcella received an urgent summons from Stanley Sporkin, the CIA's new
general counsel. In his Langley office Sporkin told Barcella and
Bruce that President Reagan had called William Casey, the recently appointed director of the agency, and said that he wanted
to get to the bottom of the charges contained in the Hersh
articles.

Sporkin had come into the CIA with Casey and he asked
Barcella if he was receiving all the help he needed. Barcella said
that he'd like a little faster action on some of his queries. An
agency lawyer, a woman who had been acting as liaison with
Barcella, was present, and Sporkin instructed her to give top
priority to whatever information Barcella requested. She did her
job too energetically. In six months, an annoyed clandestine
directorate succeeded in having her replaced. It wasn't about to
let outsiders pry into its affairs, no matter what the reason for
the inquiry was or who ordered it. CIA directors and general
counsels came and went, but the directorate remained.

4

There had been twists of fate that Wilson could never have
anticipated—Mulcahy stealing the secret proposal on terrorist
training, Barcella happening to see a Justice Department memo
declining prosecution of Wilson and Terpil and remembering
Wilson's remark about not knowing a timer from a coffeepot, a
BATF agent in an adjoining cubicle overhearing a discussion
between Pedersen and Wadsworth about some Remington
rifles, Jerome Brower completely misinterpreting what Barcella
had meant by a "big" C-4 shipment.

None, however, was stranger that the train of events that
would begin to unfold when a man named Ernest Keiser, then
living in Larchmont, a suburban community north of New York
City, read the first of Hersh's articles.

Keiser was in deep trouble. But now, suddenly, he thought
that he saw a way out of all his difficulties. And after reflecting

on it for a while, he had a loyal employee of his, Dan Drake, put in an exploratory call to Tripoli, to Edwin P. Wilson.

Drake said he had to speak cautiously. He was phoning for his boss, Ernie Keiser. Wilson and Keiser had met one another south of the border around twenty years ago while they were working for the same firm. Wilson remembered, didn't he?

Well, yeah, maybe, Wilson said, he wasn't certain. Keiser, said Drake, was still consulting at the highest levels in the "community." The thought was that Wilson could be of immense value where he was. Did that interest him? Suddenly Wilson's memory improved. Yeah, right, he did recall Ernie, he said, and he was more than interested. That was good, Drake said. He'd be back in touch.

In Tripoli, Wilson shook his head in wonderment at it all. The timing couldn't have been better. Practically on the eve of his trip to Rome.

TWENTY-ONE

The Rome meeting was set for Wednesday, July 7, 1981.

Barcella flew out of Dulles on the night of July 5. With him were Bruce, Pedersen and Bill Hart of the FBI. Normally one of the agents in the Rome legal attaché's office would have been at the meeting, but Barcella had lobbied for Hart's presence. Hart had supervised the original investigation into Mulcahy's accusations. He liked Hart and respected his insights, and he wanted his expertise about Wilson, which dated back nearly five years, instantly available.

They checked in at the Jolly, a modest hotel abutting the gardens of the Villa Borghese, within easy walking distance along the Via Veneto of the U.S. embassy, and then went to the legal attaché's office. He was away on a business trip. His assistant told Barcella that a meeting room had been reserved at the Jolly for three days, starting Wednesday.

Keats flew in on Tuesday morning, registering at the Cavalieri Hilton, where Wilson, due to arrive late that afternoon, would also be staying. Around midday, Barcella, Pedersen and Hart went to see Keats, leaving Bruce behind; five months pregnant, she was still fatigued from the journey.

As comfortable as the Jolly was, it remained a far cry from the Hilton's hilltop luxury, with spectacular views of Rome and a pool swarming with gorgeous women in bikinis. Pedersen sighed and whispered, "Larry, I've always told you, private practice has its advantages."

Keats said that Wilson hadn't been able to get a flight out of Tripoli and would not be in until the following afternoon. "Hell," Barcella snapped, "that means we can't get started till Thursday," and Keats said, "Come on, Larry, how sore can you be? You're in Rome!"

"Okay, John, you've got me there." Keats was right. He was getting too keyed up, he thought. The weather was as splendid as one could ask for and he was excited about being in Italy. It was his first visit, and he only wished that Mary could be with him. So the next day they took a guided bus tour of the city. Around six P.M. Keats called and said, "He's here."

The four of them had dinner in a small restaurant on the Piazza Navona and later, after Bruce and Hart retired, Barcella and Pedersen had a nightcap in a sidewalk café on the Via Veneto. "What do you truly think's going to happen?" Pedersen asked, and Barcella said. "I don't know. At least we'll get a look at him."

"He's probably thinking the same thing. Know your enemy."

What Barcella didn't say was how much he ached for a line on the Letelier fugitives.

2

Wilson had purposely delayed his arrival, as if to show that he wasn't that desperate, that he was not coming hat in hand.

John Heath later remembered how up Wilson got in Tripoli as the Rome meeting approached, how confidently he prophesied success with that asshole Barcella. "I'm going to solve all my problems," he boasted. "We're really going to go from here."

He brought along John Dutcher as his bodyguard. And he decided to use his Maltese passport to enter Italy. It was as good a time as any to try it out, he thought. If there were any problems, he was covered by the immunity clause in Barcella's letter to Keats. But the passport worked just fine.

Keats was at the airport. He had gone there a couple of hours earlier to scout it out. While he trusted Barcella, there was always the possibility of the Italian police making a grab for the publicity. When they returned to the Hilton, Roberta Barnes, in from London, was on hand to embrace Wilson.

All the gaiety that evening disturbed Keats. Wilson was too expansive, too manic, and he was drinking too much. Keats hoped that it was simply an explosion of relief at being out of Libya. He attempted to bring a sense of realism to the gathering. He said he wasn't so much concerned about the count of conspiracy to murder the Libyan defector Umar Muyhashi in Egypt as he was about Brower's shipment of binary explosives in August 1976 and the alleged secret terrorist training proposal that Mulcahy had supplied to the government.

He reminded Wilson that Terpil had recently been convicted in absentia and sentenced to fifty-four years on the New York gun-running charges. There wasn't a better moment than now to plea-bargain—before the C-4 indictment that everyone was expecting came down. If Wilson agreed, Keats was sure that he could work out no more than five years. Wilson wanted to know how much jail time that meant. Keats said that he couldn't say, but it was what Brower had done and he ended up serving not much more than four months, which was a hell of a deal. He kept emphasizing that Barcella was a straight guy, that his word was as good as gold, but that Wilson would be foolhardy to play games with him.

Wilson suddenly waved Keats off. "Don't worry, no problem," he said. "I know what I'm doing. You let me handle this."

3

Barcella slept fitfully and was down in the lobby by seven-thirty just as Wilson was coming into the hotel with Keats. Barcella recognized him immediately. His hair was a little longer, his face fuller than in his photograph. Next to the short, wiry Keats, he appeared even larger than advertised. "Larry," Keats said, "this is Ed Wilson," and Barcella watched his hand vanish in Wilson's massive grip.

Wilson asked if he could join him for breakfast. He wanted a chance to talk to him alone before the meeting. "Sure," Barcella said, "if 'alone' means with John. I think you ought to have your lawyer present."

When they were seated, Wilson said, "Larry—can I call you Larry?" and Barcella said, "Of course," and then Wilson leaned forward and said that he could be of real intelligence service to him in Libya—what Qaddafi was up to, what the Russians were doing there.

That was something they might discuss later, Barcella said, but frankly he wasn't in the intelligence game.

Wilson persisted. He'd heard how unorthodox Barcella's methods were, that he ran all kinds of "source" networks. "You could source me as an 'undisclosed businessman' and pass the information along. It could help you out and, you know, if it helps you, it helps me."

He appreciated the offer, Barcella replied, but to prosecute criminal cases in the District of Columbia, he didn't need an undisclosed businessman source in Tripoli.

"I understand that," Wilson said. "But you ought to think about it, the ramifications. I could be of real value to you. Look, I'm here to talk about whatever you want, Larry. I think you've had a lot of misconceptions about me and what I was doing and I want to be as open and candid as I can."

The stroke job's starting, Barcella thought. He already had a sinking feeling about where this whole thing was headed. Then Bruce, Pedersen, Hart and the assistant legal attaché, FBI agent Lee Flosi, entered the breakfast atrium and Barcella excused himself to go over to them.

"So that's big Ed, huh," Pedersen said. "What's happening?" Barcella said, "Don't react and don't laugh. But he wants to be my secret agent."

The meeting was held in one of the hotel's first-floor rooms. Barcella sat at the head of a rectangular table, Wilson on his immediate left. Wilson was the only one without a note pad, his huge hands planted flat in front of him.

Barcella began by saying that he assumed Keats had given Wilson the letter laying out the ground rules. "Right, no problems," Wilson said. Barcella reminded him that he was under an indictment and expressed the hope that no one's time would be wasted. First was the quid pro quo. Where were the Letelier fugitives?

"Uh, my man isn't here yet," Wilson said. "He's on his way and I'll give you that as soon as he gets in. Tonight, tomorrow morning tops."

"Ed, I made it crystal clear that we had to have this up front."

"I know, Larry. You'll just have to trust me. Now let me tell you something you'll really—"

Annoyed, Barcella interrupted him. "Before we go any further, where's your passport?" and Wilson said, "That's something I wanted to talk to you about. I mean, it's the only one I've got. How am I going to get back into Libya?"

"It'll be stamped canceled, but the date won't be effective until after we've finished our business."

"Gee, Larry, I've got to be careful. I could be really stuck without it."

"The passport," Barcella said.

"Okay, okay," Wilson said. Then, undaunted, like an old-time door-to-door salesman hawking his wares, he plunged on. Right off the bat, he said, he had something hot for them. There'd been rumors that he was illegally supplying Libya with C-130 spare parts. It was another bum rap against him. The real culprit was a company in Chicago called Tencom. The parts were picked up by Qaddafi's personal pilot whenever he brought one of the colonel's two Jetstar planes to the United States for servicing. He had already informed the State Department's Office of Munitions Control about Tencom in an anonymous letter.

As it turned out, a letter had been received. It had been written by Roberta Barnes and its arrival coincided with a U.S. customs investigation into Tencom that had just started. What Wilson forgot to mention was that this was his way of eliminating some competition.

This was going all wrong, Barcella thought. Wilson was talking about everything except what they wanted to hear. So he said, "Why don't you give us some background about yourself? Start from the beginning."

"Right, Larry, whatever you want," Wilson said. "You're the boss here." As he highlighted his agency exploits, he said with a theatrical wink, "A lot of this stuff is classified, but I guess you've all been cleared." He described his negotiated severance with the CIA before joining Task Force 157 as a bonus in recognition of his service. The money, he said, had helped him get his first, 700-acre Mount Airy acquisition.

"Oh, yes," Barcella said, "tell us about your property holdings," and Wilson said, "Like I told you, land means a lot

to me. I've been close to the land ever since I was a kid farm-
ing in Idaho." Actually, he confided, it was his wife, Barbara,
who put the initial nest egg together, buying and selling bits of
real estate here and there, piggybacking them, he said, into
bigger things.

That was some piggybacking, Barcella thought, but he
didn't challenge him. The game plan was to get him talking
without challenges. Don't give him any idea of what they already
knew.

What about his relationships with Theodore Shackley and
Thomas Clines? Well, they were just old friends from his agency
days, Wilson said. He was now a little down on Clines. He had
lent him several hundred thousand dollars to start up a couple
of companies when Clines retired, and later on Shackley had
become a consultant to them, and Clines had yet to pay back the
money. He was unable to recall the details.

Ed Coughlin, his Geneva lawyer, had all the papers. The
trouble was, Coughlin had gone off on some trip and was out
of reach. He was sorry about that. "John," Wilson instructed
Keats, "make a note. Let's get hold of Ed on this as soon as
possible."

"Are you still in the CIA, or any part of the U.S. intelligence
network?" Barcella asked, and Wilson said, "No, no. I just try
to help. Be useful when I can."

He had, he said, thrown Shackley quite a few tidbits about
Libya, until Shackley resigned in '79. Shackley had said that he
would source him as an unidentified businessman, but he
really didn't know if he'd been given due credit. "That's what
I was trying to explain this morning, Larry," he said. "I could
do it for you." He really wanted to get out of Libya and return
to the States, but he'd be willing to stay there another two
years and feed back intelligence for some consideration on his
case.

And he could deliver plenty—inside profiles on Libyan
higher-ups, possible coup information, Qaddafi's nuclear capability plans, Libya's buildup along the Egyptian border, its overall military strengths and weaknesses. The Libyans, for instance,
had around fifty Soviet MiG-25 fighters; they came in crates and
were assembled by Russian technicians, but lacked sensitive
electronic gear that Moscow didn't want exported. "I'm tell-

ing you, Larry," Wilson said, "you're missing a big bet here."

At the lunch break Barcella said, "Don't forget that Letelier guy," and afterward Wilson reported, "He's in the air. I checked. He'll be in tonight."

Libya, he claimed, was "all Frank Terpil's deal." All he got was a fee to manage the contract. There was no bomb factory. That was baloney. As far as he knew, the contract was for a mine-clearing project. It wasn't till much later that the Libyans wanted a simple explosives ordnance school so that they could arm and disarm booby traps in villages along the Egyptian border in case of an attack. He acknowledged the August 1976 meeting in Washington with Terpil and Brower to ship explosives. Brower was supposed to obtain the proper licenses. "It wasn't my problem," he said.

Wilson's eyes suddenly went dead cold. As Barcella saw his affable mask drop, he could easily imagine the fear and intimidation Wilson was capable of creating. "It's that drunk Mulcahy," he said. "My wife took a shine to him and I took him under my wing, and he ends up stealing money from me and I had to fire him. Then he goes to the FBI with a pack of lies and everybody starts running off on a tangent."

Wilson blinked, as if he realized he had revealed too much of himself. He turned toward Bill Hart and said, "Don't get me wrong. I'm not saying anything against you fellows. I mean, I know you have a job to do."

He said that he had split with Terpil when he discovered he was being cheated out of his fees. There also was another reason why he was glad to be rid of Terpil. The first person recruited to teach explosives ordnance to the Libyans, an old agency man named John Harper, whom Tom Clines had recommended, had a serious drinking problem and he had brought some Cubans to Geneva to replace him.

The next thing he knew, Terpil, in his cups, was telling them that they'd be working with Russians in Libya and that they would have to go to Cairo "to blow away some goddamn Libyan defector" named Muhayshi. "Hell, I didn't know what Frank was talking about," Wilson said.

After the split with Terpil, a new company based in Geneva, called Services Commerciaux et Financiers du Moyen-Orient, was formed to take over the Libyan contracts. Again, he was just its representative, operating on commissions. The backers were

Saudi Arabians interested in speculative ventures. It wasn't any-thing illegal, but part of his agreement with them was that he could not reveal their names. "Larry, you understand how they are," he said.

The Green Berets were all under contract to Services Com-merciaux. He had even retained a lawyer, Ken Conklin, to make sure it was legitimate and aboveboard. All they did was provide the Libyans with basic training, what you'd find, say, in any boot camp. Mostly, though, they had sat around with time on their hands.

Barcella glanced at Bruce, Pedersen and Hart. He could see that they were thinking the same thing. Wilson's version of what the Berets were doing matched almost word for word the testi-mony of all those called before the grand jury—except for Luke Thompson.

Wilson's face hardened again. "We only had one bad apple," he said. "A liar and a flake named Thompson. A really sick guy. Believe me, we never did any terrorist training."

He couldn't be much help about the C-4 out of Houston. It was a deal that Jerry Brower had cooked up directly with the Libyans. Brower had gotten the stuff on his own and flew it over disguised as drilling mud in a chartered DC-8. At least that was what he had heard. Brower's lawyer—"I don't know his name," Wilson said—had even been on the plane. He'd also heard that the Libyans paid Brower somewhere between $600,000 and $700,000 through a bank in Geneva.

Dick Pedersen couldn't restrain himself any longer. "I don't get it," he said. "Everyone's a drunk or a flake or a crook, and you didn't know what any of them were doing. They were your people, weren't they? Didn't you hire them?"

"I'm not here to crucify myself," Wilson replied.

Walking out with Barcella when the first day's session was over, he asked, "What do you think?" and Barcella said, "Ed, I think you're missing a golden opportunity."

4

That evening at the Cavalieri Hilton, Keats told Wilson, "This isn't going right."

"I'm telling the truth."

"I can't say you're not. But I can tell you they're not buying it."

"They're just fencing," Wilson said. "They can't turn down my offer."

At dinner Carol Bruce said to Barcella, "We're not going to get anything from him," and Bill Hart said, "Maybe he's just trying to see where we are."

Wilson's whole performance, Barcella thought, was pretty slick—if they didn't know so much of what he had actually been up to. But they did. "It's possible he's selling us short," Barcella said. "We'll see what happens tomorrow."

For Barcella, the bottom line right then was the Letelier fugitives. He'd walk the last mile to nab them.

5

"He's here," Wilson said. "But he got in late and he's knocked out. He'll be with us after lunch."

Barcella asked him about Eugene Tafoya. The news of Tafoya's arrest in New Mexico and apparent connection with Wilson had filtered back to him not long before he left for Rome, but he still didn't know all the details.

"Listen," Wilson said, "talk about flakes and weirdos, he was number one." Tafoya had been just another Green Beret. The only reason he knew about him was that he hadn't gotten along with the rest of the Special Forces people and he had had to pull him out of the Bengazi training camp. In Tripoli, he assigned him to write up some training programs.

Tafoya, though, had failed at that as well. He'd drifted off, and the next Wilson heard, Tafoya had hooked up with a Libyan intelligence officer named Abdullah Senussi, who ran all of Qaddafi's international hit squads. "That's something else I could be a lot of help on, Larry," he said. The next thing he heard was that Senussi had sent Tafoya to the States. What he might have done there absolutely did not involve Wilson in any way.

Would Wilson identify the Green Berets and other former U.S. military men he had recruited? "Ah, hell," he said, "I can't remember. Coughlin must have them. John, make a note on that, too. Whatever Larry wants."

He jumped back to his intelligence-gathering potential. Qaddafi was going all out to support Iran in its fight with Iraq. A British outfit was supplying Iran with spare parts for F-4 and F-14 fighters left over from the shah's days—the parts were disguised as oil-drilling equipment supposedly destined for

Libya. He'd heard that a California firm was in with a West German company to provide the Libyans with sophisticated radar-jamming gear. Jeeps, manufactured under U.S. license in Spain and fitted with .106 recoilless rifles, theoretically headed for Jordan, went to Libya instead.

He said that end-user certificates for restricted weapons and electronic technology were a snap to get. For anywhere from five to twelve percent of the gross sale, about half the foreign military attachés in the world were for hire. If Barcella gave him a break, he'd get right on that. He would devote himself to ferreting out American corporations and individuals violating U.S. arms laws. Barcella could count on it.

Wilson, Barcella noticed, only dealt in futures.

6

His mystery man turned out to be Rafael Quintero.

That was the last straw for Barcella, although the truth was that he'd had a nagging suspicion it would wind up like this. In the summer of 1978, after Seymour Glanzer announced that he was Wilson's new lawyer, he had asked Barcella whether a deal could be made for his client if he produced the Letelier fugitives —whose names were Dionisio Suarez and Virgilio Paz—and then Glanzer had said that they were in Guayaquil, a city in Ecuador, and an FBI agent, one with good Latin American contacts, was sent down to check out the information. The evidence was inconclusive as to whether Suarez and Paz had ever been there, but in any event, they weren't anymore.

About a year later, when Wilson was being detained in Malta, Barcella had brought Quintero from Miami to go over his testimony for the expected trial. Quintero appeared nervous. He explained that the previous August Glanzer also had called him in and told him that he had caused Wilson a lot of trouble.

If Quintero took the stand as a government witness against Wilson, Glanzer said, he would have to ask him a great many embarrassing questions about his intelligence activities—*and* those of his good friend Ricardo Chavez, the boat captain now living in Mexico who had saved Quintero's life during one of the anti-Castro raids in the 1960s. If the Letelier fugitives were caught, however, a deal could be made with the government and Wilson wouldn't have to be tried at all.

So that was why Quintero had come up with the Ecuador tip. "I just made it up," he told Barcella in his heavily accented English, "but if I could get Wilson an accommodation, I would do it to protect my friend Ricardo."

Glanzer said that Quintero had greatly embellished the circumstances of their encounter, but now, in Rome, Barcella was sure that the same pressure was being applied to Quintero again. Quintero said that he had heard that one of the fugitives, Suarez, using a Costa Rican passport, was in Guatemala under Argentine auspices helping to train rebels to fight the Sandinista regime in Nicaragua. That was more than two months ago and he didn't know how solid the information was.

Barcella drummed his fingers on the table trying to contain himself. He could figure out for himself that the fugitives were somewhere in Central or South America. For sure, they weren't hiding out in Iceland.

"Do you have a specific location?" Barcella asked, and when Quintero said no, he told him he could leave. Then Wilson said, "Look, Larry, we'll find them. I'll get those guys at my own expense. You should have moved when I had Keats contact you last May."

"Let's get something straight," Barcella said. "We don't use fugitives to get fugitives. You told me you *knew* where they were."

As far as Barcella was concerned, it was all over. But Hart had a list of names to go through with Wilson to complete his report and Pedersen had other questions about arms traffic. At the day's end they still hadn't finished. There would be one more session in the morning.

"Larry, you haven't been saying anything," Wilson said, and Barcella said, "Well, that evens us up. You haven't said anything for the last two days."

"I tried to be as honest as I could."

Barcella finally blew up. "Frankly, Ed, I can't wait to get out of here. Except for a couple of good meals, it's been a total waste. You've told us very little that we didn't already know, and what you did say that we know about wasn't true."

"You want the PLO?" Wilson said. "I'll give you the PLO."

That evening John Keats spoke to Barcella. "You came down pretty hard on him," he said. "What kind of plea would you take?"

"Are you saying he's thinking about it?"

"No, I'm just asking what you'd take. Five years?"

"John, I don't have the foggiest idea. Like I said in the letter, we'll have to review everything. But based on today, he hasn't given us anything."

"Okay, suppose he came back voluntarily. What would you want for a bond?"

"The farm," Barcella said. "Mount Airy. Nothing less." Barcella wondered whose idea all this was.

In fact, Keats had suggested it. "I have to get this back on track," he had told Wilson, and Wilson said, "All right, see what you can do. But no jail time." It was astounding, Keats thought. Wilson appeared to have no conception of what deep water he was in. He seemed convinced that his eloquence would win the day, that he was the smart guy and everybody else was a dummy.

The last meeting with Wilson, Saturday morning, July 11, took place in a lounge off the Hotel Jolly's lobby. Carol Bruce was booked on a noon flight home. Barcella, Pedersen and Hart would go on to London, where Inspector Bendle of Scotland Yard had dug up two men worth interviewing. One was a former NATO C-130 repair chief specialist who had worked for Wilson in Libya and could confirm his illegal importation of parts. The other was a source who had seen Frank Terpil about ten days earlier in Grenada, Spain.

Barcella settled in a sofa slightly away from the rest of the group. As Hart continued his name queries, Wilson kept glancing in Barcella's direction. Barcella knew what he was thinking about. The passport. Barcella had it in his pocket, with a cancellation stamp dated July 15, but he was determined to make Wilson ask for it, and at last he did. Barcella flipped it on the table without a word, got up and started to walk off.

"Larry," Wilson called.

"Yes?"

"Can't we shake hands and come out fighting?"

Oh, am I going to get your ass, Barcella thought.

7

On their way to London, Bill Hart said, "We don't believe most of what he told us. Should we believe him about not being with the agency?"

"You've put your finger on it," Barcella replied. "We don't know for sure."

Still, Barcella reflected, in retrospect the meetings hadn't been a complete loss. He'd gotten a chance to size up Wilson firsthand and he had learned something important. Wilson was dangerous and he was cunning, but he wasn't that smart, at least not as smart as he thought he was. Wilson's biggest fan was himself.

In London, on Monday, July 13, as Barcella was leaving to see Bendle, the assistant legal attaché in the Rome embassy called to say that Wilson was being kept under surveillance. They'd make certain he didn't board a plane other than one going directly to Libya.

"Yeah, fine," Barcella said.

Then that afternoon came the most bizarre twist yet in his pursuit of Edwin P. Wilson. Carol Bruce phoned him from Washington. "Larry," she said, "I know this sounds incredible, but I just found out that Kevin Mulcahy's been at the White House. He met with the president's national security adviser, Richard Allen."

THE TRAP

TWENTY-TWO

In Larry Barcella's pursuit of Edwin P. Wilson, no figure was more mysterious than Ernest Keiser. When I asked Barcella about him, he told me, as he had told every reporter who approached him, "I really don't feel I can go into that. You'll have to ask Ernie."

So the only source for Keiser's involvement with Wilson has been Keiser himself. And his version, dotted with mysterious references to past intelligence efforts on behalf of the United States, was a simple tale of altruistic patriotism—of a loyal American who stepped forward voluntarily to help bring to justice a nefarious fugitive threatening his country's national interests, if not its security.

One writer went so far as to put Keiser at the center of an elaborate CIA plot to catch Wilson, thereby ending "the ongoing embarrassment" he was causing both the agency and the "American intelligence community as a whole." Neither the CIA nor Keiser did anything to discourage this line of thought.

But as I would finally discover in a number of confidential documents, the reality of Keiser, or perhaps his unreality, was a lot better than that—a mixture of truths, half-truths and outright falsehoods so artfully whipped up by him, so deliciously blended, that they merged into a nearly indecipherable, outra-

geous whole. Six feet tall, blond, impeccably dressed, he spoke
with a soft Teutonic accent, his voice, depending on the circumstances, lazily reassuring or marked with dramatic urgency.

When he read Seymour Hersh's two pieces in *The New York
Times,* he was either sixty-three years old or fifty-eight. As far as
he knew, he said, he was Ernest Robert Keiser, born in New York
City on November 27, 1918.

Or, as other documents showed, he was Ernesto Roberto
Keiser, born that same day in the predominantly German settlement of Blumenau in Brazil. Or, as proved to be the case, he was
Ernest Otto Friedrich August von Keiser, born November 27,
1923, in Osnabrück, Lower Saxony, in what is now West Germany.

His explanations of his past at various times to government
agencies—among them the Immigration and Naturalization Service, the State Department, the FBI, the Manhattan District
Attorney's Office, the U.S. Attorney's Office for the Southern
District of New York, the U.S. Probation Office—were no more
enlightening than his public pronouncements.

His claim to American citizenship was based on the asser-
tion that his parents, Herbert and Hedda Keiser, en route to
Brazil right after World War I, had passed through New York,
where his mother gave birth to him in a hospital whose records
for the period apparently had been lost.

When World War II was over, according to Keiser, he jour-
neyed from Brazil, where he had grown up, back to Germany to
try to seek out any surviving aunts, uncles and cousins. It was
there, he said, that he began to work as an operative for Army
intelligence and also for the Office of Policy Coordination,
which became the CIA. The way Keiser told it, he was in and out
of Soviet-bloc countries under cover, forming resistance cells
against the Russians, bringing out important anti-Communist
leaders who had been targeted by Moscow.

Keiser never fashioned his history out of whole cloth. A
subsequent investigation, one of several, indicated that he had
indeed been engaged in intelligence activities, although there
was nothing about frequent trips behind the Iron Curtain. It was
also discovered that he was heavily engaged in the postwar black
market and that he had been in the Wehrmacht, in the quarter-
master corps. He'd been discharged from the German army on
March 20, 1946.

That was a mistake, Keiser said. He was being confused with
his brother. His brother's story was a tragic one. He had been
a member of Operation Valkyrie, the conspiracy to assassinate
Hitler, and was executed as a result.

In an interview, Keiser's first wife, the first of three, said that
she could not recall any brother. However, she couldn't be sure.
Her former husband, from whom she obtained a divorce on the
grounds of desertion, was "high born" and it would have been
"improper" for her to ask questions of a personal nature. Even
in his old hometown of Osnabrück, Keiser's image remained
blurred. Many citizens thought he'd been an officer. In fact he
was a corporal.

In the 1950s, extradition warrants were out on him
throughout Europe for fraud and forgery in West Germany and
for deserting his second wife. By then, he was in the Middle East,
again working, he said, for U.S. intelligence under a journalist's
cover, helping Jews emigrate from Egypt and other Arab nations
to Israel and aiding the Federal Bureau of Narcotics in interdict-
ing heroin traffic coming across Syria and Jordan.

It was established that he had been where he said he was at
least part of the time. There was a record of his marriage in 1958
in Amman, the Jordanian capitol, to his third wife, Bahira (Bibi)
Demachskie, a woman of German extraction who had been born
in Quito, Ecuador.

In Morocco in 1960 he received a three-month jail sentence
for passport tampering; for reasons still unknown he had forged
a five-month extension of his West German passport. In late
1962 in Beirut, he said, he had warned American authorities of
the imminent defection to Russia of the famous Soviet mole in
British intelligence Kim Philby, but nobody had listened.

In 1963, he said, he was back in Brazil reporting to the CIA
station chief about Communist subversion in Brazil. There were
no records of this, nor were there any concerning his entry into
the United States in 1964, when he bought a home in Fort
Lauderdale, Florida.

There was, however, verification that in 1966 in Bogotá,
Colombia, he escaped fraud charges by penetrating a major
drug ring for the local police and the Federal Bureau of Narcotics. Back in Florida in 1973, after trying to promote a gambling
casino in Belize, formerly British Honduras, he was arrested in
a real estate swindle. But in return for helping the FBI land an

even bigger fish then on the run—the man was collared while having a drink with Keiser at the fashionable "21" Club in New York—the conspiracy charge against him was reduced from a felony to a nolo contendere misdemeanor.

2

When the Hersh articles appeared, Keiser was a self-styled entrepreneur in African gold mines and precious gems. There was in this latter regard a small cloud on the horizon.

A New York socialite, Douglas Burden, accused Keiser of bilking him out of $135,000. In a complaint he filed with the Manhattan DA's office, he said that Keiser had told him that he was a close friend of the King of Swaziland in southeast Africa and could get millions of dollars in emeralds for practically nothing. Burden's $135,000 would go toward leasing a plane to fly the gems out of Swaziland and would give him a half interest in their resale.

Right on schedule, Burden was told that the shipment had arrived in Grand Cayman island in the Bahamas. He flew down and was met by Keiser's faithful batman, Dan Drake. In Drake's hotel room he was shown what seemed to be a satchelful of emeralds. Keiser had yet to show up, so Drake suggested that they celebrate at the bar. Still no Keiser. Drake and Burden returned to Drake's room to find that it had been ransacked, the emeralds gone.

It then occurred to Burden that he might have been victimized. Keiser wasn't at all concerned about Burden's complaint. There was no way of proving that a burglary *hadn't* taken place.

But he had plenty else to worry about. He was about to lose his American passport. He had gotten it in 1970 with the help of a sometime accomplice named William Taub. Taub was a man after Keiser's own heart. Taub's earliest known impersonation—to get free plane and train rides and hotel rooms—was in 1932, when he passed himself off as the secretary for Mayor Jimmy Walker of New York. He had since gone on to greater things, moving around as the worldwide film representative of the Vatican, the producer of the award-winning movie Z and the confidant of an array of luminaries that included Howard Hughes, Aristotle Onassis, Marilyn Monroe and Richard Nixon.

Keiser already had a Brazilian passport based on his alleged birth in Blumenau but, as he liked to say, he wanted to resolve the question of his dual citizenship. Taub, in one of his favorite roles, that of attorney, filed the papers for him, claiming that his client had been born in 1918 in Sloane's Hospital for Women in Manhattan. But there was a minor problem, he said. When the hospital was absorbed by the Columbia Presbyterian Medical Center, all of Sloane's records from 1917 through 1919 were supposedly destroyed or mislaid. Taub, however, produced an elderly Polish immigrant who swore that his late father had been a doctor at Sloane's. He had been visiting his father one day and was introduced to Keiser's mother, who was cradling an infant, and he distinctly remembered her saying, "This is little Ernie."

That was all it took. On June 5, 1970, Keiser's passport was delivered by mail in care of William L. Taub, Esq., although a more thorough search years afterward turned up the missing Sloane's records, which contained no mention of Keiser's birth in the hospital, to say nothing of the fact that since 1850 every birth in New York City has had to be registered, and Keiser's wasn't listed in the city's record either.

Like two scorpions in a bottle, Taub and Keiser then had a falling-out over money in another flimflam. Taub accused Keiser of trying to have him killed and said that the affidavit about Keiser's having been born in New York was phony. Keiser struck back. Secretly recording conversations with Taub, he helped the U.S. Attorney's Office for the Southern District of New York convict him for mail fraud and the interstate transportation of stolen property.

Keiser's passport problems were put on hold and the charges against him reduced. Obtaining a passport fraudulently was a felony, but he was allowed to plea-bargain misdemeanors, such as not having declared certain purchases made overseas. Still, that wasn't going to get him back his passport, and loss of his citizenship was a sure bet if he ever went to trial.

Any hope Keiser had of riding it out evaporated when James Moss, the assistant U.S. attorney on his case, told him that both the Immigration and Naturalization Service and the State Department were pushing hard for a court disposition.

Keiser hired Robert Hill Schwartz, a New York lawyer, and regaled him with all his "heroic" undercover intelligence and narcotics work. Wouldn't this make a difference? Schwartz gave it a try, but while Moss agreed Keiser's exploits sounded impressive, he said they fell short of being heroic. How about some

validation from the CIA? Keiser, however, wasn't too happy
about that. The people he had worked with were no longer at
Langley, he said.

The Hersh articles gave Keiser a last-ditch idea about how
to bail himself out—he'd get Wilson out of Libya. All he knew
about Wilson was what he'd read. But a sidebar sketch in
Hersh's first installment noted that he had once operated for the
CIA in Latin America, which was what prompted Keiser to have
Dan Drake telephone Wilson in Tripoli and speak vaguely of a
past intelligence association "south of the border," one that
could now be revived for their mutual benefit.

After Wilson fell for it, Keiser asked Robert Hill Schwartz
if he had seen the Hersh articles. When Schwartz said yes, Keiser
said, "I think I can help with Wilson. I know him from the old
days."

3

Schwartz got to Hersh through a friend they had in common, Jack Newfield, the chief investigative reporter for the New
York weekly, the *Village Voice*.

On July 6, while Larry Barcella was in Rome waiting for
Wilson, Schwartz saw Hersh in his office at the National Press
Club, where he outlined Keiser's past intelligence service, how
he had brought anti-Communists out of Eastern Europe, how he
had nabbed a fugitive for the FBI, that he knew Wilson and had
been in touch with him, that Wilson trusted Keiser but that
Keiser deeply resented what Wilson was doing. Keiser, said
Schwartz, was prepared to risk whatever was necessary to appre-
hend him.

Two days later Schwartz and Keiser had lunch with Hersh
and Kevin Mulcahy at the Jean Pierre restaurant in downtown
Washington. Mulcahy listened raptly as Keiser recounted his
history of secret service for the government and said that only
days ago he had been in contact with Wilson.

Mulcahy then announced that he had checked out Keiser
with his father and that Keiser was "triple A-one." His father,
he said, recalled that Keiser, while on a special mission, had
stayed with him in Tokyo—which would have been quite a trick
since Mulcahy's father had never been stationed in Japan. But
Mulcahy said that it was vital to keep all of this from the agency.

Although many of the CIA's old-line people were furious at what Wilson had done to the Company's reputation, he still had lines into Langley.

Now Schwartz brought up Keiser's passport troubles. He said they had been triggered by an enemy of Keiser's, William Taub, whom he had helped send to prison. Keiser didn't miss a beat. Aware that Hersh was writing a critical biography of Henry Kissinger, he said that Taub had once met with Kissinger in a zany scheme to send Jimmy Hoffa, the convicted Teamsters boss, to Hanoi, at the invitation of North Vietnamese trade unions, to mediate the end of the war and get the release of American POWs. He'd be glad to give Hersh the whole story.

Back in his office, Hersh said, "Let me make a call."

According to the daily telephone log of Richard Allen, the president's national security adviser, he spoke to Hersh at 3:25 that afternoon, July 8, 1981. Hersh asked if he was interested in the Edwin P. Wilson affair. Allen, who knew of President Reagan's recent concern, said, "Sure." Allen had another reason as well. He had received information that a West German company said to be trying to develop a cruise-type missile was shifting its test site from a remote region in eastern Zaire to Libya. The idea of such a weapon falling into Qaddafi's—or Wilson's—grasp was appalling.

Allen listened as Hersh said, "This may be right off the wall, but I've got a fellow here who says he has links with Wilson and can get him. I can't vouch for him, but maybe he could do it. It's something you ought to take a look at."

Allen said to call him back in half an hour. He wanted to be sure that White House counsel Fred Fielding was available. A meeting was then set for seven P.M. Because of the number of people involved, and for security, it was held in the White House Situation Room.

Schwartz went through Keiser's background again. He told Allen that Keiser wanted to put together his own group to trap Wilson, that Wilson had too many friends at the agency.

Mulcahy jumped right in on this, repeating that he had checked out Keiser with his father. Keiser was everything he said he was. Under no circumstances should Langley know about it.

Keiser said that he knew Mulcahy's father from Cairo. No one seemed to remember that the day before it had been Tokyo.

He said that he and Wilson had crossed paths quite frequently in the past. He and Wilson had recently talked and Wilson was very receptive, even eager, about getting together.

Schwartz raised Keiser's passport problem. He stressed that he wasn't asking for a direct giveback on the passport. That could be dealt with later. But a final court decision was not far off, and for Keiser to carry out his plan he had to be able to travel. Perhaps an adjournment might be arranged so that Keiser could get to work.

The meeting lasted forty minutes. Allen said that he would mull it over. But when Allen and Fielding were alone, Allen said, "I'm not going to do a damn thing about this. All that fellow wants is his passport. I don't know how I even let him in here."

To be on the safe side, however, he asked the CIA's deputy director for plans, Raymond Rocca, if he had anything on Keiser, and Rocca called back and said he had drawn a blank. About a week later Allen bumped into Richard Helms at a party. Helms had been in the agency almost since its inception and was its director from 1966 to 1973. "I never heard of him," Helms said.

Schwartz reminded Mulcahy that the clock was ticking. A probation officer had completed a presentencing report on Keiser. There were no guarantees about what the judge would do. Mulcahy got the name of Keiser's reluctant prosecutor, James Moss, and called him, pretending to be a Justice Department attorney.

He said that he would appreciate a hold on the Keiser court appearance. A matter of national security was involved. He spoke so knowledgeably about Keiser that Moss, already pre-sold, didn't think twice about it. On July 15 Schwartz got a memo from the U.S. Attorney's Office informing him that a continuance had been granted in the proceedings against Ernest Robert Keiser.

4

Carol Bruce told Barcella that all she knew was that the general counsel's office at the CIA said Mulcahy and Hersh and two unidentified men had met with Richard Allen at the White House. Chuck Ruff, the U.S. attorney, told Barcella that he would find out what was going on. Barcella was not to try anything on his own. For all they knew, the meeting might have been held right in the Oval Office.

For sure, Barcella wasn't going to ask Mulcahy. On the heels of the Hersh articles, he could see Mulcahy's handiwork in two front-page stories by Philip Taubman in *The New York Times*. The first, while Barcella was still in Europe, linked Wilson with the two employees at the secret China Lake Naval Weapons Center that Jerome Brower had recruited nearly five years before to work in the bomb factory at the palace of King Idris. The second, immediately after his return, tied Wilson in with Eugene Tafoya in the attempted murder of Faisal Zagallai. Later Barcella would learn that Mulcahy had obtained the documents in Tafoya's possession from the young Fort Collins detective on the case, Ray Martinez.

On July 26 a story in the Washington *Post* by Jim Hoagland reported the meeting in Rome. Barcella figured that the initial leak must have come from the Italian police or someone in the embassy. But there were other details that sounded as if they came from the Wilson camp—that U.S. officials had solicited Wilson's aid in "kidnapping" the Letelier fugitives in exchange for dropping the charges against him and also that he was hood-winked into giving up his American passport.

Barcella thought it might have been Glanzer. Glanzer was identified as a defense attorney in both the Letelier and Wilson cases and Barcella as the principal prosecutor. In any event, there was nothing he could do. He'd been in a tough spot when Hoagland interviewed him, unable either to confirm or to deny that there had been a meeting and at the same time having to deny that he would ever be a party to a kidnapping.

Mulcahy showed up in Barcella's office, a huge grin on his face. He'd never again question whether Barcella was working on Wilson. "Jesus! Unbelievable!" he said. "But you should have told me. I could have helped. What happened? What was he like?"

"I'm not confirming there even was a meeting, to you or anyone else."

"Hey, Larry, you're talking to me."

"Yeah, and you're talking to Hersh and that guy Taubman."

"Come on, I can manipulate them. Don't worry, I know how to handle the press."

"*Sure* you do."

Mulcahy didn't mention being at the White House. But on

July 31, convinced that nothing was coming out of the meeting with Allen, he told Keiser that their only hope now was Barcella. First, Keiser had to switch attorneys. Keiser needed a lawyer on the scene in Washington, one whom Barcella knew and trusted. Nobody, he said, was closer to Barcella than Gene Propper. After that, he called Barcella and said, "I've got somebody who can really help get Wilson. You have to meet him. It's your reward for Rome."

Why not? Barcella thought. Despite the injunction not to, he had gone ahead and called White House deputy counsel Richard Hauser, whom he had met a couple of times at a friend's house. Hauser said there had been a meeting between Allen and Fielding and Mulcahy, Hersh, a man named Keiser and Keiser's lawyer, subject unknown. Mulcahy's "somebody" must be the mysterious Mr. Keiser. "Okay," Barcella said. "Bring him down."

"No, no, we can't go to your office. It's too sensitive. We've got to meet someplace else, and you have to come alone."

"Carol has to be there, or forget it," Barcella said.

"All right, all right."

They met for a late lunch at a pub near Union Station. Barcella always remembered his instant impression of Keiser. Suave. David Niven with a German accent, he thought.

Mulcahy had never been more hyper. "Ernie here is a friend of mine," he said. "He's got some great intelligence contacts and has a great idea of how to get Ed Wilson back for you and I think he can do it. Not only that, but we ran it past Dick Allen at the White house a couple of weeks ago, and he thinks it's a great idea, too. Let me have Ernie explain what we can do."

"Yes, well," Keiser said, "when I met, you know, with Dick Allen, we discussed this, and he is very concerned about what Wilson is doing, and I told him I am very concerned as well. What Wilson is doing is disgraceful to the good people of the intelligence community, and I will help how I can."

"Okay, I'm listening," Barcella said.

As if he were a walking encyclopedia of Wilson's psyche, Keiser said, "Of course, you know, he likes property very much. He has all that money from Libya and he has to diversify. I am now in real estate myself and I have a friend of mine who has an option on some property in Monaco. What I think we can do is entice Wilson to Monaco to look at this property, and then,

when he is leaving Monaco, you catch him at the French border.
I would not, of course, want my involvement known to him."

"First, let's find out a little about you, Ernie, if you don't
mind," Barcella said. "Where are you from?"

"Well, that's a kind of funny thing. As far as I know, I was
born in New York City in 1918."

"What's that mean?"

"It is a little problem, but it has never gone to sentencing.
Look, I got my passport from this man William Taub. I thought
I was born in the United States. I was never sure myself where
I was born, but my mother was always very careful after the war
—after World War I—that her children would have no problems
and she said I was born in New York and this fellow Taub found
an old man who said that he saw me in the hospital. I cannot
swear to it. I was only one or two days old, after all. And then
Taub accused me of trying to have him killed overseas—it was
ridiculous—and he caused me extremely serious trouble when
I went to renew my passport and I got charged by the U.S.
Attorney's Office and I ended with some misdemeanors after I
cooperated with the government and I have not yet been sentenced."

It was hard following Keiser's rapid-fire delivery, the way
his *w*'s kept slipping into *v*'s. "Wait a minute," Barcella said.
"How long ago did this happen?"

"Three years."

"*Three years*," Barcella said. "That's impossible. Nobody
waits three years to be sentenced."

"It's true, Larry," Mulcahy said. "Ernie checks out. Ernie,
tell Larry all those things you've done for the agency, for the
FBI, for the narcs."

After listening to Keiser's tangled history of his intelligence
and law-enforcement deeds, Barcella said, "You won't mind if
I do some checking myself?"

"Of course not, I would welcome it. There is one thing,
however. I do not want the agency to know that you are utilizing
me. Frankly, you know that the agency has a problem with Ed
Wilson. There are people at the agency who do not want him
captured."

"See, Larry, that's what I've been telling you," said Mulcahy.

"How long have you known Wilson?" Barcella asked.

Keiser upped the ante. They'd met in the 1960s, he said. He'd seen him off and on ever since. True, they hadn't been in touch for five years or so, but he was sure that he would have no problems reestablishing relations. A phone call would do it. "I am sure he will remember our old friendship," he said. He didn't say he already had made contact with Wilson.

"Don't do anything until I get back to you."

"Of course, Larry. Whatever you wish. I am in your hands."

Afterward Carol Bruce said, "He's Mossad."

"What?"

"Remember when I asked him why he was so interested in this and he said that he had friends who weren't happy with Wilson. Larry, he's either Mossad or he's a fraud."

"Let's check him out anyway. You can't say his life's been uneventful." The thought kept noodling around in his head. Keiser might be just the guy Wilson would go for.

TWENTY-THREE

"A sentencing on hold for three years?" Barcella said over the phone to Jim Moss at the U.S. Attorney's Office in New York. "You all do things a little differently than we do down here."

"It's unusual, I admit. But when we cut the deal with Keiser, there was some confusion about his background and he promised to do some things for us and the bureau, and he delivered and promised to do a lot more."

"Do me a favor. Can you get his immigration file and send it to me? If I ask for it, all kinds of bells could go off and I want to keep this quiet for now. And one more thing. Would you mind kicking over his sentencing for a while?"

"I already did after I got that call from Justice."

That didn't make sense. Barcella had just met Keiser and was certain that nobody in the Justice Department knew about him. "*Who* in Justice?" he said.

"Tom Mulvaney. He seemed to know what he was talking about."

"Hang on a second." Barcella flipped through the department's personnel register. No Thomas Mulvaney.

"Is something wrong?" Moss asked.

Mulvaney? Or *Mulcahy*? "No, it's okay," he said. "I think I just figured it out."

Propper called. Mulcahy and Keiser had come to him about representing Keiser. Barcella agreed that there was no conflict of interest since Keiser would not be appearing as a substantive witness in any prosecution of Wilson. But he insisted on one condition if he decided to use Keiser. Mulcahy *was* a witness and he had to be kept out of it.

A few days later, Propper dropped off a fourteen-page narrative summary that Keiser had prepared about himself. It read like a Robert Ludlum thriller. An intrepid Ernie spiriting people at night through land mines and barricaded borders out of Hungary, Czechoslovakia and East Germany. Ernie, his life in constant peril, the bane of machine-gun-toting drug traffickers in the Colombian jungles.

Barcella asked a friend of his in the FBI to pull Keiser's file. It was like a good-news, bad-news joke. His role in capturing a fugitive wanted for fraud was there. So was his help in thwarting the planned kidnapping of a wealthy businessman several years back. On the other hand, so was the Florida land swindle and his alleged part in the conspiracy to murder Taub.

He wondered what the CIA had on him. Barcella didn't want the agency to know what he had in mind. He used the excuse that Keiser was the unidentified man who had gone to the White House with Mulcahy and Hersh and gave the general counsel's office his personal history. Did any of it add up? But the returns were inconclusive. The agency couldn't corroborate eighty percent of what Keiser said he had done.

By the same token, though, much of it could not be definitely disproved either. There were no active records on Keiser. A search of dead files did reflect some intelligence work between 1947 and 1955 in Europe and the Middle East. The trouble was that records for the period weren't all that complete.

The Immigration and Naturalization dossier was considerably more extensive—and far more damaging. But in comparing it with Keiser's version of events, Barcella couldn't helped noticing how adroitly Keiser explained things away. For instance, he wasn't personally swearing he had been born in a New York hospital; he had to depend upon the testimony of others.

When Barcella challenged him about black market activity in postwar Germany and Austria, Keiser said, "I had a wife and child to support. Believe me, to survive, *everyone* was in the black market then." Asked about his previous arrests, he said, "Larry, you must understand, I had to place myself in jeopardy to achieve my missions."

Clearly Ernie was an accomplished con artist, maybe not world class, but still pretty good. In all his scams, Keiser had wanted either to get something or to save himself from something. Now with Wilson, they came together nicely: duck a possible jail sentence and retrieve his passport.

The trick would be to take Wilson where he wanted to go. Barcella remembered from the Rome meeting how desperate Wilson was to get out of Libya. How John Keats had said that Wilson was like "a caged lion down there." How anxious he'd been to trade off his intelligence capability in exchange for a deal.

"Yes," Keiser told Barcella, "Ed is very interested in the intelligence aspect. Of that I can assure you."

"How do you know that? Listen, Ernie, I said not to talk to him until I made a final decision on this. You start doing anything on your own and I'm going to cut you off at the legs."

"Oh, absolutely. No problem, Larry. I felt, yes, I have to make contact once or twice, you know."

You never got a straight answer out of him, Barcella thought. He rather enjoyed the prospect of Wilson trying to pin Keiser down.

2

The media blitz had begun. After the Hersh pieces, *The New York Times* had assigned Phil Taubman, an investigative reporter in its Washington bureau specializing in intelligence matters, to follow up.

First Taubman, as he told me, had to pass a sort of "litmus test" with Mulcahy, and it was only after his first piece linking Wilson to the China Lake employees that Mulcahy volunteered his help.

Then, after the Washington *Post* scoop about the Rome meeting, Dale Van Atta, a reporter for Jack Anderson, wrote an Anderson column asserting that Wilson had met with Barcella and the local CIA station chief to plot Qaddafi's assassination. A poisoned dart shaped like a black fly common in Libya was how it would be done. At least one of Van Atta's sources, if not the only one, was Mulcahy.

Van Atta had called Barcella to find out if he was still not commenting about Rome. But when he explained what he intended to write, Barcella became livid. Any meeting with the CIA station chief was "absolutely, utterly false," he said. "You could get Wilson killed and I don't want a dead defendant."

It ran anyway, quoting Barcella as refusing comment. The Anderson column apparently was required reading for the Qaddafi regime. The next day security troops stormed into Wilson's place swatting every fly in sight. He was hauled off to be interrogated by Major Hajazzi and Captain Senussi. "I thought they were going to put me against the wall," he told John Heath. But he talked his way out of it. The Rome meeting was only to try to mend fences between Qaddafi and Washington. The clincher was that he would hardly be plotting to do away with the colonel while he still had millions coming to him on his contracts.

At the insistence of the Libyans, Wilson appeared for the first time on national television in an interview with ABC news. He fell back on his honest-businessman role. Ordinary "export and import," mostly "military clothing" and "commodities," he said. "Various, uh, various requirements that Libya has." All his problems were being caused by "garbage made up by journalists that are too lazy to go out and check the facts."

Another reason for his difficulties was the strained relations between Libya and the United States. "I think they [the Libyans] could do a better public relations job in the United States . . . Libya has a great story to tell," he said. "I mean they have, well, they spend billions and billions each year in agriculture. They've moved people in from the desert . . . I mean Colonel Qaddafi's done a lot for the people. Americans think it's a desert kingdom run by one man and that everyone's afraid to talk and so on and so forth. It's not that way at all."

And in Geneva, as the press coverage on Wilson intensified, Tom Clines suddenly appeared in the office of Wilson's Geneva lawyer, Edward Coughlin, to pay back the $500,000 that had been advanced to him and three other unnamed "U.S. citizens," and to sever on paper any business connection he had with Wilson.

Wilson had to waive all rights to his share in the offshore Bermuda corporation Clines had formed to receive the advance. Although Clines "declined to disclose any financial records," Coughlin wrote in a memo to himself, that he "stated that neither he nor any of the participants had made any money out of it." Coughlin couldn't understand why Clines would go to such lengths "to protect a worthless company." He also noted that Clines demanded that he retain the original copy of the release, dated August 20, 1981, because he had to show it "to some other people right away."

3

The Washington *Post*, the *Wall Street Journal* and the wire services joined the hunt. Taubman, though, continued to lead the pack. After interviewing Detective Martinez in Fort Collins, he went to Hawaii, where Luke Thompson was now living, and turned in another front-page story about how a team of ex–Green Berets, believing themselves to be part of a CIA mission, were recruited by Wilson to train terrorists.

Tipped off by Mulcahy, Taubman next flew to Houston to track down details about the C-4 shipment. The Los Angeles *Times*, belatedly picking up on Brower's plea-bargain sentencing the previous January, beat Taubman by two days. But its focus was on the hometown Brower angle, while Taubman's report was aggressively displayed in the August 30 Sunday edition with a lead saying the shipment had been "organized by a former agent for the Central Intelligence Agency."

The New York Times assigned a second investigative reporter, Jeff Gerth, to work with Taubman. Using Tafoya's notes about Clines and EATSCO as a springboard, they started tracking other corporate records. Coughlin's name was one of the names Tafoya had written down, and Gerth flew to Geneva to interview him.

The story, published on September 6, sent shock waves through Washington. For the first time EATSCO appeared in print, along with the "emerging puzzle" about Wilson's relationship with Clines and Theodore Shackley. It reported that Clines first denied, then admitted, that Wilson had helped him set up an international oil-drilling supply company whose officers included two ex-CIA Cubans, Rafael Quintero and Ricardo Chavez, with Shackley as a consultant.

Shackley was also listed as a consultant for two other companies Clines had, and it was noted that one of them, Systems Services International, was a corporate partner in EATSCO. Clines was quoted as saying that "his former ties to Mr. Wilson had 'hounded' him and hurt his business." Shackley, described as having occupied one of the CIA's most powerful and sensitive positions, was said to be looking for "separate office space."

The waves in Washington were nothing compared with what was going on in Cairo. The Egyptian government exhibited not the slightest doubt that Edwin P. Wilson, a man now publicly identified with Libya, Egypt's bitterest foe in the Arab world, was involved with EATSCO.

Hussein Salem was ordered to cut all relations with Clines. The seemingly endless millions Clines and his anonymous partners had looked forward to went down the drain. Still, at least Clines did pretty well. Salem already had given him a million-dollar "loan." Negotiations for a buy-out came to another million and a half.

On Capitol Hill, the House Select Committee on Intelligence announced that it was going to conduct a full-scale investigation into Wilson's activities and would "examine" the way both the CIA and federal law-enforcement agencies had handled, or mishandled, the matter.

The upper echelon of the Department of Justice, after having ignored Wilson for so long, got very attentive. But it could have been worse, Barcella thought. A task force chaired by Mark Richard, deputy chief of the Criminal Division, would meet weekly. Although Richard had a tendency to look to his bureaucratic hindside, Barcella knew him and trusted him.

He told Richard about Ernie Keiser and the idea of using him somehow to lure Wilson out of Libya. Richard responded with a noncommittal "All right, but keep me informed."

Carol Bruce was less than enthralled. She called Keiser "Bela," after Bela Lugosi, Hollywood's version of Count Dracula. She warned Barcella that he was making a big mistake. She didn't trust Keiser one bit. They'd all wind up with egg on their faces.

4

"*If* we go ahead on this," Barcella told Keiser, "I want all the calls recorded."

"Oh, absolutely, Larry."

But then on September 20, when Gene Propper arrived in Barcella's office with the first cassette tape of a phone conversation between Keiser and Wilson, it was obvious that there had been prior calls.

"I'm sorry, did I wake you?" Keiser was heard saying.
". . . I promised I would call. I finished my meeting—"

"*Yeah?*" Wilson interrupted.

"—and I believe very strongly that everything is going to be all right."

Barcella said to Propper, "What the hell's this?"

"Ernie felt that he was in a difficult situation and—"

"Come on, Gene, his only difficult situation is his passport. You and I have been friends too long for this."

"What can I say? He said he had to keep the contact going. This was news to me, too."

"You tell him I don't want a repeat performance. I want to know what's going on *before* it happens, not afterward."

Mostly, Keiser later explained to Barcella, it had been his man Dan Drake making the calls. To keep Wilson interested. He himself had talked directly to Wilson only once without recording it.

"Okay, what meeting were you talking about? What's going to be 'all right'?"

Well, it was because Wilson was very keen on the intelligence aspect of their relationship, Keiser said. In the first unrecorded call there had been an "exchange of pleasantries" for a few minutes and then Keiser happened to mention that he'd been engaged in some troubleshooting for Dick Allen at the White House as a consultant to the National Security Council. He said he had spoken to Allen about Wilson and was going to meet him again. All he had suggested to Wilson was that perhaps they could do some business which would be mutually beneficial.

"You said you were meeting Allen and you were a consultant to the NSC?"

"Larry, you will remember I did meet Dick Allen in the White House."

"It's me you're talking to, Ernie. You're not trying to tell *me* you're working for Allen!"

"Ah, well, anyway, Wilson could believe it."

There was no question about that. Barcella could hear the eagerness in Wilson's voice on the tape. "Okay," he said, "use it to break the ice, but don't push it too far." Barcella saw Wilson citing covert intelligence activity as his defense in a jury trial. Something like this could give it apparent credibility.

The strategy at this stage would be simply to use the national security angle in the vaguest way to coax Wilson out of Libya for further talks in a country where he could be arrested and extradited.

"Absolutely," said Keiser. "No problem whatsoever."

5

"Fantastic!" Wilson exclaimed to Dan Drake when he learned that Keiser was willing to brief John Keats about his intelligence connections. Further proof that Keiser was on the up-and-up.

But when he met Keiser, Keats immediately wanted to check his wallet to make sure it hadn't been lifted. "So you're a consultant to the National Security Council and you want to get together with Ed Wilson? Okay, let's run right over to the White House and discuss it in a little more detail."

"No, no," Keiser said, "we can't do that. This is a matter of extreme delicacy."

"I'll bet," Keats said. To his surprise, when he telephoned his reaction to Wilson, Wilson claimed never to have heard of Keiser. "He sounds like some kind of flake," Wilson said.

As far as Keats was concerned, that was the end of it.

In Tripoli, Wilson berated himself. He should have known better than to think that a criminal lawyer like Keats would understand the nuances of a high-level clandestine operation.

On October 5, Barcella let Dan Drake go into Tripoli as Wilson's advance man to explore how Wilson could best help U.S. interests. And now a more definitive plan to entice him out of Libya began to evolve. Wilson was the one who suggested it. He said that he had great contacts with the leaders of the Palestine Liberation Organization. They were in and out of Tripoli all the time. He'd arrange a secret meeting between Richard Allen and the PLO's Yasir Arafat in some neutral spot. Nothing would be more crucial in resolving tensions in the Middle East.

The best part, Barcella thought, was that it had been Wilson's idea. And right in character—a grandiose move designed to bowl everyone over. Barcella told Mark Richard that the time had come to alert the FBI. They would need the overseas presence and local connections that FBI legal attachés had in whatever country Keiser could get Wilson to go to. Barcella said that he already knew what was in Keiser's file and didn't see any problems. The bureau had successfully utilized Keiser more than once.

But the response to Richard from the FBI was stunning. The bureau wanted nothing to do with Keiser. He was too "untrustworthy." The decision was irrevocable.

Barcella couldn't believe it. The FBI had relayed only negative material that it had on Keiser. Richard said that the real reason probably was that the bureau hadn't come up with the idea of Keiser first. It wasn't anything personal. "You know how they are and there's nothing we can do about it," he said. After all the work put in by Pedersen and Wadsworth, why not try the Bureau of Alcohol, Tobacco and Firearms?

Then Barcella was blindsided again. Carol Bruce showed him a lengthy memo against using Keiser that she intended to send to Richard. "I'm not trying to throw a monkey wrench into your carefully made plans, Larry," she said. "I am just genuinely concerned about all the developments in this operation."

In the memo, she first attacked Kevin Mulcahy and his relationship with Keiser. She accused Mulcahy of indiscriminately selling himself and his information to newsmen, most recently in a story by Taubman and Gerth that revealed the existence of Wilson's two country retreats in England, both of which had remained under surveillance. It also was Mulcahy, she pointed out, who brought Keiser to Barcella. Undoubtedly he had kept the press informed of Barcella's plans to use Keiser and was now busily arranging a huge scoop for *The New York Times* so he could grab all the glory.

She warned that Keiser was a consummate con man. It would be one thing if he was acting on his own, but he was seeking the imprimatur of the federal government. What were his true motives? Was he really acting for a foreign power, like Israel? Keiser had been throwing around Richard Allen's name. There had been suggestions that Keiser, purporting to be Allen's representative, might even meet with Qaddafi. The results could be enormously embarrassing to Washington. Under no circumstances, she wrote, should Keiser be given any official support.

Barcella was aghast. If Bruce's memo started floating around after the turndown from the FBI, his whole plan was dead. U.S. attorney Charles Ruff agreed with Barcella that nothing should go over to the Justice Department in writing.

Barcella and Bruce would have to battle it out orally with Richard.

In Richard's office, Barcella argued, as he had with Bruce,
that Keiser was the only game in town. He said that despite
Keiser's checkered past, he was too smart to chance losing his
passport for good by leaking any advance information to Mulcahy.

After some hesitation, Richard sided with Barcella. But with
all these complications, Barcella would now have to draft a
memo of his own to obtain the okay of the attorney general,
William French Smith. In it, he acknowledged that there were
certain hazards involved with Keiser but said he believed the risk
was worth taking. Two days later, the memo came back approved. Richard was pleased. They were all covered.

Next, Keiser had to have a passport to travel. Barcella
drafted another memo about the problem, and it went from
French Smith's deputy to Secretary of State Alexander Haig's
deputy, William P. Clark. The issue was bucked down to the
head of Consular Affairs. He archly informed Barcella that the
Department of State did not provide passports to individuals
who had fraudulently obtained them in the first place.

Barcella reminded him that technically the case had yet to
be decided in court. This was a matter of grave law-enforcement
concern. What was wrong with giving Keiser a passport that was
about to run out—say, one of the Bicentennial passports from
1976, which would have only a month or so left before it became
invalid?

"Mr. Barcella, we are not in the business of mounting operations. Our people evidently believe this is all quite illegal."

Barcella, with Richard, went to the CIA. The agency would
love to be of help, they were told. But this was really a State
Department affair. And very delicate. They were advised to try
State again, and if it didn't come through, Langley might recon-
sider the request.

Obviously it would be a long hassle and time wasn't with
Barcella. Wilson had grown increasingly impatient on the
phone. Through Dan Drake, Keiser was resorting to excuse after
excuse. He was in Florida on a big land deal. He had the flu. Dick
Allen was abroad. Then his free use of Allen's name paid an
unexpected dividend. The president's national security adviser
had been caught in a ballooning scandal that alleged his receipt

of a cash payment from a Japanese magazine to arrange for an interview with Nancy Reagan, as well as the gift of a wristwatch, all of which would finally lead to his resignation.

Keiser told Wilson that Allen's troubles in the press were causing an unavoidable delay. If worse came to worst, he would go to Ed Meese or Michael Deaver, two of the president's closest confidants.

Barcella listened in amazement to the tape as Keiser got Wilson into a conversation about which of them would be better. "Meese would be the best, yes, definitely," Keiser said, and Wilson replied, "I'll get you a meeting with the, uh, colonel if you want one. If you can go in and talk to Meese, Meese will talk to the president. This thing has to be done with the president."

"Right," said Keiser.

Gene Propper apologized for the way Keiser had over-reached, but Barcella, still smoldering over the State Department's intransigence about the passport, had decided to give him his head. Keiser's instincts about Wilson appeared to be flawless; this was just another of the swindles he was so expert at, except he had a lot more than money at stake.

Barcella was trying to figure out what to do now when Keiser revealed that he also had a Brazilian passport. "Remember, Larry," he said, "how I told you my mother would look out for her children at all costs." The problem was that it hadn't been renewed for years. Barcella, though, had an idea.

He and Richard convinced the Immigration and Naturalization Service to give Keiser a "green card," which normally granted permanent U.S. residence. By itself, it didn't make him eligible for an American passport, but it would offer a reasonable explanation of why he had let his Brazilian one lapse.

Within a week Keiser called. He'd been to the Brazilian consulate in New York. "I have it," he said.

TWENTY-FOUR

As these events were taking place in late October and into November 1981, Eugene Tafoya went on trial in a Colorado state court for attempting to murder Faisal Zagallai. John Heath had been right about Tafoya; he didn't crack. He swore that he had been recruited by a CIA agent named "John." His assignment was merely to "rough up" Zagallai and to warn him to stop stirring up Libyan dissidents. The government was trying to improve relations with Qaddafi. Zagallai pulled a gun and in the ensuing struggle was shot.

His lawyer said he was a "forgotten patriot, a soldier left out in the cold." State prosecutors charged that Tafoya was a paid assassin of the Libyan government who had been hired by Edwin P. Wilson. Jurors were quoted as having been confused about just whom Tafoya was working for, and a compromise verdict was reached in which the ex–Green Beret was found guilty on two misdemeanor counts of assault and then was acquitted of attempted murder. Tafoya was sentenced to two years, the maximum. He was subsequently convicted in a federal court for tax evasion on the unreported income he had received from Wilson and got another six years.

2

The previous August, Doug Schlachter's name had been added to the original indictment against Wilson and Terpil. The change, however, was kept sealed. Nobody knew where Schlachter was.

His whereabouts were finally discovered when he applied for a U.S. passport for a newly born daughter. Along with his girl friend, Tina Simons, he had fled to Burundi, a central African country bordering on Lake Tanganyika, which had no extradition treaty with the United States. He had set up an air-freight-forwarding operation there and was said to have influential connections with high Burundi officials.

And on October 24, to put pressure on Schlachter, the indictment was unsealed; in it he replaced Jerome Brower in the original conspiracy "to supply covertly and for a profit the government of Libya with personnel, explosives, explosive material and other goods necessary to make explosive devices and to teach others how to make explosive devices in a terrorist training project."

When the indictment became public, Kevin Mulcahy, now a "paid consultant" to CBS, flew into Burundi and got Schlachter on camera for the network's evening news. During the interview Schlachter stated that all through his employment by Wilson in Libya he believed that he was actually working for the CIA, and that he had regularly reported his activities to CIA officials, including Thomas Clines.

In overseas calls from Burundi, Schlachter began dickering with Barcella. He was innocent, he said. What kind of treatment could he expect? That, Barcella replied, depended on what he had to say.

After arriving in Washington, Schlachter corroborated the true purpose of the time-delay detonators and the C-4 shipments. He also declared that Clines knew all about Wilson's Libyan venture, that he had personally briefed Clines and believed that Clines in turn was passing this information on to Theodore Shackley.

He said that he had carried Clines's wish list of Soviet weapons in Libya to Wilson and that on another occasion he had been present when Clines, while still with the CIA, met with the Nicaraguan dictator, Anastasio Somoza, to create a private security operation to prop up the tyrant's tottering regime. Schlachter also disclosed that Waldo Dubberstein, the Pentagon intelligence analyst, had been on Wilson's payroll.

Schlachter's insistence that he initially thought he was working for the agency was persuasive. In return for his cooperation he was allowed to plead guilty to one conspiracy count and one violation of the Munitions Control Act. Facing a possible seven years in prison, he went into the federal witness protection program and was sentenced to five years, all but six months of which was suspended, along with a $10,000 fine.

3

Peter Goulding was scared, more scared now of Barcella than of a Wilson trapped in Libya. From England, he asked for and got "safe passage" for a secret weekend trip to Washington in late October.

While Barcella and Pedersen waited at Dulles International Airport for Goulding's plane, Pedersen stepped away to speak to a distinguished-looking black man.

Who was that?" Barcella asked.

"The Sudanese ambassador."

"No kidding. How'd you meet him?"

"In a shoe store," Pedersen said. "We started talking. Had lunch. He's a nice guy."

As a result of this accidental encounter, Wilson's last hope of escaping Barcella would vanish.

4

Goulding was the first to tell Barcella that Shackley and Clines were on Wilson's secret code list of names.

When Barcella had interviewed them earlier in the year, he noticed how different their personalities were—Shackley so precise and reserved, Clines friendly and on the garrulous side. But both were careful to take notes and keep their answers exactly confined to a question, never volunteering more than was asked.

Shackley had acknowledged that he and Wilson were friends at one time. As associate deputy director of the CIA's clandestine operations, he had been determined not to be a "prisoner of the intelligence system" and while he was not by nature gregarious, he had made it a point to get around socially as much as possible to sponge up information. Wilson was a perfect example; he traveled a lot and you could pick up some interesting tidbits from him. Shackley said that he had perhaps made a judgment error in letting his daughter's horse be boarded at Mount Airy Farms.

In the spring of 1981, when Keats first started trying to arrange a meeting between Wilson and Barcella to retrieve the Letelier fugitives, Keats had said that Wilson wanted Barcella to check out his "credibility" with Shackley.

So Barcella had Shackley in again. He told Barcella that he didn't have the faintest idea of what Wilson meant. Then, for once, Shackley dropped his cool façade. If it hadn't been for Barcella, he could have been either the CIA's director or its deputy director. "I understand you had me blackballed at the White House," he said.

"You flatter me," Barcella said. "I'd like to think the White House calls me on intelligence matters, but it hasn't."

"I've heard this on good authority," Shackley insisted.

Clines, meanwhile, conceded that he had put Wilson in touch with some former agency technicians to help him in his Libyan business venture but said he was never aware of anything illegal. All he knew then about Wilson's activities was what Wilson told him, and it wasn't much.

Soon afterward, Kevin Mulcahy said that a secretary at EATSCO he'd been "working on" had told him that Clines and Wilson were meeting somewhere in Europe. There appeared to be something to Mulcahy's tip. Clines, it turned out, was traveling overseas. Barcella and agent Hart met him at the airport on his return. He denied having seen Wilson.

"Okay, did you speak to him?"

Well, yes, he'd done that. It had been by phone from London, but it was only small talk. How life was going for them and so forth. Nothing more.

Later, in the summer, when Tafoya's notes about Clines and EATSCO finally reached Barcella's desk, he questioned Clines and Shackley again. Clines said that, as a matter of fact, Wilson had lent him money to go into business, but he'd paid it back. Wilson, though, had no connection with EATSCO. He had met an Egyptian, Hussein Salem, by chance at a CIA hangout in Tysons Corner. According to Clines, Salem needed an American partner, someone who knew his way around the government.

Shackley said that he had entered into a business relationship with Clines because he had to start thinking about career opportunities outside the agency after Admiral Stansfield Turner's vendetta against him. As for any funding Wilson had provided Clines, Barcella would have to ask Clines. "I left the details up to Tom. You'll have to get the particulars from him." Shackley added that he was launching his own independent international consultancy firm and all the bad press he was getting hadn't helped.

In one of the interviews with Shackley, Dick Pedersen couldn't restrain himself. "How could you have had anything to do with Wilson after you knew what he was doing?" he said, and he would remember that Shackley just looked away.

In October Barcella decided to put Shackley and Clines on record before a grand jury. Because of their bitter complaints about being excoriated in the media, he had sent them letters advising them that they were not at present targets of an investigation.

Now this all changed with the arrival of Goulding and Schlachter. And besides Shackley and Clines, other new targets were added as well. Goulding said that there was also someone called "Redhead" on Wilson's code list. Goulding said he didn't know who he was. Only that Wilson had kept his identity closely guarded.

Barcella had been interviewing Clines's former girl friend and he took a wild shot. "How come you didn't tell us about 'Redhead?'"

Her eyes widened. "You know about Erich von Marbod? That's the one name Tom said had to be protected."

"Ever hear of him?" Barcella asked Mark Richard at the Justice Department, and Richard said no. But Richard's secretary, thumbing through a directory of high-level government employees, exclaimed, "Oh, here he is. Deputy Director of the Defense Security Assistance Program."

And according to Schlachter, Shackley, Clines and von Marbod had frequently been at Mount Airy, huddled with Wilson. Schlachter added still another name, Air Force general Richard Secord. When Barcella looked Secord up, he found that he was now chief Middle East arms-sales adviser to Secretary of Defense Caspar Weinberger.

As the FBI launched background checks, von Marbod abruptly resigned on December 1, 1981, pleading narcolepsy, a condition characterized by sudden attacks of deep sleep. Barcella learned that people who knew von Marbod were astounded. Nobody he could find had ever seen him nod off.

5

In December, Barcella's plan to use Keiser to get Wilson received another setback. The Bureau of Alcohol, Tobacco and Firearms, after consulting with its parent body, the Treasury Department, decided that it would participate only if Keiser was placed under the most stringent controls, which included wearing a secret recorder at all times and having a BATF agent accompany him wherever he went.

Barcella wanted as much control over Keiser as anyone did, but by now he had realized that there were limits if Ernie was going to be effective. That was when he turned to Howard Safir and the U.S. Marshals Service.

Safir, thirty-nine, had come out of the old Federal Narcotics Bureau to become operational chief of the marshals in 1979. His biggest coup in revitalizing the service, then something of a joke in law-enforcement circles, occurred when the FBI decided to relinquish so-called garbage fugitive cases, like walkaways from halfway houses. Safir grabbed this opening and wound up with primary authority in the apprehension of all federal escapees and parole violators.

Barcella had met Safir during the Letelier prosecution, when Barcella spent months under the protection of the marshals because of death threats from right-wing Cuban exiles. He liked his hard-nosed, no-nonsense manner. When Barcella approached him about Keiser, Safir wanted to know what the hook was. Why wasn't the FBI in on this? Barcella's explanation got Safir very interested. There had never been any love lost between narcotics agents and the FBI, and Safir hadn't forgotten it. Besides, Wilson would make for an exciting operation. Just what Safir needed to keep building morale.

Even so, he was shaken when he examined Keiser's dossier. And was less taken when he viewed a photograph of Keiser in his German army uniform. But what caught his eye was Keiser's claim to have helped break a major drug ring operating out of

Colombia. He contacted a narcotics field supervisor who had been down there at the time and was told, "Keiser's good. A great con guy."

"You really think he can pull it off?" Safir asked Barcella.

"So far, so good. We're not going to get Wilson out of Libya using Mother Teresa."

"All right. Count us in."

6

The tension between Barcella and Carol Bruce was relieved when she left on maternity leave. Rick Otto, another assistant, succeeded her. Otto loved the Keiser idea.

But in Tripoli Wilson was getting edgy. For two months, ever since Dan Drake's visit, he had been pushing Keiser to come himself. Keiser's new excuses were that American relations with Libya were at an all-time low after planes from the Sixth Fleet had knocked down Libyan fighters in a dispute about international waters in the Gulf of Sidra. Now there were rumors that Qaddafi had sent his teams to America to assassinate President Reagan and the White House had temporarily banned travel to Libya.

"As you can imagine," Keiser told him, "we have a little difficulty about my trip." Finally Wilson insisted that Keiser at least meet with Diane Byrne and John Heath in London so they could look him over. Barcella decided to let Keiser go. The plan was for him to arrive the day after Christmas.

Then a dramatic new development occurred. Around six P.M. on December 21, Barcella picked up the phone. A man with a big drawl identified himself as an assistant in the U.S. Attorney's Office in Dallas and said, "You interested in a woman by the name of Roberta Barnes?"

"I sure as hell am."

"We popped her coming through the airport a couple of hours ago. They punched her up on the computer and saw you-all have a lookout for her. So they did a search on her and found she had a little more money than she was supposed to."

"How much?"

"Well, not a whole lot. Maybe about forty-odd dollars. Hold on. I misspoke myself. What I mean is she had five thousand in American currency, which she declared, and that's the okay legal limit, but tucked inside a little old eyeglass case she had twenty-three pounds in British pounds sterling. Now that's a felony, technically, but we usually charge a misdemeanor. If this woman is important to you, though, we'll do whatever you suggest."

"Please hit her with the felony," Barcella said, "I'll have a material witness warrant down to you the first thing in the morning."

She had flown in to spend Christmas with her son, her parents and her sister and brother-in-law in Austin. Her bond as a material witness was set at $500,000 on the grounds that she might flee the country, and when she could not meet it, she was remanded to the local county jail. Barcella didn't like doing it, but he had to deliver a serious message to her. And to Wilson and his organization—that the great man couldn't even protect the one person presumably the closest to him.

And it was working. From London Keiser reported that everything was going well with Byrne and Heath. Then Wilson had called, greatly disturbed by the arrest of Barnes. He asked Keiser to use his influence to help her. "I want her to think I'm in her corner," Wilson had said, "so she doesn't end up saying things until she checks with me."

Keiser returned to Washington New Year's Eve and Barcella drove to Dulles airport to meet him. Mary Barcella was furious. She'd had enough of Wilson. For the last six months, Barcella might as well have moved out of the house. She acidly reminded him that he'd missed attending school interviews for their daughter because Peter Goulding decided to come to Washington. At least she had looked forward to the round of parties they were invited to. Now even that small respite was out. "I'll just touch base with him and be right back," he said.

But Keiser's plane was late because of a snowstorm that had swept in earlier than expected. Then, when he arrived, they spent hours in a lounge until the highway was plowed. "Look at this, Larry," Keiser said with a grin as he reached into his briefcase. It was Wilson's Maltese passport in the name of Giovanni Zammit. And next was his Irish passport bearing Philip McCormick's name. And finally his U.S. passport, the one that had been canceled in Rome. Heath had passed them on to him.

Barcella's ploy had worked. He had instructed Keiser to tell Wilson that a conference between National Security Council representatives and the PLO in Libya was impossible. While Wilson wouldn't need a visa for a meeting in Europe, some out-of-the-way nation that required one might be picked.

Those passports were irrefutable proof that Wilson had bought Keiser hook, line and sinker. For a fugitive, they were like gold. It was the best New Year's Eve Barcella could remember. Even Mary was mollified when he told her what Keiser brought back.

7

The Dominican Republic as a meeting place was Howard Safir's idea. He'd been down there in the fall for an Interpol conference and had gotten friendly with its top police officials. He was confident he could get a visa for Wilson.

On January 6, 1982, Keiser tried it out in a call to Tripoli. "Ed, I have some very good news. I don't know, do you want to talk over the phone or not?"

"Double-talk a little if you can."

"If everything goes okay, I think for our meetings it should be close to our country. How about the Dominican Republic?"

"Good. That's very good."

"So it will be arranged. I'll give you the details when I see you.
Could you make a reservation for me at the hotel that's near you?"

"You'll stay right with me. I've got plenty of room. It'll be fine."

"Oh, thank you very much," Keiser said. "I appreciate that."

The next day he left to see Wilson face-to-face for the first time. One of Safir's most experienced marshals, Phil Tucker, flew to Madrid to stand by as backup on the slight chance that Wilson might suddenly decide to come out immediately. Unknown to Keiser, a second marshal, Jimmy Reina, adept in disguises and fluent in five languages, was on Keiser's plane. "Let's make sure he goes where he's supposed to," Safir said. And from Athens, before joining Tucker, Reina reported that Keiser had been met by a man who answered to John Heath's description and then boarded a direct flight to Tripoli.

Wilson was anxiously waiting for Keiser at the airport. The arrest of Roberta Barnes had him more jumpy than ever. She had been freed on Christmas Day on a reduced bond of $200,000 guaranteed by her father and her brother-in-law, an Austin attorney. In his first contact with her by phone, figuring that her line was tapped, Wilson said to cooperate fully with Barcella. That meant tell him as little as she had to. What concerned Wilson at first was her letting anything slip about a secret plan he had to get out of Libya—to next-door Sudan.

Before Wilson's indictment, a Sudanese intelligence officer stationed in London expressed interest in having Wilson provide some of the same services to Sudan as he was to Libya. Well, maybe, Wilson had said, and gave him his card; but it was only to be polite. At the time, compared with the Libyan money machine, Sudan wasn't worth the trouble.

But then, stuck in Tripoli, the Sudan started looking good, and when Roberta Barnes telexed that the Sudanese officer had been calling her, Wilson sent Heath into Khartoum to negotiate a deal that would grant him "safe haven." He had Barnes follow up. "You have to go," he told her. "You're the only one I trust." And she pulled it off. It was going to cost him a million bucks in bribes just to get in, but she came back with a letter from the Sudanese minister of national security that said, "I was particularly pleased with the results obtained in my conversations with your representatives and wish to confirm my complete acceptance of their proposed concepts and projects for our mutual benefit."

Still, there was a problem: Libya and Sudan were engaged in constant border skirmishes. So he pointed out to the Libyans what a marvelous spy he would make for them. They appeared delighted at the prospect.

Only Roberta had misgivings. Once again she thought of how Wilson's isolation in Libya was bending his perceptions out of whack. He was entranced by the theory that if he could only get the Libyan monkey off his back, all his troubles would be over.

Ed always blamed everyone except himself when something went wrong; now he was blaming a whole country. The stress of having to go into Khartoum personally to arrange for payoffs was too much. And in London and Geneva reporters were at her heels wherever she turned. She needed a rest and she told Wilson she was going back to the States for a while. To be with her family over the Christmas holidays.

Now Wilson hoped that none of this mattered anymore. Ernie Keiser was on his way to fix up everything.

8

Keiser spent three days in Tripoli. He was whisked past customs and immigration by Wilson and taken to his villa. Wilson was worried that Richard Allen had been replaced as Reagan's national security adviser by William P. Clark.

"It is true I am closer to Allen than Clark," Keiser told him, "but believe me, Ed, it is nothing to be concerned about." The main thing, said Keiser, was to get going with a secret meeting between Clark or one of his top deputies and Yasir Arafat and other leaders of the PLO to ease Middle East tensions. He'd have them all there, Wilson said. Even the heads of extremist splinter groups, like Naif Hawatmah of the Popular Democratic Front for the Liberation of Palestine, whose grandest exploit to date had been the slaughter of twenty-one schoolchildren in a raid on the Israeli town of Maalot.

Wilson wanted to impress upon the Libyans that, despite the bad press he was getting in America, he still had valuable high-level contacts there. So he brought Keiser in to meet Nassir Ashur, Libya's chief of political and foreign intelligence. But all at once Ashur asked Keiser to explain on paper why he was in Libya to see Wilson.

Keiser outdid himself. *At the beginning of the Reagan Administration,* he wrote, after describing his intelligence background, *I volunteered to be a consultant to the National Security Council under the Chairmanship of Mr. Richard V. Allen. Mr. Allen recently resigned to become a consultant to the President in foreign affairs. William P. Clark, former Deputy Secretary of State, became the new Chairman and in my capacity as a consultant to the NSC I report directly to Mr. Clark and corroborate my duties with Mr. Allen which covers Latin America exclusively.*

At the present time I am a guest in Tripoli of an old friend of mine, Edwin Wilson. I consider my advising and helping Mr. Wilson in connection with untrue accusations in the United States as a moral duty and I am very hopeful and certain that I will be able to bring this outrageous situation under control, and that he will again be a free person acknowledged and respected by his own country.

"I am sorry, Larry," Keiser would later say, "but there I was in downtown Tripoli and there wasn't a lot I could do. I have to write what they wanted, no?"

Afterward, Wilson had said, "Boy, that was great!" Back in

his villa, he was full of new schemes, besides the PLO meeting.
He began talking about how he could set up corporate fronts in
Central America to mount assault teams against the Commies
that would be untraceable to Washington. He spoke of using his
contacts in Libya to find James Dozier, the American general
then being held by the Red Brigade in Italy. He even boasted
of having a sanctuary in Sudan and showed Keiser the letter he
had received from the Sudanese security minister. He'd be able
to settle a tinderbox situation between Libya and the Sudan,
which threatened to blow up North Africa.

Close to midnight on January 10, Barcella got a phone call
at home from Gene Propper. He said he had just been talking
to Keiser, who addressed him as "Dick."

"*What?* What did you do?"

"I played Dick Allen. What do you think I did?"

"What'd he say?"

"That it was a very productive trip and that he was coming
out alone, but he'd be going back in a couple of weeks."

"Was he alone?"

"He said Ed was standing right by him."

Among the documents Keiser returned with was a sealed
envelope, "Personal and Confidential to William P. Clark." In
the office of Jeff Harris, the deputy associate attorney general,
Richard, Barcella and Rick Otto sat staring at it, wondering what
to do. Harris had contacted the White House and was informed
that Clark had no desire to receive any communication from
Wilson. "Well, I have a solution," Barcella said and slit it open.

The letter, dated January 10 and signed by Wilson, said,
*After meeting with Ernest Keiser in Tripoli, I would like to have the
opportunity to meet with a representative of the National Security Council
at a suggested site or place like the Dominican Republic. I assure you full
cooperation in disclosing all of my activities in Libya and my contacts with
other highly important political groups in the Eastern Hemisphere.*

*It is my honest desire to clear myself of all accusations directed at me
and I sincerely believe the U.S. Government will appreciate and greatly
benefit by giving me a chance for a dialogue with one of its representatives.*

Keiser, in his debriefing, found it irresistible to add a dramatic touch. He had met with Qaddafi himself for half an hour.
Much of it had been lost in translation, but Qaddafi had denied
sending in hit teams to assassinate President Reagan and said he

hoped that through Clark relations between their respective countries would improve.

That sent a quiver through the Justice Department's executive suites. Nobody had counted on meetings with Qaddafi—*if* Keiser had actually talked to him. Barcella argued that whether Keiser had or hadn't seen Qaddafi was irrelevant to getting Wilson. So far, Keiser had delivered. He had even brought back Nassir Ashur's personal card. Why insult Keiser at this point? Over his protests, however, he was informed that Keiser would have to take a lie-detector test, or all bets were off. If Keiser felt insulted, it was too bad.

The first try was a disaster. The polygrapher made the mistake of asking Keiser a normal control question, "When and where were you born?"

"That's a long story," Keiser replied, and twenty minutes later he was still talking about it. A second polygrapher did better. Keiser's account of what had gone on in Libya appeared to be truthful, except for his meeting with Qaddafi. And even on that score, the polygrapher confessed that he could not be positive. "I've been in the business for twenty-five years," he said, "and I never had a subject like him. This guy's got nerves of steel."

Keiser also had pocketed a copy of the letter about Wilson's Sudanese deal and reported that Wilson had referred to Sudan as a sanctuary. Right away, Barcella asked Dick Pedersen if he could set up a meeting with his friend the Sudanese ambassador.

Over lunch, Barcella explained the situation. If Wilson got in to the Sudan, he would like to have him arrested and deported to America as an undesirable alien, and if that was not possible, to bar him outright. "You can rest assured of my government's cooperation," the ambassador said. A month later he confirmed it to Pedersen. "Please tell Mr. Barcella that the matter has been taken care of." Pedersen said that he got the impression that some heads were going to roll in Khartoum.

Barcella pleasurably fingered a neatly trimmed beard he had started growing during the Christmas holidays, vowing not to shave it off until he had Wilson and Terpil in hand. It gave him a somewhat devilish look. Many of his friends kidded him unmercifully that the beard was really there to make up for the rapidly diminishing hair on his head.

"You'll see," he said.

TWENTY-FIVE

In Tripoli, to keep Wilson from getting suspicious, Keiser had returned his three passports. He explained that the American one hadn't been revalidated to keep questions from being asked at the State Department. If anybody there found out about the proposed conference with the PLO, it could raise a real stink.

So Wilson agreed to use the Irish passport in the name of Philip McCormick and Keiser took it back with him from Libya. Then on February 3, once Howard Safir had obtained the Dominican Republic visa for the McCormick passport, Keiser flew with it to London.

Before Keiser left, he said, "Larry, would you mind if I made some money off Ed?"

"How?"

"You know, just a few deals. To make a dollar here or there. It's cost me a lot working with you people."

The more Barcella thought about it, the better it sounded. All of Keiser's stings, of course, were artfully designed to make the other fellow think he was going to walk away with a mountain of money. He'd be right at home, and if nothing else, Wilson was greedy. Then, too, it might help downplay the national security angle that was making everyone at Justice so nervous. "Okay," he said, "but it's got to be legal and it can't screw up the recovery."

Barcella's instinct was correct. The one document Keiser
hadn't shown anybody when he came out of Libya was a joint-
venture contract with Wilson. They would share the profits fifty-
fifty in investments that Wilson helped to finance. He had told
Wilson that he knew of many wonderful opportunities in the
Dominican Republic, and on January 21, Dan Drake went to
Tripoli to pick up a check from Wilson for $150,000.

In his conversations with Wilson, there had been occasional
references by Keiser to this or that international real estate
project that he was involved in beyond his national security
consultancy. Marshals had installed a voice-activated recorder
on Keiser's home phone, but he was obviously bypassing it
whenever he wanted to. Some calls were partially garbled and
it was evident in listening to the tapes that other conversations
with Wilson hadn't been recorded at all. This was making Howard Safir nervous, so he insisted that Phil Tucker accompany
Keiser to London, posing as a business associate.

Keiser was upset. "Larry," he said, "it's not that I have
anything personally against Phil, but it is hard for me to work,
you understand, with someone looking over my shoulder." But
Safir was adamant.

The plan was to convince Wilson to leave Libya immediately for London. Then he and Keiser would go on to the Dominican Republic. On February 4 Tucker reported that it looked
good, he was on the verge of coming out. The next day bad news
arrived. Tucker telephoned to say that John Heath and Diane
Byrne were urging Wilson to be cautious. Before venturing from
Libya, he should have a letter of immunity from the National
Security Council—the same sort of letter he got from Barcella
for the meeting in Rome.

When Tucker phoned, Barcella was with Mark Richard and
the deputy associate attorney general, Jeff Harris. They agreed
that a letter from the council was out of the question. Even
informing the White House at this late date about what was
going on was something Harris and Richard didn't want to con-
template. And now the calls began—between Keiser and Barcella, and Keiser and Wilson.

Barcella instructed Keiser to use Richard Allen's replacement by William Clark as the reason why a letter from the
council was impossible. Clark, as a former judge, was conscious

of legal niceties. The criminal charges against Wilson had to be settled before a meeting with representatives of the council took place and only the Justice Department could do that.

Keiser naturally added some fillips of his own when he spoke to Wilson. The truth of the matter, he said, was that Clark was a nervous Nellie, afraid of bad publicity, of a scandal like the Watergate cover-up, if word leaked about a meeting with Wilson and the PLO.

At first, Wilson hesitated. Finally he said all right. Ring in the Justice Department. But he wanted to deal with someone higher than Barcella, someone who understood the stakes, who was able to grasp the big picture. Keiser said he would do what he could, warning, though, that Barcella would inevitably learn about this and be involved.

In Washington, Barcella, Richard and Harris worked quickly on a letter. They couldn't assure Wilson of blanket immunity in the Dominican Republic, since he would be nabbed the second he set foot there. It not only would look tawdry to a jury but also could give Wilson a platform to argue that he'd been acting in an intelligence capacity all along.

Besides, for Barcella, there was a more important consideration. He had built his career on keeping his word. Bringing the PLO leadership together with National Security Council members had been Wilson's idea; if he thought he could pull it off by going to the Dominican Republic, that was *his* problem. But Barcella would not be a party to lying to him outright. If Barcella had wanted to take that route, he could have had Wilson taken into custody in Rome.

At the moment, the best Barcella and the others were able to devise was a two-paragraph letter signed by Mark Richard as Deputy Assistant Attorney General, Criminal Division, advising Wilson that the Justice Department was aware that he was in communication with Keiser "as to your situation," but "we are not able to pursue these matters with you while you remain in Libya." They knew it was pathetic; Wilson would never buy it, and he didn't. But it wasn't a total loss. Wilson was impressed that Keiser could obtain a response on such short notice from a Justice Department official at Richard's level. The door was still open.

From London, Keiser called Wilson in Tripoli and said that

it was too awkward to handle this through overseas phone calls and cables. He would fly back to Washington and straighten everything out.

2

Now the recovery of Edwin P. Wilson was on two separate tracks. Track A, as it was called, would have Barcella arrange a second meeting with Wilson to iron out his legal difficulties. He'd draft another "safe passage" guarantee for Wilson in a country other than the Dominican Republic, with no reference to the National Security Council or the PLO. This time, though, if Wilson so much as jaywalked in violation of the letter's conditions, he'd be collared, and knowing Wilson, Barcella had no doubt that it would happen. Track B, the fallback, would continue the national security gambit in case Wilson got desperate enough to meet Keiser without a letter from Barcella.

Barcella also sent word to Wilson through Keiser that he would only deal with his lawyer, John Keats, on the details of another meeting. Keats couldn't believe that Keiser had reemerged from the woodwork.

"Just keep after Barcella," Wilson said to Keats. "Keiser's working on something else. Barcella doesn't know about it. It's too high up for him."

Still, in the guise of doing Barcella a favor, Wilson made one last stab at getting him off the case. Keats was the messenger. Wilson was claiming that his old partner Frank Terpil, then believed to be in the Syrian-occupied part of Lebanon, was egging on PLO killers to knock off not only Barcella but also his wife and daughter.

About an hour later Keiser relayed the same story. He quoted Wilson as saying, "I don't give a fuck whether the son of a bitch goes down, but I'll get the blame for it, so I thought I better do something."

Marshals were assigned to guard the Barcellas. When a neighbor saw the big Winnebago van parked in their driveway, she said, "I see you've got visitors again. What's it like?"

"Like being in jail," Mary Barcella replied.

"Well, at least there won't be many burglaries around here for a while."

For Larry and Mary, however, it wasn't very funny to see Laura go off to school every morning guarded by marshals.

Barcella's anger began to build. It was personal now, this thing between him and Wilson.

3

At the time when the FBI was investigating Shackley, Clines, von Marbod and Secord, auditors from the U.S. Maritime Administration had uncovered massive abuses in EATSCO bills to the Pentagon. General Secord, the only one still in government service, was removed from his key position in the sale of arms to the Middle East, pending a polygraph. But he never took the test. Instead, without any prior notification to the Justice Department, he was abruptly reinstated by Frank C. Carlucci, a former deputy director of the CIA who had become the number two man in the Defense Department.

Then one night near the end of February 1982 Barcella got a curious visitation at home from Michael Ledeen, the State Department's expert on terrorism. Barcella knew Ledeen; he had bought the first house that Larry and Mary owned.

As a writer on political and intelligence affairs before his State Department job, Ledeen had published a *New York* magazine article savaging Admiral Stansfield Turner for forcing Theodore Shackley out of the agency. And now, in Barcella's den, Ledeen was saying that he had heard disquieting rumors about an investigation of Shackley and von Marbod. Especially von Marbod. He was a man of impeccable honor, practically his idol, said Ledeen. He had saved countless lives and equipment after the fall of Saigon and of the shah in Iran. Ledeen couldn't explain why von Marbod had suddenly quit the Pentagon, because he had always been such a "fighter," but Larry could be barking up the wrong tree. Any billing abuses that were being questioned might have gone for a covert operation.

"If that's so," Barcella said, "I wish somebody would trust me enough to spell it out."

For Barcella, though, it quickly became academic. Mark Richard informed him that he and his new assistant Rick Otto were overworked, what with trying to get Wilson, debriefing Schlachter and Goulding, dealing with Roberta Barnes and putting together the final touches on the C-4 indictment. So the U.S. Attorney's Office in Alexandria, whose jurisdiction included both Langley and the Pentagon, would take over Barcella's probe into EATSCO, Waldo Dubberstein and any poten-

tial charges against Shackley, Clines, von Marbod and Secord.
But not to worry, Richard said. Barcella would retain overall
supervision.

The assistant U.S. attorney in Alexandria assigned to work
with Barcella was Theodore Greenberg, a rather short, aggres-
sive, somewhat abrasive prosecutor with a large ego. But Barcella had an ego, too. They managed a workable if slightly
uneasy relationship. As time went on, however, Greenberg
made it increasingly clear that his cases were his.

What especially concerned Barcella about the new arrangement was that there were "people" prosecutors, who sent criminals to jail, and "paper" prosecutors, dealing mostly in fraud
cases, where victory more often than not was signaled by a guilty
plea bargain and a fine, and Greenberg's reputation was that of
a "paper" prosecutor.

"You said everything was to go through me," Barcella pro-
tested to Richard, and Richard, gulping another Tums to quell
a chronically troublesome stomach, said, "Look, this had got to
be divided equally, but you're more equal because you know
more. Come on, Larry, you know how it is."

4

Throughout March and into April Barcella vainly attempted to find a Western European country where he could
meet with Wilson again. By now stories about former CIA agent
Edwin Wilson were appearing regularly in the European press.
He was too hot. Various nations that were approached—including Italy, France, West Germany, Austria and Greece—had commercial ties with Libya that they did not want endangered. Who
knew what Qaddafi's reaction would be to Wilson's arrest?

Keiser kept Wilson up-to-date on each of these efforts. Wilson, though, told him that he was fed up with waiting. He had
to get moving. He had other options, he said, and resurrected
his plan to go to the Sudan.

But to his bewilderment and anger, Wilson would learn that
Khartoum was no longer interested in his services. He fired off
a letter to Major Hajazzi, charging that the Sudanese must have
been tipped that he'd be spying for the Libyans. There had to
have been a leak at the highest levels of Libyan military intelligence, and the CIA had notified the Sudan. For days afterward,

downing glasses of flash and grapefruit juice, he ranted about it to John Heath.

Seized by the fear that he would never be able to leave Libya under any circumstances, Wilson committed an act bordering on treason. In a second letter to Hajazzi, he declared that he had confederates in U.S. intelligence and military circles—citing Shackley, Clines, von Marbod and Secord by name—who could tell him about every tank, every missile, every plane being shipped to Egypt.

5

Oh, by the way, Richard said one day to Barcella, the FBI was developing a source in the Arab world that might be instrumental in prying Wilson out of Libya. Although he experienced a moment of foreboding, Barcella didn't really make much of it at the time. He welcomed all the help he could get.

Besides, that same April, he finally got Roberta Barnes's cooperation.

When they had first met after she was out on bond, she could barely bring herself to speak to him. "You didn't have to keep me in that stinking jail," she said. "I wasn't going anywhere."

"How could I know? If you had told me you were coming in, like some others did, we could have worked it out."

Actually, there wasn't much of a case against her that would stand up, although he did his best to keep this from her and her lawyer. She more than anybody else, however, knew about Wilson's array of corporations, bank accounts and contracts. He didn't want to put her away on conspiracy charges unless he had to, he said.

The problem, of course, was that she was still in love. In February, when Keiser went to London, she gave him a letter to pass on to Wilson. Keiser opened it, but all it turned out to be was a mash note. Wilson had asked Keiser to keep an eye on her, to keep tabs on what she was saying. And even after she caved in, when she was given immunity, Keiser told him that she was holding fast. "You're a lucky man, Ed," Keiser said. "You've got a wonderful girl there. Wonderful."

Then the Justice Department came up with a country that appeared willing to accept Wilson for a meeting with Barcella.

The deputy minister of justice in Turkey had granted provisional approval. The minister himself, away on a trip, would have to confirm it formally, but no hitches were anticipated.

"I want to give you some good news," Keiser told Wilson on April 22. Wilson was elated, but he wanted direct, personal confirmation from Barcella about the letter guaranteeing that he was safe from arrest.

It was weird, Barcella thought. He'd been pursuing Wilson all this time, and now here he was picking up a phone, directly dialing his number in Tripoli and saying, "Hello, Ed, this is Larry Barcella."

The letter was delivered by Dan Drake to John Heath in Brussels on April 29. It was essentially the same as the one for the Rome meeting, except that Wilson's safe passage was specifically limited to travel from Libya to Turkey and back, and solely to see Barcella. This provision was added because Wilson had been talking to Keiser about going on for a second meeting, about the PLO, in the Dominican Republic—or even right there in Turkey.

Keiser kept telling Wilson that it was only a matter of days before Turkey officially said okay. In a call on May 8, Wilson sounded amiable and relaxed. Keiser had said that he was moving from Westchester County in New York to the Washington area, perhaps to McLean, in Virginia. Running his real estate enterprises and commuting to Washington on national security business was getting to be a terrible burden.

Wilson urged him to take a look at a farm he had in Middleburg. It was beautiful, and very convenient to Dulles airport. Might be perfect for Keiser. And while he was at it, Keiser ought to go on to Mount Airy. "Just drive by and tell me what it looks like," he said. "It'll give you a chance to see the countryside."

Listening to the tape, Barcella couldn't resist thinking how close they were getting. He started envisioning Wilson coming off a plane in handcuffs. But by May 11, Wilson had become querulous. Why couldn't the sessions with Barcella and with Clark's representatives both be in Turkey? It'd be an easier trip for the PLO people. Or why couldn't he meet Barcella in the Dominican Republic before proceeding to Turkey for the PLO end of it?

Barcella had told Keiser that he didn't want the two meetings anywhere near each other. It would just complicate things if and when Wilson went on trial. So Keiser explained, "That wouldn't be good, Ed. As you know, I try to keep the two, ah, parties apart. For obvious reasons."

Still there was no definitive answer from Turkey. And on May 13 Keiser emphasized that Barcella was doing everything he could. Sending telexes left and right.

"Is he really?"

"Yes, truly."

To Barcella's relief, Wilson suddenly surmised that the delay must be because Secretary of State Alexander Haig was in Turkey. He told Keiser that the Turkish minister of justice probably was worried about letting in a "known terrorist" while Haig was still there. "What we're talking about is the Middle East mentality," he said.

"Ah, the Middle East mentality," Keiser said. "That's right. Yes."

6

Barcella was just as sore as Wilson was. To begin with, the whole bureaucratic procedure for locating a host nation was so cumbersome, embracing both the Justice and State departments. And instead of making the request in one shotgun cable, it had been done country by country, which was why all this time had passed.

On the morning of May 20, he was about to grab the phone to demand what the hell was going on with Turkey when his contact at Justice called first with the news that Turkey had declined. No reason was given.

He gazed at the receiver. What else could possibly go wrong? Then he found out. Mark Richard summoned him.

The undercover "asset" the FBI was using to retrieve Wilson had reported that a man named Ernest Keiser was completely bollixing up his efforts. The bureau was insisting that Keiser stop communicating with Wilson. Its man was on the verge of success. All he needed was a week or ten days to have Wilson ushered out of Libya, most likely to neighboring Tunisia, where he'd be taken by plane directly to the States, and not some clumsy plan like Barcella's, in which Wilson at any moment could take off on his own, or a dozen other things could go wrong.

Affronted, Barcella also began to be suspicious. He knew

that the FBI's man had widespread contacts in the intelligence community. And offhand, he could think of an awful lot of people in that community who might not want Wilson back—*ever*.

He argued with Richard that he personally didn't give a damn who got the raves for recovering Wilson—that was why he hadn't minded a parallel FBI operation—but to eliminate Ernie just to satisfy some prima donnas at the bureau was senseless. Keiser had delivered over and over again, and the FBI's guy had not done anything except make promises.

Well, that was the way it had to be, said Richard. The bureau was being very tough about it.

Barcella brought in Keiser on May 28. He told him that he would have to phone Wilson right now from his office and say that he was going to be out of touch for at least ten days. He couldn't explain why, but from the look on Keiser's face, Barcella could see that he knew another plan was in the works.

Under the circumstances, it wasn't Keiser's best performance. "What's the ten days for, why ten days?" Wilson had yelled, and Keiser said, "Ed, I simply cannot go into details."

"As far as I'm concerned, you know, the hell with it. Forget it. I'm done with these people. It's been three months since they've said we're going to have a meeting in Turkey, or we'll have a meeting in whatever, and they haven't kept their word . . . I don't give a shit if I ever come back."

"It has nothing to do with Barcella," Keiser said.

"The hell with them. They're all a bunch of rabbits!"

It was all over, Barcella thought. Nearly a year of planning and maneuvering down the tube.

For Ernie Keiser, though, it wasn't over. That night he told Roberta Barnes to phone Diane Byrne in London with a message for Ed. She was to say that his call earlier in the day had been monitored. It wasn't the way it had sounded. Something big was afoot. But he was under strict instructions not to discuss it personally with Wilson. Tell Ed, Keiser said, that he should know how crazy the intelligence business gets sometimes.

Then he sent Dan Drake to a printing shop in Tysons Corner. Drake said he was with the National Security Council, which desired new stationery. The proprietor, delighted at the prospect of such prestigious business, promptly made up a variety of NSC letterheads to choose from.

In Wilson's Washington townhouse, which Keiser was

using until he found a permanent residence, Keiser started drafting a letter, using one of Wilson's typewriters.

Barcella knew none of this.

7

To prove how much clout its man on the scene had, the FBI promised that all of Wilson's communications to the "outside world" would be cut off. But by June 4, Barcella had learned from Roberta Barnes that he was still talking to her in Washington and to Diane Byrne in London. And he proposed to Richard that they ought to let Keiser at least try to reestablish some sort of contact with Wilson, or Wilson would be off the hook for good.

"All right," Richard finally said. But he warned that Keiser would have to drop the national security dodge. All they had to have was something leaking out of the Middle East that National Security Council representatives were secretly going to meet with the PLO.

When Keiser heard about the new restriction, he said that it wouldn't be easy, but there was still one other possibility of enticing Wilson out. "Di" and "Bobbi" had been saying how desperate he was for a reprieve from Libya, that he might risk using the McCormick passport for a Caribbean vacation in the Dominican Republic.

With that, Keiser then secretly phoned Wilson. At last, he said, he was able to explain what the hiatus had been all about. William Clark and the rest of the council had decided to take up Ed's recommendation that he set up fronts to mount covert military actions against Communist guerrillas in Central America. It had become top priority, more important than the PLO. That would come later.

He said that he had a letter from the National Security Council outlining everything and also guaranteeing Wilson immunity from arrest in the Dominican Republic. Soon he would be calling Wilson again, but it would be for Barcella's benefit. Wilson was to *ignore* whatever he said. Barcella was not to know anything. Not even the CIA would be in on it for the time being.

"That's fantastic," Edwin P. Wilson said.

Keiser made his next call in Barcella's presence. After dutifully informing Wilson that the council was out and that a meeting place to negotiate his indictment remained up in the air, he raised the possibility of going to the "island" anyway, and Wilson said, "Okay. Fine."

There was always the possibility that the Libyans might not allow Wilson to leave, and Keiser said, "You have no difficulties over there?"

"No, none whatsoever."

It seemed odd to Barcella and Rick Otto that Wilson was taking it so calmly. Keiser reiterated to Barcella Wilson's desire for "a little rest and recreation." Also, he admitted that he might have mentioned at one point or another the possibility of a meeting with Barcella somewhere in the Caribbean. "It was very vague, Larry," he said. "Nothing specific."

Afterward Otto said, "You think he has something up his sleeve we don't know about?" and Barcella said, "Probably. Ernie's Ernie. But I don't care. He's come through so far. Let's ride with him all the way."

Keiser had one more chore. Wilson had demanded that he show the letter from the council to Roberta Barnes, and that night they met in a restaurant in Virginia. As she remembered, the letter was quite official, the paper heavy and cream-colored with a light blue heading that said "National Security Council" and underneath that, "The White House."

It began by acknowledging awareness of Keiser's discussions with Wilson. Wilson would be granted immunity from arrest in the Dominican Republic for forty-eight hours. If the discussions with Keiser and other representatives of the NSC were fruitful, Wilson would receive a probationary passport good for a year. The thrust of the discussions would be in regard to covert operations in Central America. Another item would be the creation of a clandestine relationship with the Palestine Liberation Organization.

It was signed "Frank B. Henderson," a name Keiser had made up.

In the morning, Keiser and Barnes met again, this time at National Airport, and from a pay phone she summarized the contents of the letter to Diane Byrne in England so they could be passed on to Wilson in Tripoli.

8

Everything was moving fast. By June 8 Wilson was talking to Keiser about meeting him that weekend, on Sunday, the thir-

teenth, in Zurich. Keiser would bring the passport and visa with
him. Then on to the island.

Barcella told Richard, "It's now or never."

The FBI went berserk, claiming that its man had been temporarily stymied because of Israel's invasion of southern Lebanon to wipe out PLO strongholds after an Israeli diplomat was
shot down in London. The entire Arab world was in turmoil.
More time was needed.

"How much more time?" Barcella said. "Come on, Mark,
the Arab world's always in turmoil. This can go on forever."

Oliver ("Buck") Revell, an assistant FBI director, told Richard that if Barcella's harebrained idea wasn't stopped, not only
Barcella's head but Richard's would be served up on a platter.

Rudolph Giuliani, then associate attorney general of the
Department of Justice, hadn't seen anything like it. He and his
immediate deputy, Jeff Harris, got "informal" calls from assistant FBI directors John Otto and Frances Mullen warning of the
terrible media embarrassment that was in the offing. Harris said
he'd been told, "When the shit hits the fan, it's going to be all
over you and Rudy."

The FBI's pitch to Giuliani was that Barcella was going to
use U.S. marshals to help him and they weren't up to it. Giuliani
was diplomatic enough not to ask how any embarrassing leaks
might get out. He figured the bureau was still mad that the
marshals had gotten into the fugitive business, especially after
they had beaten the FBI in tracking down Christopher Boyce,
the famous runaway Falcon in the *Falcon and the Snowman* case.

Personally, Giuliani thought that the marshals under Howard Safir's field lead were doing a pretty good job. He thanked
the bureau for its concern and said he'd stick with what his own
people decided. He had confidence in their judgment.

9

Howard Safir had assured Barcella that everything was set
in Santo Domingo, the Dominican Republic capital. Once Wilson arrived, he wouldn't even get through immigration; officially, he would not have entered the country, so extradition
proceedings could be skipped.

The trick was to make sure Wilson was on the plane when
it landed. The schedule called for him to depart Libya for Zurich
Sunday afternoon, June 13. There would be a four-hour layover

in Zurich. The next leg was to Madrid, where he would board
a connecting flight across the Atlantic to Santo Domingo. The
Madrid stop was about two hours.

Barcella's big worry was whether Wilson had something
else in mind—that he'd been using Keiser simply to bemuse the
Libyans so he could leave the country, and that he would take
off the minute he was in Zurich or Madrid. And that wasn't the
half of it. Wilson could accidentally wander out of the international zone in either airport, and with the Interpol alert on him,
he might be apprehended. Extradition, especially in Switzerland, could be interminable. The C-4 indictments hadn't come
down yet and some of the other counts weren't extraditable in
Switzerland at all. Legally, moreover, the counts Wilson could
be tried on in the United States were limited to those allowed
in the extradition warrants.

In Madrid, the Spanish judicial system presented other
problems. When Frank Terpil was sentenced in absentia to fifty-
four years on the gun-running charges in New York, so was a
partner of Terpil's, a man named Gary Korkala. Like Terpil,
Korkala had fled, and was finally located in Spain. After lengthy
negotiations, Korkala was extradited, but on the condition that
he be retried, and he was eventually able to plea-bargain down
to where he could get out in six years. Who knew what Wilson
might manage in Spain with the right lawyers?

As backup, Phil Tucker would openly go with Keiser to
Zurich for the trip to Santo Domingo, while Jimmy Reina, the
other marshal assigned to Wilson's retrieval, would travel in his
customary undercover role.

But Barcella also was determined to be on hand himself—
to precede Wilson at the Zurich and Madrid airports to scout the
layout, to ensure the cooperation of local authorities and to
guard against any slipups, anticipated or unexpected.

When Mark Richard found this out, he said, "Listen, Larry,
you're a prosecutor, not a cop," and Barcella replied, "On this
one, I'm the cop, too."

TWENTY-SIX

At the last minute, serious hitches developed.

First, Keiser reported that Roberta Barnes wanted to be in Zurich for Wilson's arrival. She had already asked Barcella for her passport to visit Diane Byrne, but Wilson, of course, was the real reason. All Barcella needed was for the two of them to run off to some hotel.

"Can't you talk her out of it?" he said to Keiser, and Keiser said that both he and Wilson had tried, to no avail.

But there was a flip side to it. She would be finishing up her initial round of grand jury testimony just before Zurich, so he could hold the passport over her head to assure her cooperation. Besides, she was capable of kicking up a fuss if he didn't let her go, maybe enough of one to scare Wilson off. In any event, Barcella had no choice; he would have to live with it.

Then, even worse, the four-hour layover in Zurich that frazzled Barcella's nerves to begin with now had to be extended to *twenty-eight* hours.

In the final phone call between Keiser and Wilson confirming Sunday in Zurich, Barcella heard Wilson say mysteriously that while his "friend in Geneva" had most of the cash in hand, he wasn't going to be able to get the rest of the money till Monday, when the banks were open.

"Ed, we can talk about this later," Keiser interrupted, staring warily at Barcella.

But Wilson kept on. The problem, he said, was that it had to be taken out of "yellow hard stuff."

Afterward, Barcella said, "What was that all about?" and Keiser said well, it was part of the business deal that he mentioned to Barcella in February. Remember? The one Barcella had said was all right.

"Yeah, and I also said that it had to be legal and couldn't screw up anything."

"It won't," Keiser said. It was an investment opportunity that he and Wilson had been kicking around at length and to stop it now would make him suspicious.

Barcella thought of all Keiser's unrecorded calls. "Okay," he said, "but I'm telling you, Ernie, if Wilson gets out of the international zone, I'm going to have your scalp. And you'll have to declare any cash you bring into the States."

"I have to declare it?" Keiser said, as if his best friend had just mugged him.

"You heard me."

"Right, of course, Larry," Keiser said. "I wouldn't have it any other way."

As a hedge against Wilson's suddenly bolting with all that time on his hands, Barcella told Phil Tucker to carry the Irish passport with the Dominican visa and not to show up physically at the Zurich airport until Monday. And Jimmy Reina, undercover in the international zone, would keep his eyes pinned on Wilson's movements.

2

On Friday afternoon, June 11, 1982, before Barcella left Washington, Mark Richard said, "Please, Larry, no cowboy stuff over there."

"Go get him," said Safir.

In New York, Barcella boarded Swissair 101, seat 30 G, in the smoking section. For months he'd toyed with the idea of giving up cigarettes, but now it was unthinkable.

The night before there'd been another crisis, a domestic one. For two years he had been promising to build Laura a playhouse, but every time he was about to begin, some new wrinkle in the pursuit of Wilson cropped up. This weekend, he had sworn to her, the playhouse would finally materialize. Well, he thought, that was one more score to settle.

Along with Tucker and Reina, he was accompanied by Lawrence Chamblee, a Justice Department attorney from the Office of International Affairs. Chamblee knew many senior law-enforcement officials in Switzerland and Barcella might need his help.

For sure, he couldn't count on much from the FBI agent attached to the embassy in Bern. Richard had told him that while the bureau's evaluation of the plan still stood, nothing would be done to "thwart" it.

"That's nice of them," Barcella said.

Keiser was to fly to London the next day on the Concorde; there he would be joined by Barnes, traveling separately from Washington, and Diane Byrne. On Sunday the three would go on to Zurich. Wilson was due in Sunday night at six P.M. The two women were to return to London on Monday, while Wilson, Keiser and Tucker took off for the Dominican Republic via Madrid that night.

And now, on Swissair 101, as Barcella briefed him on the plan, Chamblee said, "It sounds great, but have you ever heard of one that went off like clockwork?"

"That possibility has occurred to me," Barcella said.

He started reading a spy novel. Quite appropriately, it was about snaring a fiendish terrorist in the Middle East. The difference was that the novel's hero had a series of exotic women swarming around him. Barcella thought about Mary and everything she'd had to put up with, and about his broken promise to build the playhouse for Laura. Then he dozed off. It was practically the only sleep he would have for the next four days.

3

The FBI legal attaché met them. "Just what can I do for you?" he said, not looking all that happy, and Barcella said they would like to meet the airport police chief. When they were introduced, it was obvious that the chief hadn't been forewarned. "Anything else?" the legal attaché asked, and Barcella said thanks, but no, they'd take it from there.

While Chamblee started phoning his Swiss contacts, the chief and some of his men stared stolidly at Barcella, Tucker and Reina. Barcella had always thought of Switzerland in terms of musical-comedy cuckoo clocks and quaint chalets. These cops didn't look so picturesque.

Finally, though, a call came in for the chief and afterward he broke out his best smile. "I am at your service," he said.

Barcella explained that a man would be arriving from Libya Sunday evening. Although there was an Interpol warrant on him, he was expected to stay in the international transit zone. He'd be met by another man and two women, and then by Tucker on Monday. He would be leaving Monday night. Barcella also said that he would appreciate any courtesies shown to Reina, who would be conducting a surveillance in a variety of disguises.

"As long as the subject remains in the international zone," the chief said, "my instructions are to ignore him." He took them on a tour of the airport. Down some stairs, still in the zone, he pointed out a nursery for children between flights. There were rooms as well for adults who wished to rest. The area was locked from midnight to six A.M.

All at once Barcella thought Roberta Barnes's presence might be a big help. The chief agreed to set aside a room. Keiser had the name of the airport hotel Tucker would be at, and Barcella told Tucker, "When Ernie checks in, tell him to tell Wilson that he knows a perfect place where he can shack up with her for the night."

4

For three days now, ever since Nassir Ashur of Libyan intelligence had told him he could leave, Wilson had been pouring down glass after glass of flash. Ashur controlled all the comings and goings at the airport in Tripoli. Having Ashur meet Keiser when Keiser had been over was the smartest move he'd ever made, he told John Heath. He mimicked Ashur saying, "Ah, yes, I recall Mr. Ernest Keiser. An interesting man. I trust you are not making a mistake."

Heath watched and listened as Wilson lurched around, filled with visions of Caribbean beaches, of the Central America deal, of maybe even being let back into Libya so he could collect some of the goddamn money he was still owed. By God, he'd pull off the PLO thing, too.

"Are you?" Heath said.

"Am I what?"

"Making a mistake with Keiser?"

Wilson slumped in his chair and looked up at Heath and said, "I'll tell you something, John. I don't care. I'd rather spend two years in jail than two more days in this fucking sandbox."

That was Saturday. In the morning, as Heath helped him pack, Wilson said, "Look, if Keiser's doing a number, I've arranged for you to get fifty K to knock him off."

5

In Zurich Barcella remained up past midnight with Chamblee, Tucker and Reina, hashing it over, worried that there was a loophole they had missed. Then he was so keyed up he couldn't sleep. He finished the spy novel. In the end the terrorist leader was killed. That was another difference. He wanted Wilson alive. The FBI guy had said that Wilson would be executed if he tried to get out of Libya on his own, and Barcella had been truly concerned until Wilson told Keiser on the phone that there wasn't any problem.

Finally he managed to grab a couple of hours before going to the airport with Chamblee to catch a plane for Madrid to set up things there. A Swiss cop who had driven them in from the airport said that an airport train departed regularly from the station right by their hotel, so they took it in the morning, to save per diem money, but wound up in a cab anyway. On the train Barcella asked a conductor who spoke English how long it was to the airport, and the conductor said they weren't going to the airport. There had been two trains on the same platform and they had taken the wrong one. The conductor arranged to have the engineer radio ahead for a taxi at the next stop. He gave them back their fare. "We are to blame," he said. "There should be a better sign."

The airport in Madrid was bedlam. It turned out that the World Cup soccer matches were about to kick off in Spain and thousands of people were streaming in. But when Barcella tried to go through immigration with his government passport, he was stopped. "Visa?"

"No visa," Barcella said. "You don't need one."

Neither Barcella nor Chamblee spoke Spanish. Chamblee said he had his regular tourist passport as well, so he tried it and went right through. Barcella was taken to a room by a member of the Guardia Civil while Chamblee looked for the State Department security officer who was expected to meet them.

In about twenty minutes, Barcella was sprung. The security officer, John Swafford, explained that Spain was in a snit because the United States required visas on all Spanish passports, but rather than harm its tourist trade, Madrid decided to save face by requiring Americans entering Spain on official business to have visas.

Barcella and Chamblee didn't have any Spanish currency. Since it was Sunday, Swafford personally exchanged all the pesetas he had, about a hundred dollars' worth. "Nothing shabby about this operation so far," Barcella said to Chamblee.

Late in the afternoon at the embassy, Swafford introduced Barcella to Rich Dunnegan, who headed up a U.S. narcotics squad stationed in Spain. Dunnegan, an old friend of Howard Safir's, had set up an appointment in the morning with the commanding general of the Spanish police to work out procedures when Wilson came through. "If there's anything else I can do," Dunnegan said, "just give a holler."

Barcella called Phil Tucker. "Everything's cool," Tucker said. Reina had reported that Keiser, Barnes and Byrne had arrived. Wilson's plane was delayed but it was in the air.

6

Close to seven o'clock in Zurich airport, Jimmy Reina watched as Wilson, wearing a dark blue suit and blue raincoat and carrying a briefcase, strode into the international zone, where he was greeted by Keiser, Barnes and Byrne.

Reina, in a knitted sweater and cap, a knapsack slung over his shoulder, looked like another Alpine hiker. He was of average height and weight with pleasantly conventional features and light brown hair. Safir called him "my invisible man."

Roberta Barnes hugged Wilson as they all went to the bar. He immediately ordered drinks for everyone, a double Chivas Regal for himself. Keiser raised his glass to toast a new life and new success for Wilson, and Wilson, laughing, said, "I'll drink to that." After about an hour at the bar, the group went into the transit restaurant.

Wilson and Keiser left the table briefly to stroll along the concourse. "Where's the passport?" Wilson asked, and Keiser

said that it would be there on Monday. His associate, Phil
Tucker, was bringing it. He did not want to chance having it on
his person, in case Barcella got wind of what was up. Tucker also
would be traveling with them to the Dominican Republic.
Tucker really knew his way down there.

They talked about the Central American project. Something had been added to it, Keiser said. Ed would have to sign
a contract to stay on board for at least a year. "Great! Fantastic!"
Wilson said. He'd brought a comprehensive proposal for it.
They'd love what he had to show them.

Back at the table, Wilson told Barnes that she was going to
have to help organize a new front company in Washington. She
was all aglow. By now, Barbara Wilson had obtained a divorce
decree, and on the flight from London, Keiser confided to
Barnes that Ed was thinking of marrying her on the island.

Suddenly Diane Byrne asked if she could see the letter from
the National Security Council. "Yeah, I forgot about that.
Where is it?" Wilson said. After he glanced at it, he started to
put it in his jacket pocket, but Keiser said, "It must remain in
my possession. You understand how these things are, Ed."

Reina observed them returning to the bar area. He had
switched to an airport janitor's outfit. At the bar, Keiser took
Wilson aside and told him about the nursery. "Hey, buddy, you
think of everything," Wilson said.

7

Around two A.M. Madrid time, Barcella learned that Wilson
and Barnes had been safely tucked in for the night. Then he put
in a call to Rick Otto in Washington and said, "Tell Mark and
Howard everything's looking good."

At eight, Tucker called. He'd given Keiser the passport and
had met Wilson. "I hear we might be doing some deals together," Wilson had said jovially.

"You ought to see Reina," Tucker told Barcella. "He's
borrowed one of the policewomen. They're pretending to be
young lovers."

At the embassy, Rich Dunnegan had unsettling news. The
police general had canceled his meeting with Barcella. The first
match of the World Cup was on in Barcelona and he had taken
off to attend it. "Look, Larry," Dunnegan said, "maybe it's for
the best. Spanish surveillance isn't so subtle. I know those peo-

ple at the airport. If you say the word, I'll have my guys out there and if Wilson tries to leave the transit area, we'll jump him. We'll just say we happened to spot a fugitive we were after."

It was a good thing Mark Richard wasn't around to hear this, Barcella thought. "Okay, fine," he said.

A little after two P.M. Tucker called again. Wilson's lawyer, Edward Coughlin, had come in from Geneva with a suitcase that Wilson handed to Keiser. Tucker had glimpsed the contents. It was filled with stacks of hundred-dollar bills.

"How much?"

"I don't know, but it's a lot of money."

If everything went according to plan in the Dominican Republic, Tucker and Keiser were to fly from Santo Domingo to Miami. "Listen, Phil," Barcella said, "when Ernie takes it in, make sure he declares it."

Barcella went out to look over the Madrid airport. He figured it should be a lot simpler than Zurich. Even with the schedule change, Wilson would be there no more than three hours. But then he saw that there was considerable construction work going on in the transit area, all sorts of detours. Christ, Ed could wander out by accident.

The urge to be on hand to view him was overwhelming. Since Rome, Barcella had grown his beard and he had glasses to replace the contact lenses he usually wore. Finally, though, he decided the risk was too great.

Wilson, Keiser and Tucker, ticketed first class, were due to depart Zurich at eight-forty. Reina also would be on board in tourist. About six P.M. Tucker called in and said that they had a problem. Wilson had been at the bar all day. "He's so drunk I don't know if they'll let him on the plane," he said. "I'll try to get some coffee in him and walk him around."

At nine, with no further word from Tucker, Barcella couldn't stand it. From his hotel room, he put in a call to the chief of airport police in Zurich. It took nearly an hour to get through. At last the chief was on the line, and despite the language barrier, Barcella was able to ascertain that yes, the subject had left on schedule.

8

On Iberia flight 281 to Madrid, Phil Tucker was amazed that they had allowed Wilson on board. Now he was ordering more drinks. He was so drunk, he didn't seem to know where he was. When Tucker heard what he was saying, he was positive of it. Wilson and Keiser were in aisle seats across from each other. Tucker was right behind Keiser. Leaning toward Keiser, Wilson said he was going to take care of that son of a bitch Barcella, for what he'd done to him and the way he'd mistreated Barnes. He would buy a Washington law firm and make Barcella an offer he couldn't turn down. And after a year, he'd call him in and tell him who he'd been working for all the time, and then he would have that "dago bastard" killed.

In Madrid, close to midnight, John Swafford phoned to say the plane had landed. An hour later, he said Wilson was asleep in a lounge chair. It looked as if their biggest problem would be to wake him up for the next leg.

As Barcella paced alone in his hotel room, Swafford called again to say the departure was delayed, but Wilson was up and walking around, a little bleary-eyed. Then about three, he called for the last time and said the flight had left with Wilson on it. "Don't worry about the D.R. once he gets there," Safir had assured Barcella, and in his room, Barcella yelled, "Whoopee!" at the top of his lungs.

After Swafford dropped them off, Barcella met Chamblee and Jimmy Reina in the deserted hotel lobby. The night porter got them six bottles of beer and they all went back upstairs to celebrate. "Piece of cake," Chamblee said.

9

On Iberia 945 to the Dominican Republic, Wilson revived somewhat. He began reminiscing about his CIA career. He'd done a hell of a job supporting covert operations around the world, and now he would do the same for the National Security Council.

He talked about how he had gotten boats for Cuban hit-and-run raids even after the agency dropped out. He talked about Task Force 157 and what a farce it was when active-duty officers retired with pensions and were rehired as civilians in 157's proprietaries. He spoke of how he had formed Swiss and Liberian corporations, retaining Coughlin at $60,000 a year even though he was a drunk and basically a bagman.

He lamented the bad advice he'd gotten in the gold market. He brightened up about his property acquisitions. He knew this guy in the government's farm agency who advised him. "I ought to put you two together," he told Tucker. "You could probably work something out." Then he said that as soon as the Central American operation was set, they'd go on to the PLO. He could pick up a phone and talk to Yasir Arafat anytime he wanted to. He admired and sympathized with the PLO, he said. The fucking Jews had had it their way too long.

Wilson had gone full cycle. From the Great Gatsby of the spook world, he had become like the madman Kurtz in *Heart of Darkness.*

At the airport in Santo Domingo, the U.S. marshal for Puerto Rico, José A. López, stood by, waiting with Dominican Republic immigration officers.

Keiser told Wilson, "It's better, yes, that Phil and I go first to make sure everything is in order."

As Wilson stepped up to passport control, he was told, "Come this way, sir."

Unshaven, Wilson looked dazed. "I have a visa. Is there something wrong with it?"

"Don't worry. It's only a routine check."

Keiser and Tucker took off at once for Miami. Going through customs there, clutching his suitcase of money, Keiser tapped it and said, "It's all cash," and handed the customs agent a declaration that said he was carrying $250,000. The agent began to laugh. Tens of millions of dollars from drugs were being sneaked into Miami to be laundered and here Keiser was, declaring $250,000 just like that. "You've made my day, friend," he said, and waved him through without looking in the suitcase.

10

Wilson sat in a room, still befuddled, surrounded by armed guards. "I don't understand. Where's Mr. Keiser?"

A Dominican officer looked blankly at him. "We will have to send you to New York. Your papers are insufficient to enter our country."

"But I don't have a visa for the United States."

"Do not concern yourself. You will not have any problems."

Wilson was escorted to a nonstop flight to New York. López and two deputy marshals were on the plane. López watched Wilson closely. He had started looking skittish, and López was afraid he might harm himself. He saw him open his briefcase, take out some papers, tear them, slip them into an air sickness bag and place it on his breakfast tray. When a stewardess took the tray, López retrieved the bag. The torn papers inside were a rundown—incomplete, as it turned out—of Wilson's current assets and liabilities, listing his net worth at $14,097,366.

Later, when his briefcase was examined, it was found to contain a comprehensive forty-page proposal for the covert Central American operation, featuring a 1,500-man Special Mobile Airborne Reaction Force called SMARF.

Other items in it included $5,000 in cash; 1,570 German marks; blank Swiss bank checks; the names of his PLO contacts; his Maltese passport; an article by Frank Snepp, a former agency analyst, pointing out the double standard the CIA used in hounding Snepp for writing an unauthorized book called *Decent Interval* about intelligence failures in Vietnam while doing nothing about Wilson and Terpil; a numerical telex code for people and places; and the prospectus for a company called Executive Protection Services, which would guard "individuals, corporate executives and government representatives" against terrorist attacks.

11

In Madrid Barcella boarded a plane for New York just as Iberia 945 was landing in Santo Domingo. All the way across the Atlantic he was left to wonder how it had gone. He tried fitfully to concentrate on another spy book, but now reading offered no relief.

At JFK he was met by a customs investigator he had worked with before. "Son of a gun," the agent said, "now I know what you've been up to. It was on the radio while I was driving to the airport."

"What was?"

"That a big fugitive had just been brought in. Didn't know exactly who. Either Robert Vesco or Edwin Wilson."

Television crews, reporters and photographers were swarming all around the the federal courthouse in Brooklyn where Wilson's bail would be set at $20 million. Barcella made his way through them unnoticed.

Standing dejectedly in the courtroom, Wilson suddenly

TWENTY-SEVEN

"Larry, I assure you it was quite legal," Keiser said. And it was. He produced a loan agreement for $275,000, signed by Wilson and dated June 14. In return, Wilson would have a five percent interest in property in Florida near Disney World that Keiser wanted to option. If Keiser couldn't resell the land or get development financing, the loan was supposed to be repaid in three yearly installments, beginning in 1987, the ten percent interest on it due the third year.

The difference between the amount of the loan and the $250,000 Keiser tried to declare in Miami was because in Zurich Wilson had helped himself to some of the cash, which he shared with Barnes, Byrne and Coughlin. "It was terrible to watch," said Keiser, "but there was nothing I could do."

It took Wilson several days to realize how he had been duped. He kept babbling about a National Security Council letter that guaranteed him immunity from arrest. At first Barcella didn't take him seriously.

But then Roberta Barnes spoke about it. She didn't understand, she said. She'd seen a letter. Keiser had shown it to her. What was going on?

This could turn into a legal matter, so Barcella called Gene Propper, who remained Keiser's attorney. The sky outside Barcella's office window had turned dark and threatening, exactly reflecting his mood. But Propper said he didn't know what Barcella was talking about. He'd never heard of any such letter. He promised to report back as soon as he spoke to Keiser.

Barcella told Mark Richard what was happening, and Richard came unglued. Suppose Keiser had committed an illegal act? He saw Wilson walking right out of jail.

Propper then called in with Keiser's version. There was no letter; Keiser and Wilson had only talked about it. "Why believe Barnes?" Propper said. Like Richard, he was worried that his client had committed a criminal violation.

"Because I do. Stop acting like a defense lawyer, Gene. I want the truth. Tell Ernie he isn't dealing with Wilson now."

Propper called Barcella again. There'd been a misunderstanding, he said. What Ernie had meant to say was that there no longer was a letter.

Barcella said he wanted to see Keiser right away. They met at Propper's house. Keiser then admitted having the stationery made up. He said that Wilson had been really upset that the council was out of the picture, so he told him he had gone to his people at the White House and railed at them until they relented. Barcella couldn't help admiring Keiser's slickness. "I am sorry there was confusion about this," Keiser said. "I only wanted to do what was best. I did not want you in trouble if I overstepped."

Barcella was concerned that the letter also had promised Wilson immunity from prosecution. That could influence a jury, maybe even a judge. Where was it?

But Keiser had covered all bases. "Ah, well, Larry," he said. "I tore it up, you know, in Zurich and flushed it down a toilet."

After reviewing the situation, Barcella calmed Richard down. What Keiser had done conceivably could muddy things up, but Barcella said he didn't think so. Trickery wasn't a crime in collaring a fugitive. A fugitive could even be physically abducted. Short of lighting matches under someone to force his return, federal courts didn't care how a fugitive came into their jurisdiction; what counted was a fair trial. Besides, Keiser had been operating under Barcella's aegis. If Wilson's defense went after Keiser as an individual—charging him with fraud, say, for forging the letter—Barcella said he'd accept full responsibility as a federal law officer, even though he hadn't known everything

Keiser was doing. It was like using an informant to make an otherwise illegal drug buy to arrest a narcotics trafficker.

2

Wilson wanted a big-time attorney. He asked one of the marshals guarding him if he had any suggestions, and the marshal mentioned Herald Price Fahringer. Fahringer had just come off a sensational trial in which he had defended Claus von Bülow for the attempted murder of his wealthy socialite wife in Newport, Rhode Island. Even Wilson, in isolation in Tripoli, knew about the case. It didn't seem to matter that Fahringer had lost.

John Keats would stay on to assist Fahringer because of his background knowledge about Wilson's situation, but Wilson wasn't listening to his counsel anymore. Although Keats had warned him not to leave Libya until he had a firm guarantee signed by Barcella, Wilson appeared to blame him somehow for his capture. And Fahringer, with his prematurely white hair, his erect, elegant bearing, his cultivated speech, his tailored clothes and gleaming shoes, made Keats look, well, a little seedy.

Keats argued that Wilson's only hope was to make a deal. Barcella wanted to know who Ed's confederates were, who in government had helped him. Keats was sure he could get a commitment from Barcella for no more than five years. And even if it turned out to be more, it would be a lot better for Wilson than spending the rest of his life in prison.

Fahringer asked Barcella if he had any particular names in mind, and Barcella said that was up to Wilson. He wasn't going to place himself in a position where he could be accused of putting words in Wilson's mouth. He would, though, give Fahringer an idea of the areas he was interested in—conspiracy and bribery, conflict of interest, undisclosed violations of restricted arms shipments and treason.

To Keats's astonishment, he heard Fahringer, who had gotten an initial retainer of $250,000 from Wilson, tell his client that he didn't have to do a thing. He'd beat the charges on the grounds that Wilson had been brought back to the United States illegally.

He would also use a "CIA defense," so-called graymail tactics that had been successfully practiced by other defendants in cases involving national security where the government had

to weigh a criminal prosecution against possibly embarrassing
and damaging revelations. But Congress had recently passed
the Classified Information Procedures Act. A defendant was
now required to submit this sort of sensitive material in closed
pretrial hearings. A judge would then decide whether it was
relevant and admissible.

Still, in a press conference, Fahringer declared, "If the government makes us go to trial, my client will be forced to reveal
information that will shake the CIA to its foundations."

My God, Keats thought, you dangle what Ed wants to hear
in front of him long enough and he'll go for it like a guppy.
Wilson had bought the CIA defense strategy. He was never
going to learn. And being locked up wasn't helping his stability.
He actually believed that some of his old pals—Ted Shackley
and the others—would rush to his rescue.

3

On July 19 an indictment was returned against Wilson on
the C-4 shipment out of Houston. Although the other counts
against him—conspiring to kill the Libyan defector Umar Abdullah Muhayshi and shipping the initial round of explosives for
a terrorist training center—had come first, the task force that
gathered daily in Mark Richard's office decided they were too
amorphous to start off with. Barcella himself recommended that
they start with the Houston C-4 charge. It meant that he would
have to give up being the courtroom prosecutor, because another federal jurisdiction was involved. But the case was far less
complicated, almost cut-and-dried in its criminality.

Dick Pedersen tried to get everybody interested in still an-
other case against Wilson. The same day he had been brought
back to the United States, more than two years after the fact, a
tracer request for the Magnum .357 that had been used to kill
Omran el-Mehdawi in Bonn, Germany, arrived at the Bureau of
Alcohol, Tobacco and Firearms. The trail led to the Bonnie
Doone Volunteer Fire Department in Fayetteville, where Wally
Klink, the former Green Beret then in Wilson's employ at Mount
Airy Farms, had bought it.

A subsequent FBI report said that Klink denied knowing
about any guns. But Pedersen recalled Reginald Slocombe, Wilson's freight forwarder, saying that in addition to bringing the
sample M-16 rifle overseas, he had delivered maybe four or five

pistols. Couldn't remember the details, however. Pedersen hit Slocombe again, and he said that come to think about it, the fellow he got them from was named Klink.

Since Klink had been in Virginia when Wilson ordered the purchase, within the jurisdiction of the U.S. Attorney's Office in Alexandria, Barcella told Pedersen to see Theodore Greenberg about getting a grand jury subpoena.

When Klink arrived at the Alexandria courthouse, another case was being heard. Pedersen could see that Klink was becoming more nervous by the minute as he waited to be called. "Look, Wally," Pedersen said, "you're in way over your head. We're not after you. You went down there to North Carolina and got some guns for Ed Wilson. You didn't know what you were involved in. You don't want to get caught up in this, but you will be if you keep saying you don't know anything. We know what happened. I'm just telling you that we're not interested in Wally Klink. Be smart."

An hour later Pedersen ran across the street to Greenberg's office. Klink had admitted that he got the guns on Wilson's orders. Greenberg could hardly believe his luck. As a newcomer to the case, he'd been trying to figure out how to enlarge his role. "Did you read him his rights?"

"I didn't have time," said Pedersen. "He was already confessing. Honest."

So now the gun-running charges got precedence. Even cleaner and simpler than the C-4. And it would take Fahringer by surprise. The indictment was handed down on September 21.

4

On the morning of October 26, Kevin Mulcahy's body was found slumped outside the door of his motel room in the Shenandoah Valley. He had been dead for several hours. He was forty.

Barcella rushed to the scene. Rumors circulated, and were printed and reported on television, that Mulcahy might have been the victim of some exotic drug administered by the CIA or by agents of Wilson fearful of testimony he would give in open court. He had been asked to leave by the motel's proprietor after he blew out a cabin window with a shotgun. In the cabin more than a dozen empty jugs of wine were found.

A preliminary medical examiner's report indicated that he

had been suffering from bronchial pneumonia and advanced emphysema. While alcohol was found in his blood, it was not enough by itself to have been fatal. Exposure to the elements could have contributed to his death. After an autopsy and an exhaustive analysis of his vital organs, it was determined that he had died of natural causes, specifically of bronchopneumonia.

The truth was a good deal more sorrowful. From a suitcase found in his cabin, Barcella sifted through stacks of documents, many of them FBI and BATF reports that Mulcahy had taken, others from the desk of Barcella's secretary, along with scribbled and typed comments on the investigation. There were notes for his book that had never gotten off the ground. And an incomplete script for a movie.

Friends said that he had begun drinking again not long after Wilson had been taken into custody. In the two weeks before his death, he had appeared deeply depressed and had talked about suicide. "I don't count anymore," he had said. Getting Wilson had become the focal point of his life and now he was on the periphery of events.

During the past six years, he had played one federal agency against another, reporter against reporter. He had become devious and deceitful, spiteful, a real pain in the ass. But the hard fact was that if it hadn't been for Kevin Mulcahy, there would have been no pursuit of Wilson to begin with.

5

Wilson would go on trial in Alexandria, in Houston, in Washington and eventually in New York.

In Alexandria, with Greenberg the chief prosecutor, Herald Price Fahringer claimed that his client was operating in Libya under CIA sanction when he had conspired to smuggle the handguns and an M-16 rifle out of the country, and if he had committed what normally would be construed as crimes, they were to fulfill his mission.

But in trying to prove this, Fahringer committed a tactical error by using Roberta Barnes as a defense witness, enabling the prosecution in cross-examining Barnes to demonstrate what Wilson really had been up to in Libya, forcing her to tick off all the contracts he had with the Qaddafi regime and the vast amounts of money he had made.

The trial lasted less than two days. Wilson did not take the

stand. Nor would he in subsequent trials. The jury deliberated
for about four hours before finding him guilty on seven of the
eight charges, the exception being whether he knew that Wally
Klink would have to cross state lines, from Virginia to North
Carolina, to buy the handguns. He was sentenced to fifteen
years.

In Houston, at a pretrial hearing, Fahringer attempted to
show that Wilson had been returned illegally. He put Barcella
on the stand and demanded to know if he had been aware that
Keiser was a notorious confidence man with a string of prior
arrests. "Yes," said Barcella, "that's why I thought he'd get
along so famously with your client."

During the trial itself, Fahringer's basic defense was Wilson's old story that Jerome Brower was responsible for flying
over the twenty-one tons of C-4. He hadn't had a thing to do
with it. But Barcella had convinced John Heath to return to the
United States and testify. Barcella phoned Heath, alone and
nervous in Tripoli, and said, "Isn't it time you came home?"
The statue of limitations had run out on many of the acts Heath
might have been prosecuted for, and in exchange for his cooperation, Barcella agreed not press any more charges.

And on the stand in Houston, Heath tied Wilson directly to
the C-4 shipment, testifying that Wilson had complained about
how the Libyans were dragging their heels in paying him for the
explosive. He also testified that on orders from Wilson he had
helped to smuggle some of the C-4 from Rotterdam to the
Libyan embassy in London. The jury found Wilson guilty on all
counts. He was sentenced to another seventeen years.

After the Houston trial, Theodore Greenberg was ready to
prosecute Waldo Dubberstein for passing military secrets to the
Libyans. On the morning of April 29, Dubberstein was sched-
uled at the Alexandria federal courthouse to answer a grand jury
indictment. When he didn't show, Greenberg, fearing that he
had fled, sent out an airport alert and also contacted the State
Department to have his passport revoked.

About an hour later a body identified as Dubberstein's was
found in the basement of the apartment house in nearby Arlington where he lived with his mistress. Greenberg hurried over to
make sure that it was Dubberstein. And it was, an apparent
suicide, the result of a blast from a shotgun he had placed in his
mouth.

Most of the damage was in the back of his head. His face was clearly recognizable, looking, Greenberg remembered, like a collapsed Halloween mask. At first there was concern about foul play. But he had left suicide notes both to his mistress and to his wife. And it was learned that he had bought the shotgun himself three days before, along with a single box of shells.

In Washington, Barcella and Carol Bruce then proceeded on the counts contained in the original 1980 indictment against Wilson. Of all the cases, it was the most esoteric. Were the Triex and Quadrex compounds that Brower had first shipped to Wilson actually explosives when they left the United States or were they merely the components for explosives? There was also the conspiracy to assassinate Umar Abdullah Muhayshi in Cairo—a murder that in fact had never taken place.

Barcella hoped to use the explosives part of the indictment to dramatize how Wilson had been aiding and abetting worldwide terrorism. But the presiding judge ruled that the explosives shipment and the assassination conspiracy had to be tried separately and that the would-be murder of Muhayshi was first on the docket.

Even worse, on the eve of the trial, Barcella's star witness, Rafael Quintero, revealed that he had accepted a $135,000 loan from Wilson *after* he had reported the plot to both the CIA and the FBI. The money was for a construction project in Mexico. Tom Clines, his old agency case officer, had arranged it, Quintero said. He trusted Clines. Tom told him it was a good deal. And Quintero had not paid back the loan.

Herald Price Fahringer said he was too busy appealing Wilson's first conviction in Alexandria, so he brought in a savvy criminal lawyer named Patrick Wall to handle the Washington trial. Wall hammered at the loan. Wasn't that the reason why Quintero was testifying, so he'd never have to repay it? Quintero's response was pretty feeble. The peso in relation to the dollar had dropped precipitously; he'd been waiting for it to regain its value.

The jury found Wilson not guilty. Barcella went out alone to confront the waiting television cameras. "Look," he told Bruce, "I'm always out there when I win one. I'm not going to duck them because I lost."

Wilson, though, would be tried a fourth time—in New York. In the most bizarre twist of all, Wayne Trimmer, a fellow inmate at the Metropolitan Correctional Center and a government informer, reported that Wilson, while awaiting his Alexandria and Houston trials, had approached him with an extensive hit list of people he wanted killed.

The list had nine targets. Topping it were Barcella and Bruce. For their demises, Wilson agreed to pay a quarter of a million dollars each. Others on the list included Keiser, Quintero, John Heath, Reginald Slocombe, Jerome Brower, Edward Coughlin and Francis Heydt, the Oklahoma clothing manufacturer who Wilson believed had cheated him on the Libyan uniform contract. The price per head for them was $50,000.

Trimmer, wearing a hidden recorder, got some of the hit list particulars on tape; he also had handwritten notes from Wilson and notes of his own about the victims, with information that only Wilson could have given him. An FBI agent posing as a hired killer was brought into the act. After he said that he had to have a down payment for the first person to be murdered, Jerome Brower, Wilson called Roberta Barnes and said he needed $10,000 for legal expenses. He asked her to have his younger son, Eric, fly up from Washington with the money, which was handed to the undercover agent.

Wilson was transferred to federal prison in Otisville, in upstate New York, where he then conspired with two other convicts, one of whom pretended to be a member of a vicious national gang of current and former prisoners known as the Aryan Brotherhood, to assassinate Trimmer for $500,000.

For reporters covering the trial, it was hard to believe that Wilson could have been so stupid. A hack television writer wouldn't dare turn out a scenario like this. *Newsday* columnist Murray Kempton wisecracked, "Wilson must have thought that the Metropolitan Correctional Center was just another CIA station."

Herald Price Fahringer, after suffering humiliating defeats in Alexandria and Houston, had had enough of his client. Michael G. Dowd of Queens, New York, one of the city's best defense lawyers, took on the case. But it was hopeless.

Dowd at least got a new count against Wilson—conspiring to obstruct justice by having his former wife killed—thrown out on the grounds that she had never been named as a witness in any of the trials. Wilson supposedly had added her to his hit list so he wouldn't have to share his assets in a final divorce settlement. Still, he got twenty-five more years for his multiple murder plots.

6

Roberta Barnes told Barcella and Theodore Greenberg what Wilson had said to her—that the $500,000 he had advanced to Clines was seed money for a plan to grab off the huge contract to ship arms to Egypt. Clines would be the front man but von Marbod, Shackley and Secord were all in on it. There'd been many meetings to set things up, at Mount Airy, at Shackley's home, in a hotel in Crystal City, Virginia, near National Airport. Von Marbod, according to Wilson, was the mastermind. Originally, Wilson had wanted to put up only $100,000 but von Marbod had insisted on more.

Barnes also said that she had been at a dinner in London, in January 1980, with Wilson, von Marbod and Secord, when Wilson had passed an envelope to von Marbod. On instructions from Wilson, she had previously placed $10,000 in cash in the envelope, but she couldn't swear it still contained the money.

She said all of this, but she told Barcella that he wouldn't be able to corner any of them. "They were too smart," she said. "There is no paper trail." And then, of course, this part of the case was no longer Barcella's.

Of the four men, only Major General Richard V. Secord ever took the stand in one of Wilson's trials. In Houston, he was called as a defense witness by Fahringer. He identified himself as deputy assistant secretary of defense for the Near East and South Asia. He had known Wilson about ten years. Tom Clines had introduced them.

Later, he had met Wilson in Iran when Secord was head of the Air Force's military assistance program there. He also met Wilson in 1979 and 1980 in Brussels while Secord was attending NATO conferences, and he acknowledged that on other occasions he had been together with Wilson and Shackley, whom he knew to be a senior CIA official, in the early and late seventies.

Fahringer, trying to show that his client had been working for U.S. intelligence, asked if Wilson discussed obtaining a Soviet MiG-25 fighter from Libya, and over the prosecution's objection, Secord said, "The answer is yes." In cross-examination, Secord was asked if his encounters with Wilson and Shackley were social occasions. "Yes," said Secord. That was as far as this line of inquiry went. The trial judge ruled that it really didn't have much to do with the question before the jury: whether Wilson had shipped twenty-one tons of C-4 from Houston to Tripoli.

By now it was known that Wilson had bailed Secord out of a bad real estate deal, a house Clines had sold him as an investment, and that Secord had used Wilson's Beech Baron plane almost as if it were his own. He quietly resigned from active duty, just when he would have been up for another star.

But as far as implicating Secord—or others—in Wilson's machinations, none of this meant a thing in court. The "smoking gun," as they say, wasn't there. Wilson, convinced that appeals would reverse his convictions, remained defiantly silent.

Although memos of Edward Coughlin regarding the $500,000 referred to three "unnamed" American partners that Clines had, Clines claimed that they didn't really exist. They were just John Does required for the filing of incorporation papers. Von Marbod's denial of wrongdoing, meanwhile, was absolute; he didn't know anything about anything. The same went for Secord. The one common thread binding each of these men was an uncertain relationship with Edwin P. Wilson, and that by itself was not a crime.

As long as they hung tough, nothing could be proved—if, indeed, there was something to prove. Barcella always thought that the most likely candidate to crack was Clines. Then the chance to find out arrived.

Auditors finally determined that EATSCO, during a period when Clines was still a visible partner, had fraudulently billed the Pentagon for some $8 million, in addition to the big profits it was already making. Barcella argued for all-out prosecution. Not only were jail terms merited for Clines and his Egyptian codefendant, Hussein K. Salem, but the thought of a cell door clanging shut behind him might do wonders for Clines's memory.

But this was getting into the ozone layers of American foreign policy. And rather embarrassingly so. With President Sadat dead, U.S. relations with Egypt were at a tender stage. Rightly or wrongly, the U.S. Attorney's Office in Alexandria was widely perceived as an extension of the offices of the general counsels at the CIA and the Pentagon. Nothing now happened to change this impression.

After a plea bargain, it was announced that Salem had signed a check for $3 million in claims and fines. I was able to learn, however, that in a sealed court agreement, the money went right back into the Egyptian arms pipeline. The Pentagon and the State Department didn't object. Neither did the Justice Department, according to Greenberg.

Although he had taken out at least two and a half million from EATSCO before being forced to depart because of his publicized connection to Wilson, Clines in his own plea bargain also was let off with a corporate fine. On behalf of Systems Services International, which had owned a forty-nine percent interest in EATSCO, he paid $10,000. Another hundred thousand went to settle civil claims.

In addition, Clines got a letter from the Alexandria U.S. Attorney's Office informing him that no further indictments against him were contemplated. For all practical purposes, that ended the investigation.

The feeling seemed pervasive. Everyone was out of government service; careers were cut short, reputations to some degree tarred. Time to move on. Just what Wilson had foreseen at worst for himself—until Barcella came along.

TWENTY-EIGHT

After his trials were over, I visited Wilson, on November 28, 1983, at the federal penitentiary at Marion, Illinois, which had replaced Alcatraz as the toughest one in the country. Its site was incongruous, in the middle of a wildlife preserve. Outside the prison's double walls topped with coils of razored wire, deer and fox abound in a lovely pastoral setting, ducks streak across a string of lakes and ponds.

Because of the vicious gangs that composed so much of Marion's population, with memberships extending beyond its walls, the prison was designed as much to prevent break-ins as breakouts. Surface-to-air missiles were in place in case of a helicopter escape attempt. Among these gangs were the Aryan Brotherhood, the D. C. Blacks, the Texas Syndicate and the Mexican Mafia. They were in a continual battle for violent preeminence. The day before I arrived there to see Edwin P. Wilson, two guards had been slain, the gang killers making no effort to hide who they were. Additional time they would receive was of no consequence. They were in Marion for the rest of their lives anyway.

Wilson was in an isolated area of Marion called the K wing. Other inmates in the wing included Jack H. Abbott, the author of *In the Belly of the Beast*, who, after most of a lifetime in jail, had been released, only to knife to death a waiter in a New York restaurant over an imagined slight; the famous "Falcon," Christopher Boyce; and Joseph Franklin, a white supremacist who had indiscriminately murdered blacks around the country.

They were housed in solitary cells, really more like rooms, behind steel doors with slots in them for the passage of food. The cells were in the wing's basement and contained a cot, a desk and chair, a toilet and shower and a black-and-white television set. A slit window just above the ground level of a small courtyard allowed some daylight to enter.

Like the others, Wilson was locked up twenty-three hours a day. One hour was allotted for exercise in a small gym, for walks in the courtyard and for making collect, monitored phone calls. While all these men were considered highly dangerous, they were in large measure kept away from the general prison population for their own protection.

"Why would Boyce, say, be a target?" I asked an assistant warden guiding me through a series of bolted steel doors to the K wing. Were there super patriots in the yard ready to kill him because he'd sold spy satellite secrets to the Russians? "They don't need a reason, just an excuse," he said. "But I'll tell you one thing. That Wilson's a fast talker. You give him two minutes with the Aryan Brotherhood and you don't know what would happen."

Wilson and I met in a room off the K wing's infirmary. He was brought in with his wrists handcuffed behind him. After he was inside, he stuck his hands back through the door slot so he could be uncuffed. "You see how they treat me," he said.

He was wearing an orange prison jumpsuit. He was slightly bent and thinner than I had seen him in court during his trials. His face was gray. Still, he retained a commanding physical presence. It was easy to see how menacing he could be in other circumstances. His huge hands rested in his lap, flying up now and then to emphasize a point. His voice was big and resonant.

He knew I was writing a book and he wanted to relate his side of the story. He appeared most upset about his conspiracy-to-murder convictions in New York. "Did you listen to those tapes?" he demanded at once. "That wasn't me."

I said that I had, and it sounded like him.

"Well, look, did you study the transcripts? Did you see how they changed the words?" Only a moment ago it hadn't been his voice at all and now it was some words that had been doctored.

When I disagreed again, he stared at me and said, "If you're going to be so fucking hostile, what the fuck good is it talking to you?" For a moment I thought he was going to summon the guard stationed outside. But he did not. At least I was better than the cell he would have to return to.

"Why don't you tell me about your childhood growing up in Idaho?"

That broke the tension. He began to speak about his father's farm—"thirteen cows, a hundred chickens and a thousand debts." His father was a "dreamer who could never make any money." It had been hard on his mother, who was "educated."

He began laughing when he recalled the turnout for his father's funeral. "I thought maybe everyone was there to try to figure out how to collect the money he owed," Wilson said. Then he grew somber. "No, it was because they liked him. He really was a tremendous guy. He liked and got along with all kinds of people, but he couldn't put it together. The fact that I had to do it gave me the realism I needed to achieve success later on."

He talked about having to miss half his classes from the seventh grade through high school to work the farm, having to work the farms of neighbors so he could borrow their equipment, earning his own way through the University of Portland, where the Holy Cross fathers were the first men he had ever seen who wore dresses. These seemed to be important memories to him.

He talked about shipping out and how he despised homosexuals. He recalled in detail being beaten up when he tried to defend an alcoholic carpenter against a ship's bully, only to discover that the carpenter hadn't given the incident a second's thought. It was the turning point of his life, Wilson said. "That's when I said to myself, Ed Wilson, get smart. Start using your head. Look out for yourself. Survival of the fittest is the name of the game."

He talked as though he had forgotten where he was—that in all likelihood he would be spending the rest of his life in prison. In Virginia, a federal appeals court had ordered a restructuring of his sentence because of overlapping counts in his conviction. When Fahringer found it inopportune to appear on his behalf, Michael Dowd, the lawyer who defended

him in New York, volunteered to represent him and succeeded
in getting five years lopped off his sentence, along with the
elimination of a $200,000 fine. Still, he had consecutive sen-
tences totaling fifty-two years. While he would be eligible for
parole after ten years, the earliest date it might actually be
considered was more like seventeen years away, and even that
was a long shot.

He told me that he was innocent of any criminality. Nothing
he had done in Libya was different from what Washington was
doing covertly in dozens of other countries. There were pro-
American and pro-Soviet sides in Libya's ruling circles, and
given time, he could have turned things America's way. In this
regard, his use of Waldo Dubberstein had been a real plus;
besides, Dubberstein hadn't told the Libyans anything they
didn't already know.

He said he had contacted Dubberstein after Shackley left
the CIA and Clines had gotten a "big head." He had always
wanted to set up a front company in Libya when he was with the
agency, and that was why he had gone in there when Frank
Terpil popped up. To do a little business and gather some
intelligence.

The common denominator I had found mentioned by everyone who knew Wilson was that he never blamed himself for
anything. It was always someone else. Prison hadn't changed
him.

He insisted that the explosives "training school," as he
called it, was all Terpil's idea. He hadn't paid much attention to
it. The C-4 shipment was between Brower and the Libyans. His
only participation was to introduce Brower to key people in
Tripoli to make sure there weren't "any fuck-ups" when the
plane landed. He'd instructed Slocombe, his freight forwarder,
to stay out of it, but Slocombe hadn't listened. He knew about
the shipment, all right, but his sole motivation was to burrow in
deeper with the Libyans, make himself invaluable, so he could
influence them.

It was the same story with Eugene Tafoya. The Libyans
wanted him to go on some special mission in the States. Wilson
didn't have a clue what it was. His main concern was simply
getting back the money he'd advanced to Clines, and he gave
Tafoya just enough information about EATSCO so that Clines
would take him seriously. He hardly knew Tafoya. He had cho-

sen him because his top kick among the former Green Berets instructing the Libyans, a guy named Jimmy Dean, told him Tafoya was a genuine thug.

I asked him about EATSCO. His great hands clenched and unclenched and finally he repeated the story to me that Roberta Barnes said he had told her some four years before. What turned out to be EATSCO, he said, was Clines's idea. Clines had kept talking about the big money to be made shipping arms to Egypt, and it was von Marbod who arranged an initial $25 million Pentagon prepayment so the money could start earning interest right off the bat.

Why hadn't he told this to Barcella when he had the chance to plea-bargain?

"It was my lawyer," he said. "He gave me bad advice. I'm going to sue him for malpractice." He looked perplexed, though, as if he really didn't understand it himself. "It was that fucking Barcella. And Keiser. You know, I could have done something with the PLO. Really helped." He spoke as though those fictional meetings with PLO leaders and the National Security Council had actually been in the works. Then out of the blue, he said, "My wife was a good woman. I treated her like shit."

His last words to me at Marion were a demand to see my manuscript when I had finished it. "I want to fix up all the garbage you're going to write," he said.

Two months later, toward the end of January 1984, he contacted Barcella. He had nothing more to lose, he said, and he now wanted to tell the whole story of how EATSCO had come about and who had been involved in it. He was brought back to Alexandria and related his version to Barcella, Greenberg and Pedersen in detail. But if any of it was true, it was too late. There was no paper trail, as Roberta Barnes had predicted. Nothing that would hold up in court. And by now Wilson had lost all credibility. A first-year law student could have picked him apart in cross-examination.

Wilson lost all of his appeals. On January 28, 1985, he wrote me from prison, threatening me with a libel suit. "Much to date has been published about me that is not true," he said. "I plan every legal effort I can mount to assure there are not more malicious statements about me."

2

There remained Frank Terpil. In the beginning, Barcella
had perceived him as being on an equal footing with Wilson, if
not the dominant player. But then he had discovered that in
comparison with Wilson, Terpil was really small-time, a psychopathic freebooter skipping from one poisonous deal to the
next, whom Wilson had used for his own ends. Still, it rankled
that Terpil remained on the loose. When Barcella had decided
to grow a beard, vowing not to shave it until he got Wilson, that
vow had also included Terpil.

After fleeing his gun-running charges in New York, Terpil
had gone to Lebanon, changing planes in the same transit zone
at Zurich airport that Wilson would later pass through on his
way to the Dominican Republic. He had hooked up with the
Arafat wing of the Palestine liberation movement, providing it
with specialized assassination weapons and sophisticated
detonators from his old network of suppliers and helping to set
up a PLO communications system for its underground cells
around the world.

He had abandoned his wife for a young Filipino woman he
had come across working at a Bloomingdale's cosmetics counter
in suburban Washington, and in a series of self-advertisements
designed to impress his PLO clients, he had been interviewed
by Mike Wallace on *60 Minutes* and starred in a public television
documentary titled "Confessions of a Dangerous Man."

Then, when the Syrians moved into Lebanon, Terpil was
jailed by them for being a CIA agent. After six months, he was
released and rejoined the PLO.

Barcella nearly got him following Wilson's first conviction
in Alexandria in November 1982. He had been instrumental in
obtaining the release of a federal inmate in time for Christmas.
And in gratitude, the inmate reported that another convict, of
Lebanese extraction, had an uncle high up in the ruling Chris-
tian Phalangist party who knew where Terpil was hiding in the
Moslem section of Beirut.

Just before Thanksgiving, Barcella, Howard Safir and two
marshals flew to Lebanon. Arrangements were made with the
Phalangists to have local police make the actual arrest. But they
missed Terpil by two days. He had vacated his apartment. A
stakeout was started. The first night was less than auspicious.
Barcella was sitting in a car with his Phalangist driver near the

entrance to the apartment house. Safir was in another car around the corner.

Two Moslem militiamen approached Barcella. Suddenly he was looking at the wrong end of a machine gun. First in Arabic, then in broken English, one of them wanted to know what he was doing. Buying time, trying to think what to say, Barcella took out his wallet. As he flipped through it, he saw a photograph of his daughter. He pointed to it. She had disappeared, he said. He was out looking for her, and the militiamen, satisfied, moved off.

Barcella's Thanksgiving dinner was pita bread and ground-up chick-peas in olive oil, along with a skewer of undercooked lamb, a meat he detested in any event. Safir was as unhappy. He had promised his wife, Carol, that he would be home in time to carve the turkey. He had invited thirteen of his marshals and their wives for dinner, none of whom she had met. Once Barcella thought that he spotted Terpil getting into a Mercedes. He and Safir careened after him through the Beirut streets, but when they caught up to the Mercedes, it wasn't Terpil. After a week, they gave up. He was gone.

Barcella learned that Terpil had eventually left Lebanon in a Palestinian exodus forced by the Israelis. And then that he was in Prague, behind the Iron Curtain, and then on the island of Grenada before the U.S. invasion and after that in Nicaragua. In another interview, this one in *Penthouse* magazine, Terpil said that he felt no personal animosity toward Barcella. They both were only doing their jobs. "Really, if I met the guy on the street I'd probably buy him a drink," he was quoted as saying.

Terpil returned to Lebanon and then mysteriously was back in Prague. In the late summer of 1984 rumors floated that he was dead and had been buried in Damascus. But this turned out to be a subterfuge, like that used by the character Harry Lime in Graham Greene's *The Third Man*.

Sooner or later, Terpil would tumble off his highwire act. Barcella was sure of it. Either he'd have a fatal falling-out with his terrorist pals or he would finally be caught.

3

After Wilson disappeared from the headlines, Theodore Shackley was retained as a consultant for Stanford Technology, run by the Iranian Albert Hakim, now an American citizen, for whom Frank Terpil had once worked. Retired general Richard Secord was also hired by Stanford Technology.

Erich von Marbod became a consultant for Sears World Trade, a subsidiary of Sears Roebuck and Company, which had gotten into brokering advanced aerospace technology, electronic gear, heavy machinery, helicopters and spare parts to customers abroad. Von Marbod was brought into Sears by its chairman, Frank Carlucci, his old boss and former deputy secretary of the Defense Department as well as a former deputy director of the CIA.

Tom Clines tried a series of ventures, which failed, including one involving tomato paste from Colombia. He told friends that he was working on a book about the dangers of international Communism.

In Washington, EATSCO, because of its billing abuses, no longer shipped U.S. arms aid to Egypt, so the Pentagon and Cairo awarded the business to Four Winds, a freight-forwarding firm based in San Diego. To help it get the contract, Four Winds employed the services of the power broker Robert Keith Gray, Wilson's self-described "elevator buddy," who had once accompanied him on a two-week trip to Taiwan and served on the board of his old CIA front, Consultants International.

Larger interests reasserted themselves in other parts of the world. Umar Abdullah Muhayshi, whom Qaddafi wanted liquidated, had moved from Egypt to Morocco. At the time Morocco and Libya weren't speaking. Libya was supporting desert rebels intent on autonomy in southern Morocco. But in the spring of 1984, the two countries signed a peace pact and entered into an era of mutual cooperation. As part of the deal, Muhayshi was handed over to Libya. He was not heard from again.

Ernest Keiser went back to his old ways. While Barcella tried to keep his word about getting him a U.S. passport because of his role in trapping Wilson, Keiser continued his scams. In 1984, he was indicted on grand larceny charges in Westchester County, New York, and for fraud in Tampa, Florida, both having to do with money for a land deal. Keiser's wife also was charged with falsely declaring in an application for bail reduction that she and her husband were virtually penniless. On January 30, 1985, the day before she was to go on trial in Tampa, the Keisers became international fugitives. Still furious over being shut out of the Wilson recovery, the FBI began spreading rumors to selected members of the media that Barcella had shielded Keiser in his swindles.

4

There was yet one sinister footnote to the drama.

During the time Edwin P. Wilson was in the Metropolitan Correctional Center in New York, when his rage against Barcella peaked, he had also arranged to give $50,000 to a professional killer named William Arico, then being held at the center awaiting extradition for a murder he had committed in Italy.

Arico was planning an escape. Wilson made arrangements with Diane Byrne in London to pass the money to Arico's wife at a Heathrow Airport hotel. Byrne, who knew her only as "J," had handed over the cash in English pounds.

Arico, along with two accomplices, did try to escape down sheets tied together from an upper floor of the center. The first man landed safely and Arico had only six feet to go when the third, an overweight Cuban drug dealer, started too soon, caught his belt buckle in the sheets after coming out a window and plummeted on top of Arico, surviving himself, but squashing Arico to death in the process.

Wilson, when confronted by these facts, denied that Barcella had been the intended target. The money, he said, was "only a loan."

AUTHOR'S NOTE

Blind attributions, like a "close friend" or a "former colleague" or a "highly placed official," have come to plague works of nonfiction. The rationale advanced is that they serve to illuminate a subject. At best, though, they leave the reader in the dark as to the quality of the information. At worst, they are fictive projections of the author.

In this book there are no quotes, comments or thoughts of consequence from anonymous informants.

Principal players who refused to be interviewed include Theodore Shackley, Thomas Clines, Erich von Marbod, retired major general Richard V. Secord, Rafael Quintero—and Seymour Hersh.

Secord's attorney advised that his client might entertain written questions. Since this would eliminate necessary give and take, the suggestion was declined. Hersh, for his part, said that he was not in the business of helping other writers.

In very large measure, the book was based on official records, proceedings and investigative reports not normally available to outside scrutiny. The documents of course speak for themselves. Let it be specifically noted, however, that while E. Lawrence Barcella, Jr., was interviewed at length, he did not supply any classified material.

Information about Edwin P. Wilson's covert activities in the Central Intelligence Agency and Task Force 157 were derived primarily from agency career summaries and evaluations and from similar records in the Office of Naval Intelligence, as well as from reports by the Federal Bureau of Investigation, the Bureau of Alcohol, Tobacco and Firearms, the Defense Investigative Service and the CIA's Office of the Inspector General.

When it became apparent that Ernest Keiser was sticking to the same imaginative account of his past that he had related to others, I eventually put together a dossier on who he actually was and where he had come from, based on files of the Immigration and Naturalization Service, the State Department, the FBI, the Manhattan District Attorney's Office, the U.S. Attorney's Office for the Southern District of New York and Interpol. The account of Keiser's visit to the White House was taken from the notes and recollections of Richard Allen, then the president's national security adviser, and Robert Hill Schwartz, Keiser's attorney at the time.

The investigative efforts into the actions of Jerome Brower, the hiring of explosives experts for service in Libya, the shipments of explosives and arms, the recruitment of former Green Berets and other elements of the conspiracy were based largely on comprehensive files of the Bureau of Alcohol, Tobacco and Firearms. While senior BATF agent Richard Pedersen did not provide these documents, he amplified on them in a series of interviews, adding texture and a sense of the moment that would otherwise be missing, and I gratefully acknowledge his cooperation.

The original FBI report, which, with Justice Department concurrence, found little legal ground for prosecuting Wilson or Frank Terpil, was addressed to Benjamin Civiletti, then assistant attorney general in charge of the criminal division. It was dated November 17, 1977. A copy also went to the U.S. Attorney's Office for the Eastern District of Virginia for possible U.S. Customs violations surrounding Wilson's shipment of night-vision devices to Libya. Nothing came of this at the time either.

The details of the loan Wilson advanced to Thomas Clines were taken from a handwritten proposal Clines presented, dated January 5, 1979; a memorandum for the record dated January 18, 1979, prepared by Wilson's attorney in Geneva, Edward Coughlin; subsequent correspondence between Coughlin and

Clines's attorney in Washington, Barbara Rossotti; and a final agreement, dated August 20, 1980, to repay $499,934.63, contingent on Wilson's signing a general release.

The circumstances surrounding the check that was sent to the military attaché, General Abu Ghazala, at the Egyptian embassy in Washington was based on correspondence between the Federal Financing Bank, which processed funds for arms aid to Egypt, and the Defense Security Assistance Agency. The bank informed the agency that its "legal staff has advised against endorsing the enclosed check over to the Attache, as was requested in a letter dated January 25, 1980, from Attache." The agency thereupon issued a new check directly to the attaché.

The curious nature of the Egyptian American Transport Services, Inc. (EATSCO), were first explored publicly in the *Wall Street Journal, The New York Times* and the Washington *Post.*

In my research, I made a special effort to elicit the thoughts of participants during a given incident. Reconstructed dialogue in the book was kept to a minimum. Whenever there was uncertainty about the precise words, paraphrased dialogue or comments were substituted. As an example, for the period covering Jerome Brower's plea bargaining, William Hundley, Brower's attorney, and Barcella were interviewed separately. Each was then afforded an opportunity to review what the other recalled being said or done.

Verbatim dialogue with Wilson and with Peter Goulding during the BATF undercover operation to try to arrange an illegal arms shipment came from the transcripts of the conversations, which were recorded. The same applies to the many telephone calls between Ernest Keiser and Wilson in 1981 and 1982.

The discourse at the secret meeting in Rome was based on the notes and recollections of Barcella and Pedersen, a report written by special agent William Hart of the FBI, the recollections of John Keats and those of Wilson himself.

The description of Wilson's capture and the events leading up to it was written primarily from Barcella's recollections; the notes and recollections of Howard Safir, Associate Director for Operations, U.S. Marshals Service; eyewitness reports of Chief Inspector Philip Tucker and Inspector Giovanni Reina; the report of U.S. Marshal José López; the recollections of Roberta Barnes and a statement from Diane Byrne.

Besides Barnes, key Wilson associates personally interviewed in depth were Douglas Schlachter and John Heath. I also had access to statements made by Peter Goulding beyond his testimony in open court.

Wilson's attempts to seek refuge in the Sudan were documented in reports Barnes, Heath and another Wilson associate, Carl Mounts, made to Wilson following exploratory trips to Khartoum, and in correspondence between Wilson and the Sudanese minister of national security at that time, Omer Mohammed el-Tayeb.

As indicated in the text, Admiral Stansfield Turner, Robert Keith Gray and Martin McNamara, Vice President Humphrey's campaign manager, were interviewed for this book. So were Donald Nielsen and W. Don Randol, who served with Wilson in Task Force 157. Former CIA analyst Frank Snepp provided helpful data. The labor historian and writer Philip Ross graciously forwarded material he located in the archives of the Seafarers International Union pertaining to Wilson's early covert years at Cornell University, in the SIU and the AFL-CIO.

I am indebted to Stephen Higgins, Director of the Bureau of Alcohol, Tobacco and Firearms, for the courtesies he extended to me, and to BATF agents Gene Reagan, Joseph Chisholm and Rick Wadsworth, who is now with the Secret Service, for their valuable contributions.

Other law-enforcement officials who were interviewed include Theodore Greenberg of the U.S. Attorney's Office for the Eastern District of Virginia; Carol Bruce in the District of Columbia; Mark Richard, deputy chief of the Justice Department's criminal division; Rudolph Giuliani, now the U.S. Attorney for the Southern District of New York; Manhattan District Attorney Robert Morgenthau and Seth Rosenberg, chief of the rackets bureau in that office.

Defense lawyers willing to offer their perspectives within the constraints of the attorney-client relationship were William Hundley in Washington; Michael Dowd, Patrick Wall and Herald Price Fahringer in New York; John Keats in Alexandria and Marian Rosen in Houston.

Members of the news media quick to share their knowledge with me included Bob Woodward, Scott Armstrong and Phil Smith of the Washington *Post;* Philip Taubman and Jeff Gerth of *The New York Times;* the Boston *Globe's* Ben Bradlee, Jr.; Dale

Van Atta of the Jack Anderson syndicated column; Washington writer Jim Hougan; George Crile and Robert Schakne of CBS; and Ira Rosen, also with CBS, who introduced me to Barcella.

Mary Barcella kindly allowed me to see portions of the diary she kept while her husband was pursuing Wilson, and I am grateful for the insights of Reta Fletcher, Wilson's schoolteacher in Nampa, Idaho.

My thanks to Howard Kaminsky and Jason Epstein at Random House. My appreciation also to my agents at International Creative Management, Sam Cohn and Arlene Donovan, for their support.

And a particular thank you to John-Michael Maas, who unraveled the mysteries of the IBM computer used to write this book. I'm not sure if the computer is the greatest invention since the wheel. I have no doubt, though, that it is the most revolutionary turn in the history of father-and-teenage-son relations.

—Peter Maas
New York City

INDEX

ABOUT THE AUTHOR

Five previous works of nonfiction by PETER MAAS include *The Valachi Papers, Serpico* and *Marie: A True Story.* He is also the author of the critically acclaimed novel *Made in America.* His books have been translated into seventeen languages.

After graduating from Duke University and serving in the Navy during the Korean War, he achieved initial success as an investigative reporter for such publications as *Look*, the *Saturday Evening Post* and *New York* magazine.